Church of England Record Society
Volume 28

PROCEEDINGS AGAINST THE 'SCANDALOUS MINISTERS' OF ESSEX, 1644–1645

PROCEEDINGS AGAINST THE 'SCANDALOUS MINISTERS' OF ESSEX, 1644–1645

EDITED BY
Graham Hart

THE BOYDELL PRESS

CHURCH OF ENGLAND RECORD SOCIETY

First published 2024

A Church of England Record Society publication
Published by The Boydell Press
an imprint of Boydell & Brewer Ltd
PO Box 9, Woodbridge, Suffolk IP12 3DF, UK
and of Boydell & Brewer Inc.
668 Mt Hope Avenue, Rochester, NY 14620–2731, USA
website: www.boydellandbrewer.com

ISBN 978-1-83765-186-3

ISSN 1351-3087

Series information is printed at the back of this volume

A CIP catalogue record for this book is available
from the British Library

Printed and bound in Great Britain by
TJ Books Limited, Padstow, Cornwall

Contents

Acknowledgments

Many scholars have helped in the production of this volume. In particular, I pay tribute to the encouragement and help given by John Walter, Kenneth Fincham and the late Clive Holmes. I am also grateful for the help of Andrew Barclay, Nicholas Cranfield, Stephen Roberts, Paul Seaward, Christopher Thornton and Nicholas Tyacke. The support of Grant Tapsell, my editor, and of Linda Randall, the (much-needed) copy-editor, has been outstanding.

I am grateful for the permission of the University of Leicester Library to print my transcript of MS 31. In particular, I thank Simon Dixon, Head of Archives and Special Collections, for his help in accessing the manuscript and in providing information about its acquisition. I also thank the staffs of the Manuscripts Room at the British Library, the Bodleian Library, Oxford, Cambridge University Library and the Essex Record Office, Chelmsford, for their efficient service.

And, of course, nothing could have been done without the support of Margaret, Alan and Matthew.

Abbreviations

Acts and ordinances	*Acts and ordinances of the interregnum 1642–1660*, ed. C. H. Firth and R. S. Rait (1911)
BL	British Library
Cambridgeshire scandalous ministers	*The Cambridgeshire committee for scandalous ministers 1644–45*, ed. Graham Hart (Cambridgeshire Records Society, 2017)
CCEd	The clergy of the Church of England database, 1540–1835, www.theclergydatabase.org.uk
Cole MS	British Library, Additional MS 5829, folios 1–74
Commons Journal	*Journals of the House of Commons* (1507–)
CSPD	*Calendar of state papers domestic*
ERO	Essex Record Office
Fincham and Tyacke, *Altars restored*	Kenneth Fincham and Nicholas Tyacke, *Altars restored: the changing face of English religious worship, 1547 – c. 1700* (Oxford, 2007)
Foster, *Alumni Oxonienses*	J. Foster, *Alumni Oxonienses: the members of the University of Oxford 1500–1714* (4 vols., Oxford, 1891–2)
Green, 'Persecution'	Ian Green, 'The persecution of "scandalous" and "malignant" parish clergy during the English Civil War', *English Historical Review*, 94 (1979), 507–31
Gyford, *Public spirit*	G Janet Gyford, *Public spirit: dissent in Witham and Essex 1500–1700* (Witham, 1999)
HMC	Historical Manuscripts Commission
Holmes, *Eastern Association*	Clive Holmes, *The Eastern Association in the English Civil War* (Cambridge, 1974)
House of Commons, 1604–1629	*The history of parliament: the House of Commons, 1604–1629*, ed. Andrew Thrush and John P. Ferris (6 vols., Cambridge, 2010)
House of Commons 1640–1660	*The history of parliament: the House of Commons 1640–1660*, ed. Stephen K. Roberts (9 vols., Woodbridge, 2023)
Josselin diary	*The diary of Ralph Josselin 1616–1683*, ed. Alan Macfarlane (Oxford, 1976)
Leicester MS 31	University of Leicester Library, Special Collections, MS 31
Lords Journal	*Journals of the House of Lords* (1509–1767)
LPL	Lambeth Palace Library

McCall, *Baal's priests*	Fiona McCall, *Baal's priests: the loyalist clergy and the English revolution* (Farnham, 2013)
Matthews, *Calamy revised*	A. G. Matthews, *Calamy revised, being a revision of Edmund Calamy's account of the ministers and others ejected and silenced, 1660–62* (Oxford, 1934).
Matthews, *Walker revised*	A. G. Matthews, *Walker revised, being a revision of John Walker's sufferings of the clergy during the grand rebellion 1642–60* (Oxford, 1948).
Milton, *Second reformation*	Anthony Milton, *England's second reformation: the battle for the Church of England, 1625–1662* (Cambridge, 2021)
Morant, *History of Essex*	P. Morant, *History and antiquities of the county of Essex* (2 vols., 1768)
Newcourt, *Repertorium*	Richard Newcourt, *Repertorium ecclesiasticum parochiale londinense* (2 vols., 1708–10)
ODNB	*Oxford dictionary of national biography* (60 vols., Oxford, 2004; online 2008)
OED	*Oxford English Dictionary*
'Royalist clergy of Lincolnshire'	'The royalist clergy of Lincolnshire', ed. J. W. F. Hill, in *Reports and papers of the Lincolnshire Architectural and Archaeological Society* (new series), vol. 2, part 1 (1938, published 1940)
Shaw, *History of the church 1640–1660*	W. A. Shaw, *A history of the church 1640–1660 during the Civil Wars and under the Commonwealth, 1640–1660* (2 vols., 1900)
Smith, *Ecclesiastical history of Essex*	Harold Smith, *The ecclesiastical history of Essex under the Long Parliament and the Commonwealth* (Colchester, 1933)
Smith, 'Sequence of Essex clergy, 1640–1664'	Harold Smith, 'The sequence of Essex clergy, 1640–1664', typescript, 2 vols., ERO
Suffolk scandalous ministers	*The Suffolk committees for scandalous ministers 1644–1646*, ed. Clive Holmes (Suffolk Records Society, 1970).
TNA	The National Archives, London
VCH Essex	*A history of the county of Essex* (12 vols., Victoria County History, 1903–2022)
Venn, *Alumni Cantabrigienses*	J. and J. A. Venn, *Alumni Cantabrigienses: a biographical list of all known students, graduates and holders of office at the University of Cambridge from the earliest times to 1900. Part I: from the earliest times to 1751* (4 vols., Cambridge, 1922–7)
Walter, *Understanding popular violence*	John Walter, *Understanding popular violence in the English revolution: the Colchester plunderers* (Cambridge, 1999)
Webster, *Godly clergy*	Tom Webster, *Godly clergy in early Stuart England: the Caroline puritan movement c. 1620–1643* (Cambridge, 1997)

Introduction

From its earliest days, the Long Parliament showed deep concern about the condition of the church. On 6 November 1640, the House of Commons set up a committee of the whole house on religion. Soon, parliament was being bombarded with petitions demanding reforms, and over the next five years, radical measures were enacted. The main targets under attack were the powers, and soon the very existence, of the bishops and the church's courts; ceremonialism in worship and the established liturgy of the church, associated in the mind of puritan critics with idolatry, superstition and popery; and the presence within the clergy of many who failed to meet the particular and exacting standards of their godly parishioners.

In its early months, parliament received hundreds of petitions against individual parish ministers. It responded by assuming the power to summon ministers and to imprison them, and later to deprive them of their livings and to nominate their successors.[1] By the end of 1643, parliament had ejected two hundred or more parish ministers from their livings. Dissatisfied with this rate of progress, in January 1644, parliament authorized the earl of Manchester, the major-general of the Eastern Association, to carry out a thorough purge of the University of Cambridge and of the clergy in the Association's seven counties, which included Essex.[2]

The two manuscripts printed in this volume record the earl of Manchester's purge of the clergy of Essex, which took place between March 1644 and April 1645, when Manchester's commission as major-general came to an end. It was one episode in a protracted drive by the Long Parliament to transform the clergy across the whole country. In *The sufferings of the clergy*, Dr John Walker attempted to record this programme, which led to the ejection of a quarter of England's parish ministers from their livings.[3] Walker was responding to Edmund Calamy's commemoration of the ordeals of the nonconformist clergy at the Restoration.[4] In the twentieth century, both works were supplemented and corrected by A. G. Matthews, whose books, *Calamy revised* and *Walker revised*, are essential works of reference.[5] Matthews confirmed Walker's claim that the victims of parliament's purge outnumbered the ministers recorded by Calamy as ejected for nonconformity at the Restoration.[6]

Recently, as historians have re-examined the part played by religious issues in the Civil Wars, the persecution of the episcopalian clergy has begun to receive attention. An important article of 1979 by Ian Green provided a national overview of the parliamentary purge, while Fiona McCall's *Baal's priests* adds much detail,

1 Anthony Fletcher, *The outbreak of the English Civil War* (1981), p. 111; Shaw, *History of the church 1640–1660*, II, 175–7.

2 '22 January 1644: An ordinance for regulating the University of Cambridge, and for removing of scandalous ministers in the seven associated counties', in *Acts and ordinances*, pp. 371–2. The ordinance was copied into BL, Add. MS 5829, and is therefore printed at pp. 2–3 below. For the history and politics of the Eastern Association, see Holmes, *Eastern Association*.

3 John Walker, *An attempt towards recovering an account of the numbers and sufferings of the clergy* (1714). Walker's papers are in the Bodleian Library, MS J. Walker.

4 Edmund Calamy, *An abridgment of Mr. Baxter's history of his life and times* (1702).

5 Matthews, *Calamy revised*; and Matthews, *Walker revised*.

6 Matthews, *Walker revised*, pp. xiii–xxi.

particularly on the personal implications of persecution for the clergy and their families.[7] Kenneth Fincham and Stephen Taylor have suggested that the response of the episcopalian clergy to parliamentary policies in this period should be seen as more than purely defensive, and 'rather in terms of formulation and reformulation'. Anthony Milton has shown that during the 1640s and 1650s the doctrine, liturgy and governance of the Church of England were widely debated and challenged within as well as outside the episcopalian community, and argued that the events of this period should be seen as part of a much longer process running from the Henrician reformation through to the 1660s and beyond.[8]

The two Essex manuscripts printed in this book vividly illustrate the problems which beset the parish clergy and their parishioners as they sought to deal with the pressures imposed on them by higher authority: in the 1630s, as Archbishop Laud, with the king's support, drove forward a divisive programme of change which the godly could not accept, and as parliament, in the 1640s, reversed the Laudian programme and strove to bring about a religious revolution.

The manuscripts

The manuscripts printed below were the products of two distinct stages in Manchester's purge of the Essex parish clergy. British Library, Additional MS 5829, folios 1–74, printed at pp. 1–54 below, is well known to scholars but no transcript or edition of it has previously been published. The manuscript was written by William Cole the antiquary and is referred to below as the 'Cole MS'.[9] He wrote it at Bletchley (Buckinghamshire), where he was rector, in 1757.[10] Cole was transcribing a manuscript book which recorded the proceedings of a committee appointed by the earl of Manchester in February 1644 to gather evidence against scandalous ministers in north Essex. The original manuscript which Cole transcribed is no longer extant, but there is no reason to doubt that he copied the manuscript faithfully. Cole also added many notes of his own, either to record characteristics of the manuscript or to comment on the people and events recorded in it. These comments make it clear that Cole was no supporter of the purge. His additions have been printed in this volume in italics, to distinguish them from the original text.

Cole recounts that the book had been given to him by Stephen Soame of Thurlow, Suffolk, five years previously.[11] Soame in turn had been given it by 'my

7 Green, 'Persecution'; McCall, *Baal's priests*.

8 Kenneth Fincham and Stephen Taylor, 'Episcopalian identity, 1640–1662', in *The Oxford history of anglicanism*, I, ed. Anthony Milton (Oxford, 2017), pp. 457–82; Milton, *England's second reformation*.

9 A graduate of King's College, Cambridge (BA 1736–7, MA 1740), Cole continued to live in college until 1753 when he became rector of Bletchley (Buckinghamshire). As an antiquary, his main interests were the churches of Cambridgeshire and the university: his collections, in 113 volumes, were bequeathed to the British Museum (now the British Library) on his death: John D. Pickles, 'William Cole (1714–1782)', *ODNB*. As often in his collections, Cole wrote our manuscript only on the recto side of the folios: he used the verso sides to record material on different subjects.

10 Cole MS, fos. 1–2.

11 Cole MS, fo. 2. Elsewhere in BL, Add. MS 5829 (fo. 162), Cole refers to Soame as 'my very worthy friend and most accomplished gentleman', who lived at Little Thurlow and was a justice of the peace for both Suffolk and Cambridgeshire. The manor of Little Thurlow had come into the Soame family in 1582 when Sir Stephen Soame (*c.* 1544–1619) bought it: Venn, *Alumni Cantabrigienses*, IV, 120; W. A. Copinger, *The manors of Suffolk* (7 vols., 1905–11), V, 297–8.

lady Bernardiston of Kedington', Suffolk. The Soame and Barnardiston families had lived in proximity and kinship for many years. Indeed Arthur Barnardiston, who played a prominent part in the work of the north Essex committee for scandalous ministers in 1644, was the brother-in-law of Jane Soame, through her marriage of 1613 to Sir Nathaniel Barnardiston, his elder brother.[12] It seems probable that the book which Cole transcribed once belonged to Arthur Barnardiston (died 1655) and remained in the family after his death, before eventually being passed to Stephen Soame.[13]

In organizing his purge of the clergy of Essex, the earl of Manchester had appointed two committees, one for the north of the county, one for the south: Cole's book related only to twenty-eight ministers serving in north Essex. It was a working record of the charges laid by parishioners, the material being copied into the book as it was submitted. A further feature of Cole's book is that, as he noted, it was in fact two books bound up together: one of perhaps thirty-two folios which occupies folios 9–63 of the Cole MS, and a much shorter book sewn into the longer book at the back (copied into the Cole MS at folios 64–74).[14] This short book, originally consisting of eight folios, had lost its two outer leaves, and thus began and ended in the middle of two sets of articles. Judging from the content of this shorter book, it was created for hearings at Colchester, possibly by a secretariat based in Colchester and serving the town's parliamentary committee, rather than the county-based secretariat which serviced the hearings at other venues, for example Halstead, Maldon and Chelmsford.

The second manuscript, printed at pp. 55–100 below, was acquired by University College, Leicester, in 1930 as part of the bequest of Caleb Robjohns, a local hosiery manufacturer who collected books and manuscripts.[15] It is a seventeenth-century book in vellum covers, and contains articles setting out charges against twenty-one ministers serving parishes in both north and south Essex, including ten of the ministers articled against in the Cole MS. These articles occupy thirty-two folios. At the back of the book five folios, numbered A3–A7, set out records of 'his Lordshipps proceedings in the Reformation of the Universitie of Cambridge'. There follow, at fos. A13–A32, copies of warrants of sequestration and ejection of twenty of the Essex ministers.

It has been known since the early eighteenth century that parliament had once held books recording the earl of Manchester's purge of the clergy of Suffolk, Lincolnshire, Cambridgeshire, Essex and Norfolk, five of the seven counties which comprised the Eastern Association.[16] These books, along with many other documents, had been removed from parliament's keeping around 1680 by Dr John Nalson, for use in writing a history of the Civil Wars. After Nalson's death in 1686,

12 Jane Soame was the daughter of Sir Stephen, mentioned in the preceding note: Richard L. Greaves, 'Sir Nathaniel Barnardiston, 1588–1653', *ODNB*.

13 See pp. lv–lvii below for more about Arthur Barnardiston. The Lady Barnardiston who gave the book to Soame was presumably the wife or widow of one of four Barnardiston baronets who lived in the first half of the eighteenth century at Kedington, probably Catherine, wife of Sir Samuel Barnardiston Bt (dsp 1736). She 'enjoyed the estate of Ketton [Kedington] during her widowhood and was buried there 3 December 1757': *Complete baronetage*, ed. George E. Cokayne (5 vols., Exeter, 1900–6), III, 273–4.

14 See Cole's annotations at Cole MS, fos. 63 (final sentence) and 64.

15 University of Leicester Library, Special Collections MS 31, referred to here as 'Leicester MS 31'.

16 Manchester also purged the clergy of Huntingdonshire and Hertfordshire, but there is no record of comparable books for those counties.

the papers which he had taken from parliament remained in the possession of his family, at first his son-in-law and successor as rector of Doddington in the Isle of Ely, Philip Williams, and then the latter's son, also Philip, fellow of St John's College, Cambridge.[17] Williams senior contrived to lose the Norfolk book,[18] but the other four county books remained in the family's possession for many years. While the books were in the possession of Nalson's descendants they were on occasions lent to antiquaries. In 1704, Philip Williams senior lent them to Simon Patrick, bishop of Ely, who passed them on to Charles Goodall for use in his historical work.[19] Later, Zachary Grey and Thomas Baker both had access to the Essex book but did not systematically transcribe the Essex material.[20]

The Cambridgeshire, Suffolk and Lincolnshire books were in the possession of Dr George Gordon, dean of Lincoln, at his death in 1845.[21] The Essex book, however, appears to have been no longer in the family's possession; its whereabouts at that time are unknown. All we know is that by 1930 it was owned by Mr Robjohns, who bequeathed it to University College, Leicester. Baker's comment relayed in n. 20 above is sufficient to confirm provenance of the Leicester manuscript, but its identification as the missing Essex book is reinforced when it is compared with the other surviving county books.

Comparison of Leicester MS 31 with the manuscripts relating to the scandalous ministers of Suffolk, Lincolnshire and Cambridgeshire shows they are similar in content and form.[22] All four books contain the evidence given against ministers in their respective counties, but they do not contain the responses which it is known that many of the accused ministers submitted. For each minister, the entry normally

17 The history of these books is well summarized by Holmes, *Suffolk scandalous ministers*, pp. 27–8.

18 Bodleian Library, MS J. Walker c.1, fo. 94. Nalson copied extracts from the Norfolk book and these survive: *ibid.*, MS J. Walker c.6, fo. 44.

19 Letter of 1 Aug. 1704, Patrick to Goodall: Bodleian Library, MS J. Walker c.1, fo. 94, printed in G. B. Tatham, *Dr John Walker and the sufferings of the clergy* (Cambridge, 1911), pp. 94–5. Goodall returned the books to Williams. Goodall abandoned his project of writing a history of the persecution of the clergy and passed many of his papers to Dr John Walker, for use in his *Sufferings of the clergy*, but it is clear that Walker never had access to the Essex book.

20 Grey abstracted some facts about the Essex purge, which he noted down in his copy of Walker's *Sufferings*. In turn, William Cole copied Grey's notes on Essex ministers, with other material: BL, Add. MS 5829, fos. 76–88. Baker copied the material about Cambridge University three times: Cambridge University Library, MS Mm. 1.38, 459–63, MS Mm. 1.48, 19–26, and MS Mm. 1.53, 223–8. At MS Mm. 1.48, 19, Baker noted that he had taken the material 'From the Books of the Committee (129) endors'd *Essex, and the Reformation of the University of Cambridge*, … W[illiams].' '(129)' and 'Essex' are still legible on the vellum cover of Leicester MS 31. Baker also transcribed the articles set out in Leicester MS 31, fo. 5, against Francis Gouldman, rector of South Ockendon: *ibid.*, MS Mm. 1.38, 464.

21 These books came to Dean Gordon through his mother, who, before marrying Gordon's father, had been married to the younger Philip Williams, Nalson's grandson. Gordon's executors sold the Cambridgeshire book to the British Museum, while the Lincolnshire and Suffolk books passed to a firm of solicitors in Lincoln, and were donated to Lincoln City Library in 1927: 'Royalist clergy of Lincolnshire', pp. 34–5.

22 The three manuscripts are Lincolnshire Archives, MS LCL 5456 (Lincolnshire); *ibid.*, MS LCL 5458 (Suffolk); and BL, Add. MS 15672 (Cambridgeshire). The latter manuscript has been rebound in leather, apparently in the nineteenth century. All three manuscripts have been transcribed and printed: *The Suffolk committees for scandalous ministers 1644–1646*, ed. Clive Holmes (Suffolk Records Society, 1970); 'The royalist clergy of Lincolnshire', ed. J. W. F. Hill, in *Reports and papers of the Lincolnshire Architectural and Archaeological Society* (new series), vol. 2, part 1 (1938, published 1940); *The Cambridgeshire committee for scandalous ministers*, ed. Graham Hart (Cambridgeshire Records Society, 2017).

states the names of the deponents for each article, the names of the committee who heard the evidence, the date and place of the hearing and information about the income of the living and the minister's personal circumstances (private means, and whether he was married and had children). These last items had been requested by Manchester in his instructions to the committees.[23] All four books also contain copies of the warrants by which Manchester authorized the sequestration and ejection of the ministers. In some cases they are recorded as drafts, with gaps for the signature and date, in others, a date and Manchester's name are recorded, but actual signatures are not found anywhere in the books: the books are compilations made by copying original documents which are no longer extant. The warrants are invariably entered in the book in a separate section from the depositions. All four books also contain some material which does not relate to the ministers of the county in question. The books for Essex, Suffolk and Lincolnshire contain information about Manchester's purge of Cambridge University.[24] The Essex book has the fullest entry, and the book has sometimes been referred to as that of the 'reformation of the University of Cambridge'.[25] The Cambridgeshire book contains articles against an Essex minister; the Essex book contains an entry about a Cambridgeshire minister; the Lincolnshire book contains several stray entries about ministers from Huntingdonshire, Suffolk, Cambridgeshire and Hertfordshire.[26] Finally, none of the four books is the work of a single scribal hand and the same hand is found in more than one book. In particular, the scribe who wrote most of the Essex book also wrote a significant part of the Cambridgeshire book.[27]

In short, the many similarities and links between the four books make it certain that they were produced as part of a concerted procedure covering all four counties, probably by the secretariat of the Eastern Association in Cambridge. It is also clear that the papers which were copied into the four books recorded the position reached at or near the end of the process, when the county committees had heard the evidence and made a submission to Manchester for his decision. In relation to the twenty beneficed ministers who feature in Leicester MS 31, there is independent evidence for all except one of them that they were indeed sequestrated and ejected from their livings.[28] In his edition of the Suffolk book, Clive Holmes suggested that it was produced on Manchester's orders and deposited in parliament after the termination of his appointment in April 1645, for use in any appeals against his decisions. This seems much the most likely explanation of the origins of the four books.[29]

23 Cole MS, fo. 8.
24 Leicester MS 31, fos. A3–A7 (pp. 89–94 below); Lincolnshire Archives, MS LCL 5458, fo. 222; *ibid.*, MS LCL 5456, pp. 88–87.
25 BL, Lansdowne MS 1038, fo. 14. As n. 20 above indicates, Thomas Baker was careful to record the position correctly.
26 BL, Add. MS 15672, fos. 42–3 and 78v, referring to Arkesden (Essex); Leicester MS 31, not foliated (see p. lxxi below, referring to Fen Drayton (Cambridgeshire); Lincolnshire Archives, MS LCL 5456, pp. 1 and 246, and, at the back of the book, pp. 9–17, referring to several stray entries in the Lincolnshire book.
27 Leicester MS 31, fos. 1–32; BL, Add. MS 15672, fos. 29–55 and 71v–84v.
28 See John Fenwick, at Leicester MS 31, fo. 1, n. 1 below.
29 *Suffolk scandalous ministers*, p. 27; *Cambridgeshire scandalous ministers*, pp. 22–3. I am indebted to Dr Holmes for many helpful discussions of this and related questions.

The two Essex manuscripts compared

A comparison of the content of Cole's book with that of Leicester MS 31 shows that they were compiled for different purposes in different circumstances. Cole's book was kept by the north Essex committee as a working record of the charges laid by parishioners against twenty-eight ministers in their area. Leicester MS 31, while containing some similar material relating to ten of those ministers, also contains the charges against nine ministers from the south of the county, as well as two more from the north. The absence from Cole's book of these two cases is explained by the fact that they were not heard by the north Essex committee, but by one sitting in Cambridge.[30] The depositions relating to the other ten north Essex ministers listed in Leicester MS 31 also appear in Cole's book and may therefore be compared. The two sets of depositions are similar but not identical. In Cole's book, they have been entered roughly in date order and when the committee heard two or three sets of complaints about the same minister at different times, they are entered at separate places, as they were heard: in Leicester MS 31, all the evidence relating to one minister has been consolidated into a single entry. Cole's book rarely gives the date or place of the hearing or the names of the committee hearing the evidence, while MS 31 provides that information. As to the content of the depositions, the version in MS 31 has at many points been edited, but in a minor way, usually to clarify the meaning or to correct an obvious mistake in the Cole version, such as the name of the parish concerned.[31] In one case, the writer of Cole's book has struck through two articles, and they are omitted altogether from MS 31 and the subsequent articles renumbered.[32] In short, Cole's book was compiled over a period, as evidence was taken by the committee; it was kept by the committee for local use. Once the committee had decided to recommend a minister's sequestration, the case was written up for Manchester's consideration in the edited form seen in MS 31. It is significant that two-thirds of the cases entered in MS 31 are headed 'Essex', unnecessary information in a local book, but useful in documents intended for circulation outside the county. A further difference between the two books is that MS 31, like its sibling books for Suffolk, Lincolnshire and Cambridgeshire, contains copies of the warrants by which Manchester was to authorize the sequestration and ejection of the ministers.

The most interesting aspect of a comparison between the two manuscripts is that only ten of the twenty-eight cases contained in the Cole MS are carried forward into Leicester MS 31. The outcomes of all twenty-eight cases are summarized in Appendix 2, and possible explanations for these different outcomes discussed at pp. xl–xlvi below. It is clear that a significant number of ministers who had been articled against by their parishioners were able to remain in possession of their livings.

30 Edward Young and Thomas Punter, Leicester MS 31, fos. 30–2. The committee in these cases was a group of members of the Eastern Association committee which met at Cambridge: see Leicester MS 31, fo. 30 and n. 88.

31 For example, William Evett was minister not of Yeldham Magna (Cole MS, fo. 23) but Yeldham Parva (Leicester MS 31, fo. 15v).

32 Numbers 10 and 11 of the articles against Christopher Newstead in the Cole MS, fo. 20, have been struck through, and omitted altogether from Leicester MS 31, fo. 21.

The background to Manchester's purge of the Essex clergy

The strength of puritan sentiment in early seventeenth-century Essex is a commonplace, and one founded in fact. Around 1604, a puritan pamphlet estimated that about a quarter of ministers in Essex were 'diligent and sufficient preachers'. Networks of godly gentry and clergy worked together to find positions for promising young men, often graduates of Emmanuel College, Cambridge, in livings or as curates and lecturers.[33] Kenneth Shipps estimated that by 1630 godly patrons controlled entry to a hundred or so of the county's livings, a quarter of the total: twenty-two advowsons were held by the earl of Warwick alone. Dr Shipps's estimate that in the 1630s puritan ministers occupied a half of the county's benefices seems too high, as Barbara Donagan suggested, but a figure in the range of 35–40 per cent is plausible.[34]

Even in Essex, however, godly ministers were a minority: the county's clergy were divided, as two petitions sent to Bishop Laud in 1629 illustrate. William Laud, then bishop of London, the diocese in which Essex lay, regarded Thomas Hooker, the puritan lecturer at Chelmsford, as a disruptive influence and was seeking his removal. Within a few days, Laud received two petitions, one from forty-nine Essex parish ministers expressing support for Hooker, and another from forty-one ministers, which did not mention Hooker by name but asked that the bishop should enforce conformity in the diocese. By 1642, sixteen of these conformist ministers were still serving in the county: thirteen of them were to become victims of the parliamentary purges.[35]

There were also many puritans amongst the county's gentry. Dr Shipps found that puritan gentry owned the advowsons of over a hundred of the county's livings. In 1640, these godly people were strongly opposed to the religious policies of the king and looked to parliament for redress. The earl of Warwick, acting with his long-standing ally Sir Thomas Barrington of Hatfield Broad Oak, was able to secure the election to the Long Parliament of a godly member for every one of the eight seats in the county. From 1642, parliament exerted military and political control over the county: two years later, when the earl of Manchester needed to recruit godly men of standing to carry out his purge of the Essex clergy, he could call upon a large body of puritan gentry who had already served parliament in important *rôles*.[36]

33 Smith, *Ecclesiastical history of Essex*, pp. 15–20; W. Hunt, *The puritan moment: the coming of revolution in an English county* (Cambridge, MA, 1983), ch, 4; Sarah Bendall, Christopher Brooke and Patrick Collinson, *A history of Emmanuel College Cambridge* (Woodbridge, 1999), pp. 188–95; Webster, *Godly clergy*, especially ch. 2.

34 K. W. Shipps, 'Lay patronage of East Anglian puritan clerics in pre-revolutionary England', Ph.D. thesis, Yale University, 1971, pp. 141–4; Barbara Donagan, 'The clerical patronage of Robert Rich', *Proceedings of the American Philosophical Society*, 120 (1976), 390–1; Holmes, *Eastern Association*, p. 19. In his count of puritan ministers, Dr Shipps seems to have included all ministers who did not suffer sequestration in the 1640s, this being 'an ex post facto test for puritan sympathies'. This makes unwarranted assumptions. In a study of 111 Essex parishes, I found evidence that 38 per cent of the incumbents in 1640 could be regarded as 'godly preaching ministers'. In contrast, when I sought to count the godly ministers of Cambridgeshire in the 1630s, I was able to identify only a few, no more than 5 per cent of the total. The two neighbouring counties were very different in this and many other respects: Graham Hart, 'The parish clergy of the diocese of Ely and their parishioners, c. 1630–1650', Ph.D. dissertation, University of Essex, 2015, pp. 55–8.

35 Smith, *Ecclesiastical history of Essex*, pp. 30–7; Webster, *Godly clergy*, pp. 151–4. The thirteen ministers who were articled against included three who feature in our manuscripts: John Jegon, Stephen Nettles and Gabriel Honifold: Cole MS, fos. 9–10, 49–52, 66–7.

36 Shipps, 'Lay patronage', p. 142; Holmes, *Eastern Association*, pp. 20–2, 28; for the Essex committees for scandalous ministers, see below, pp. xvii–xix, and Appendix 3, pp. lv–lxx.

Once in session in November 1640, the House of Commons appointed a committee to receive the flood of petitions demanding church reform and complaining about individual clergy. Its *rôle* included inquiring into the scarcity of preaching ministers and considering how scandalous ministers might be replaced by godly preachers who had been persecuted by the authorities in the previous decades. By June 1641, this committee for scandalous ministers had received some 900 petitions, and its chairman, Miles Corbett, claimed that they showed that the church was encumbered by a corrupt clergy.[37]

Progress in dealing with these and subsequent petitions was slow. Parliament had many priorities, and there were practical problems in organizing the hearing of complaints against individual ministers. The committee for scandalous ministers, re-established in December 1642 as the committee for plundered ministers, had no satisfactory mechanism for obtaining sworn testimony from the locality in question.[38] Witnesses had to attend the committee at Westminster and the cost and inconvenience of doing so deterred many from pursuing their complaint. Moreover, once the Civil War began, parliament did not have the means to enforce its wishes in large parts of the country. In November 1643, John White, who had chaired the commons' committee, published his account of the charges against 'the first century of scandalous and malignant priests'. This summarized 100 cases selected by him, no doubt with an eye to publicizing the worst offenders, from those which parliament had dealt with.[39] All of White's *First century* cases concerned parishes in London or counties close to it. The largest number, thirty, were drawn from Essex; Suffolk accounted for eighteen cases, Kent fifteen, Hertfordshire ten and London and Middlesex nine. The large number achieved in Essex may well have owed something to the uniformly godly character of the eight members of parliament representing the county and its boroughs, and particularly to Sir Thomas Barrington, who played a proactive part in the Westminster committee.[40] He and his Essex colleagues were well placed to apply pressure both locally, to encourage the submission of cases to parliament, and in parliament for these cases to be given priority. By the end of 1643, sixty or more Essex ministers, including the thirty listed in *First century*, had been sequestrated by parliament.[41] This large cull of episcopalian ministers affected the nature of the task remaining when the next stage of parliament's purge, under the earl of Manchester's commission, took place.

On 22 January 1644, parliament approved the ordinance which empowered the earl of Manchester, as commander of the Eastern Association, to act against scandalous ministers. It gave Manchester two distinct targets: the clergy of the seven counties of the Eastern Association, and, separately, the senior membership of the University of Cambridge.[42] Under the ordinance, Manchester carried out the purge

37 Fletcher, *Outbreak*, p. 111; *Proceedings in the opening session of the Long Parliament: House of Commons*, ed. Maija Jansson (7 vols., Rochester, NY, 2000–7), IV, 679.

38 For the complicated story of how the committee for scandalous ministers evolved, and in December 1642 was re-established as the committee for plundered ministers, see Vivienne Larminie and Stephen K. Roberts, 'Committees for religion', in *House of Commons 1640–1660*, I, 673–85.

39 John White, *The first century of scandalous, malignant priests, made and admitted into benefices by the prelates, in whose hands the ordination of ministers and government of the church hath been* (1643); McCall, *Baal's priests*, p. 71.

40 See below, p. xvii, for more on Barrington.

41 See Appendix 1 below.

42 '22 January 1644: An ordinance for regulating the University of Cambridge, and for removing of scandalous ministers in the seven associated counties', in *Acts and ordinances*, pp. 371–2. The ordinance was copied into the Cole MS at fos. 3–5 and is printed below.

between March 1644 and April 1645, when his commission as major-general of the Eastern Association came to an end.[43] Thereafter, the responsibility for decisions on scandalous ministers returned to the committee for plundered ministers, relying on local committees to provide the relevant testimony.

The Essex committees for scandalous ministers

Parliament's ordinance specified that the committees appointed by the earl of Manchester should consist of ten members, of whom any five or more should have power to act. They should be people who had already been appointed by parliament as deputy lieutenants or members of a commission (a committee or panel appointed by parliament to carry out such functions as taxation and sequestration).[44] For Essex, as for Suffolk, Manchester appointed two committees: one of the Essex committees consisted of men who came from the northern part of the county and heard cases concerning parishes there, the other of men mainly from the southern area, who dealt with cases arising in the south. Of the twenty members nominated by Manchester, five are not recorded as actually having sat to hear cases, while two men who were not named in Manchester's commission (Isaac Wincoll and Sir William Martin) did in fact sit as members. Appendix 3 at pp. lv–lxx below provides biographical notes on the twenty-two individuals.[45]

It is probable that the members of the committees were chosen after discussion between Manchester (perhaps acting through his chaplains, Simeon Ashe and William Good, whom he nominated as his channels of communication for the purge),[46] and Sir Thomas Barrington. Barrington was the acknowledged leader of parliament's supporters in the county; he chaired parliament's committee for Essex, and as member for Colchester he had already played a leading *rôle* in parliament in promoting religious reform. Immensely wealthy, Sir Thomas was related through his mother, Joan Cromwell, to Oliver Cromwell, John Hampden and Oliver St John. Through his membership of the Providence Island Company in the 1630s, Barrington had become a partner of Lord Saye and Sele, Lord Brooke, Benjamin Rudyerd and John Pym.[47] Barrington was also closely allied to Robert Rich, second earl of Warwick, the county's greatest landowner, patron of twenty-two of its parish livings, and appointed by parliament as its lord lieutenant in 1642. Barrington and Warwick had long worked together to shape the course of politics in Essex. At the outset of the Civil War, parliament had appointed Warwick admiral of its

43 For the problems of the Eastern Association in 1644–5 and the ending of Manchester's commission, see Holmes, *Eastern Association*, pp. 183–219. The north Essex committee for scandalous ministers met, probably for the last time, on 20 Mar. 1645, when they ordered one of their number, Henry Barrington, 'one of the sequestrators for the said county [of Essex]' to pay John Smith, clerk of the committee, £29 so that he could pay the members of the committee the money owed to them as fees (5s a day): TNA, SP 28/227, not foliated.

44 *Acts and ordinances*, pp. 371–2.

45 Please refer to the individual biographies for the references supporting the following discussion of the committee members.

46 Cole MS, fo. 7 and n. 9 thereon.

47 Chris R. Kyle, 'Sir Thomas Barrington, second baronet (c. 1585–1644)', *ODNB*; John Trevor Cliffe and Andrew Barclay, 'Sir Thomas Barrington', in *House of Commons 1640–1660*, III, 327–39.

fleet, but he was still active from time to time in the county's politics.[48] The earl of Manchester himself had long had a close relationship with Warwick: his second wife was Warwick's daughter, Anne, and after she died in 1642, Manchester married Warwick's niece, Essex.[49]

Few of the committee members appointed by Manchester had held important public office before the Civil War. But, as required by the ordinance, all had undertaken service for parliament in 1643, either as deputy lieutenants or as commissioners. Their recruitment to such work means that they were judged to be 'well affected' and were willing to serve in opposition to the king. In Essex, there does not seem to have been any shortage of recruits of good standing.[50] The Essex committees for scandalous ministers contained four knights, all of whom played active *rôles* in the purge. All the committee members were gentry; sixteen of the twenty-two had had a university education and thirteen had studied at one of the inns of court. Eighteen of them were currently or would soon become justices of the peace.

Two further characteristics of the Essex committees should be noted. Most (probably all) of the active members of the two committees were well known to each other before the purge began. Some indeed were kin; and most lived in the same area as the other members of their committee. Seven of the eight active members of the north committee lived in close proximity. Barnardiston, Thomas Cooke and Wincoll lived within a few miles of each other in the north-east of Hinckford hundred. Robert Crane, Richard Harlakenden and Sir Thomas Honywood lived in neighbouring parishes in Lexden hundred, a few miles to the east of the Hinckford cluster. Henry Barrington was the only member from Colchester, ten miles further east, where he led the puritan faction within the town's council. The north committee had no members from the north-east and north-west corners of the county. The relatively small area in which the north Essex committee men lived was one where puritanism had long flourished.[51] A leading figure in the north committee was Arthur Barnardiston. Uniquely, he attended every meeting for which the attendance is recorded, normally listed first in the record. His elder brother, Sir Nathaniel, living just over the boundary in Suffolk, was the leading figure in that county's support for religious reform and parliament's opposition to the king. The Barnardiston brothers had

48 Sean Kelsey, 'Robert Rich, second earl of Warwick (1587–1658)', *ODNB*; Donagan, 'The clerical patronage of Robert Rich', pp. 389–90; Arthur Searle, 'Introduction', in *Barrington family letters 1628–1632*, ed. Arthur Searle (Camden fourth series, vol. 28, 1983), pp. 7–8; Walter, *Understanding popular violence*, pp. 149–51.

49 Also in 1642, Warwick conveyed all his Essex advowsons to six trustees: Manchester, Lord Robarts, John Pym, Edmund Calamy, Stephen Marshall and Obadiah Sedgwick: Ian J. Gentles, 'Edward Montagu, second earl of Manchester (1602–1671)', *ODNB*; TNA, PROB 11/276/373.

50 In Essex, by early 1644 well over a hundred men had been appointed by parliament as commissioners or deputy lieutenants. In some counties, parliament had difficulty in finding people willing to act as sequestration commissioners. And Manchester apparently could not identify enough local men to populate the Cambridgeshire committee for scandalous ministers: *Acts and ordinances*, pp. 90–1, 112, 147, 169–70, 229, 243, 292; W. L. F. Nuttall, 'Sir Thomas Barrington and the puritan revolution', *Transactions of the Essex Archaeological Society*, third series, 2, part 1 (1966), 65 and 78 (n. 33); Holmes, *Eastern Association*, pp. 191–2; *Cambridgeshire scandalous ministers*, pp. 149–50.

51 One indication of this is the number of highly regarded puritan preachers who could be regularly heard in this area. In the 1630s and 1640s, they included Richard Blackerby, Samuel Fairclough, Daniel Rogers, Matthew Newcomen and Edmund Brewer: Jason Yiannikkou, 'Richard Blackerby (1574–1648)', *ODNB*; Barbara Donagan, 'Samuel Fairclough (1594–1677)', *ODNB*; Jason Yiannikkou, 'Daniel Rogers (1573–1652)', *ODNB*; Tom Webster, 'Matthew Newcomen (d. 1669)', *ODNB*; Smith, *Ecclesiastical history of Essex*, p. 40.

been brought up in a deeply puritan household. Castle Hedingham, where Arthur lived, and Gestingthorpe, the neighbouring parish where John Elliston lived, both provided a regular diet of puritan preaching.[52]

Kinship and neighbourhood were also factors in the membership of the south Essex committee. Two close relations of Sir Thomas Barrington played prominent parts. Sir Richard Everard of Great Waltham was Barrington's son-in-law, and William Masham was the son of Sir William Masham, member of parliament for Essex and the husband of Sir Thomas Barrington's sister, Elizabeth. Other very active members of the south Essex committee were Sir William Martin and Sir Henry Holcroft, both deputy lieutenants who were also playing leading *rôles* in the county committee under Barrington's chairmanship. As in the north, so in the south members of the committee lived in close proximity. There were no members at all from the south-eastern area of the county. Martin and Masham came from the west of the county, while Holcroft, Edward Birkhead, William Atwood, Carew Hervey Mildmay and John Wright all lived within a few miles of Romford; the latter three had ties of kinship.

Finally, the common bond between the members of the Essex Committees was their shared commitment to godliness and the reform of the church. Of the committee members who were still active in the county in 1647, sixteen were appointed to be elders in their local presbyterian classis, while three more (Robert Maidstone, John Elliston, and Henry Barrington) were almost certainly Independents.[53] No doubt the individual committee members had their own views about many issues, but they could unite in their rejection of the religious policies which the king and Archbishop Laud had promoted.

In summary, the two committees which the earl of Manchester appointed to carry out the purge of the Essex clergy were well qualified for their task. Supporters of parliament, committed to reform of the church and to establishing a godly preaching clergy, they enjoyed the confidence of Manchester, Warwick and Sir Thomas Barrington. Many of the members were related to other members or knew them well through the social and religious networks in the areas where they lived. The result was two cohesive committees which were able to act quickly and efficiently.

The process

Manchester appointed the two Essex committees on 26 February 1644. In sending them their commission, he enclosed instructions for the conduct of the purge.[54] The committees were to act against ministers who were scandalous in their lives or doctrines; non-resident and lazy ministers; and any who were ill-affected to parliament. Furthermore, where a minister was to be ejected, his parishioners should nominate a

[52] Edmund Brewer, the minister of Castle Hedingham, lectured there weekly, while Richard Blackerby lectured regularly at Gestingthorpe until 1648: Smith, *Ecclesiastical history of Essex*, p. 40; Yiannikkou, 'Richard Blackerby', *ODNB*.

[53] By 1647, John Wright was dead, and Edward Birkhead seems to have left the area. Sir William Martin may have become disenchanted with the parliamentary cause, but his absence from his local classis may have some other explanation.

[54] The commission and instructions sent to the north Essex committee are found at fos. 6–8 of the Cole MS, printed below at pp. 4–6.

replacement, who must be orthodox and able to gain the approval of the Westminster Assembly of Divines.[55] Anabaptists and antinomians were to be excluded.

As to procedure, Manchester instructed that the accused minister was not to be present when witnesses were heard, 'because of discountenancing the Witnesses and disturbing the Service', but the accused was to be offered the opportunity to have a copy of the depositions (on payment), to be allowed to comment on them in writing and to defend himself in person within fourteen days or so. The accusations and any defence offered by the accused were then to be sent to one of Manchester's chaplains for decision by Manchester.[56] The instructions emphasized Manchester's concern that the purge could fail because of the reluctance of parishioners to depose, either because they were 'Enemies to that blessed Reformation so much desired by the Parliament', or because they were influenced by gratitude for past favours over tithes. Manchester therefore ordered that the committees should summon some well-affected men within every hundred and encourage them to go out and identify ministers who deserved to be ejected.[57]

The instructions were sent under cover of a letter from Manchester which put strong moral pressure on the county committees: 'If a Generall Reformation follow not within your County, Assuredly the blame will be laid upon you; And you must expect to be called to Accompt for it, both here and hereafter'.[58] They certainly responded to this call to action, although, as will appear, there were obstacles to achieving the sort of clean sweep which Manchester's rhetoric implied.

Manchester turned his attention first to Cambridge University which puritans saw as a hotbed of Arminian theology and ceremonialism. As the setting in which half of the nation's clergy were educated, it too needed to be purged.[59] Manchester's method was simple and quick to produce results. College heads and fellows could be ejected either for non-residence or for failing to take the solemn league and covenant, the oath of loyalty to presbyterianism which in February 1644 parliament had imposed on all adult men. In a rapid and draconian process, over two hundred senior members of the university, about half of the total, were ejected.[60]

By early 1644, parliamentarians in Essex could feel that real progress had already been made. The hierarchy of the church had been swept aside, its disciplinary machinery dismantled, Laud's hated 'innovations' reversed. Over the last three years at least sixty of the county's parish clergy had been ejected and replaced by new 'godly preaching' ministers. Now the commission to Manchester and his committees in the eastern counties enabled further progress to be made.

55 The assembly had been set up by parliament in 1643 to revise the doctrine, liturgy and government of the church. It also had an important *rôle* as the body which vetted candidates for appointments as ministers. For the activities of the assembly, see *Minutes and papers of the Westminster Assembly 1643–1653*, ed. Chad Van Dixhoorn (5 vols., Oxford, 2012).

56 Cole MS, fo. 7.

57 *Ibid.*, fos. 7–8.

58 Bodleian Library, MS J. Walker c.6, fos. 17–18.

59 See David Hoyle, *Reformation and religious identity in Cambridge, 1590–1644* (Woodbridge, 2007), for a detailed account of the rise of Laudian/Arminian influence in the university in the years before the Civil War. Oxford University was beyond parliament's reach at this time: a purge was carried out there in 1647–8.

60 *Acts and ordinances*, pp. 376–8; John Twigg, *The University of Cambridge and the English revolution* (Woodbridge, 1990), *passim*, especially pp. 97–8, 293–6. See pp. 89–94 below for a transcript of Leicester MS 31's record of the university's purge.

The deponents

Manchester and his committees in the county were certainly keen to reform the clergy, but they needed the support of parishioners in order to identify the victims and supply the evidence against them. To succeed, the purge needed the co-operation of hundreds of ordinary people as well as strong leadership from parliament and gentry in the county. Study of the 336 deponents who gave evidence to the Essex committees shows that most were people of no great status about whom little is now known. Nevertheless some significant conclusions may be drawn about the deponents' gender, status and motivations.

Women played an important part in providing testimony for the purge in Essex. Fifty-two of the deponents (15 per cent of the total) were women. In the simultaneous purges in Cambridgeshire and Suffolk, women deposed less often, representing respectively 6 and 10 per cent of the deponents.[61] The Essex women made charges on a wide range of issues.[62] In three parishes, they testified to sexual harassment by the minister, either on the basis of their own experience or as reported to them by other women.[63] The charges now made against John Lake and William Frost harked back to previous proceedings against them in the 1630s (see pp. xxxiv–xxxv below). Some women gave evidence based on their experience as a servant. Elizabeth Coote said that she had often seen Joseph Bird, parson of Belchamp Otten, drunk in his own house: on one occasion he was 'so unquiett for Beere that his Wife and this Deponent fetchd a Barrell of Beere and sett it in the Chimney Corner by him to drinke what he pleased'. She also heard him swear often. Apparently, Bird attempted to discredit Coote's testimony by claiming that she had been convicted of fornication and theft before Mr Oliver Raymond, a local JP and member of the north Essex committee for scandalous ministers. Raymond was asked about this and stated that he was not aware of such a conviction.[64] Joan Dennis, a servant of John Jegon, rector of Sible Hedingham, joined with Andrew Bridge, also a servant, to accuse Jegon of swearing and of very seldom praying in his family or reading the scriptures to them. This accusation provoked Cole to anger against 'the villainy of those iniquitous Inquisitors' who encouraged servants to give evidence against their masters and to breach confidentiality.[65]

Most of the women deponents were giving evidence as parishioners who had heard the minister's sermons or witnessed the everyday events of parish life; sometimes they gave evidence with their husbands, but usually they were acting alone or in company with other parishioners, men and women. At Great Maplestead, Mary Laverick and Joane Fosset asserted that the minister, Edward Shephard, was not fitted for the ministry, having 'a very bad Utterance and … a weake memory'. They were supported by a separate statement that '16 women of his parish, some of good Sort, came to the Committee to desire a godly Minister, affirming Mr Shepard

[61] *Cambridgeshire scandalous ministers*, p. 17; *Suffolk scandalous ministers*, pp. 28–101.

[62] For a fuller discussion, see Amanda Flather, 'Gender, agency and religious change in early Stuart England', in *Popular culture and political agency in early modern England and Ireland*, ed. Michael J. Braddick and Phil Withington (Woodbridge, 2017), pp. 145–63, especially pp. 151–60.

[63] The ministers in question were John Lake of Great Saling, Cole MS, fo. 16; William Frost of Middleton, Leicester MS 31, fo. 18v; and Stephen Nettles of Lexden, Cole MS, fos. 51–2.

[64] Cole MS, fos. 33, 63; for Raymond, see p. lxii below.

[65] Cole MS, fos. 9–10.

altogether unfit to be a Minister'.[66] The women may well have heard about goings-on at the vicarage which came to court later, in summer 1645, when Shephard made charges of theft against Elizabeth Spurgeon, who had been a maidservant in his house. She denied the charges, and, with four parishioners, promoted an indictment of Shephard as 'a common barrator and disturber of the peace'. Both cases ended in acquittal, but not to the credit of Shephard. His evidence that Elizabeth had stolen money, linen and clothing was weak. She claimed that he had assaulted her sexually four times and paid her money to buy her silence, and that he beat himself with white rods, saying 'cannott I curbb this sinfull flesh of mine, I will curbbe this sinfull flesh of mine'. There is also evidence that during the hearing of the case, which took place in the house of Thomas Cooke JP, Shephard struck Spurgeon in the mouth, making her bleed.[67]

At Belchamp St Paul – a parish where, most unusually, almost half of the parishioners taking the protestation in 1642 were women – four of the eight deponents were women. Mary Sparke quoted from an argument which she had had with Robert Fisher, the vicar, about the lawfulness of the parliament's taking up arms. Arguing her case, she had cited a book 'written to that purpose', which provoked Fisher to blame her for reading so much for the parliament and so little for the king, and to quote from a book by Prince Rupert.[68]

Dr Cliftlands examined the status of the deponents in twenty-seven of the parishes where the ministers were articled against in 1644, and concluded that a quarter or more had held parish office or acted as jurors at quarter sessions or in the local manorial court; and study of the ship money assessments for 1636 suggests that more than half of the deponents had been rated as liable, though in the great majority of cases for comparatively small amounts.[69] In short, the middling sort played a big part in the process, but so also did a significant number of poorer people.

There were also cases where local gentry gave evidence. Two or possibly three members of the north Essex committee themselves testified. Oliver Raymond and Isaac Wincoll gave evidence in the case against Joseph Bird. Wincoll also deposed against Rowland Steward, perhaps motivated by the hope of promoting the prospects of John Collinges, his chaplain, who did in fact take over Steward's parish after its sequestration.[70] A similar motive may have encouraged John Meade to depose against Thomas Wilson of Debden, if the deponent John Meade was the north Essex committee member of that name, a gentleman from the nearby parish of Finchingfield. It seems likely that a plan was devised to replace Wilson in the rich living of Debden with Hugh Glover, Stephen Marshall's curate at Finchingfield: this was the outcome.[71] William Harlakenden, who gave evidence against William Evett, absentee minister of Little Yeldham, was also connected to the committee: he was a cousin of Richard Harlakenden, who heard the case, and a prominent member of Manchester's administration.[72]

66 Cole MS, fos. 12, 23.
67 ERO, Q/Sba 2/57, Q/SR 325/32 and /34; *Josselin diary*, p. 40.
68 Parliamentary Archives, HL/PO/JO/10/1/91/5; Cole MS, fos. 35–7.
69 William Cliftlands, 'The "well-affected" and the "country": politics and religion in English provincial society, c. 1640–c. 1654', Ph.D. thesis, University of Essex, 1987, pp. 244–6; ERO, T/A 42/1.
70 Cole MS, fos. 63 (Bird), and 11 n. 24 (Steward). For Raymond and Wincoll, see Appendix 3, pp. lxii–lxiii below.
71 Cole MS, fos. 69–70, and n. 147 there; for Meade, see Appendix 3, p. lxi below.
72 Leicester MS 31, fo. 15v; for the Harlakendens, see Appendix 3, p. lx below.

Bartholomew Wall was another gentleman who was active in the purge. He and his wife Margaret were prominent in pressing the case against William Frost of Middleton. Margaret deposed that she had been sexually harassed by Frost, while Bartholomew was a strong parliamentarian: another Middleton parishioner told the committee how Wall had persuaded the villagers to take the vow and covenant, despite the dire warnings of the minister. Wall also deposed against Edward Strutt of Faulkbourne, and he was nominated as a sequestrator of both livings.[73] Eight other people described as gentlemen gave evidence, but none of them was of high status or appears to have played a leading *rôle* in the purge.[74]

The number of deponents in each parish ranged from twenty-one at Great Bardfield and eighteen at Sible Hedingham to three at Southchurch and Little Yeldham and two at Heydon, with an average of nine. These numbers are similar to those found in the purges of Lincolnshire, Suffolk and Cambridgeshire, numbers which Ian Green considered to be strikingly small. He also suggested that a relatively high proportion of the witnesses had a grudge against their minister and that some ministers clearly enjoyed considerable support within their parish. He concluded that '"scandal" and "malignancy" often existed only in the eyes of a small and rather jaundiced group of beholders'.[75]

It seems likely that this was the situation in Sible Hedingham, where a relatively small group of radical people was determined to remove John Jegon. When the attempt was frustrated, they disrupted church services by violent protests, which probably lost them any support they had from the great majority of the parishioners.[76] But in other parishes, the opposition to the minister may well have been widespread, for a variety of reasons. The opposition to Christopher Newstead at Stisted had its basis in a distrust of a new minister who had been championed by Laud himself, amongst parishioners who had been served for many years by a succession of young and godly curates. A group of residents proved very active and persistent in their opposition to Newstead. In fact, they had very little direct experience of Newstead's ministry, but they obtained testimony from his previous parish of Abingdon (Berkshire) relating to his record there. When finally the parishioners succeeded in having Newstead sequestrated, they could not agree on who should replace him.[77] Again, it is clear that Thomas Newcomen and Gabriel Honifold would have found it difficult if not impossible to continue serving their Colchester parishes during the Civil War, given their reputation and the degree of mistrust, hatred even, which had been engendered against them.[78]

It is less easy to make sense of the deponents' behaviour at Little Maplestead, where six men of middling status tried to make a case against John Chamberlin, based on his fondness for the alehouse and his former compliance with Laud's altar policy. The evidence was not strong and the owner of the living may have

73 Cole MS, fos. 31–3, 37, 43–4, and Leicester MS 31, fo. 19v (Middleton); Cole MS, fos. 38–41, and Leicester MS 31, fos. 16v–17 (Faulkbourne). See especially Cole MS, fo. 32 n. 86, for Wall and his wife.

74 Cole MS, fos. 13, 29; Leicester MS 31, fos. 11, 12v, 14.

75 Green, 'Persecution', 520–1.

76 Six of the eighteen deponents against John Jegon at Sible Hedingham were charged in April 1645 with interrupting church services in protest at the failure of attempts to eject the rector: see Cole MS, fos. 9–10 and 21–2, and see below, pp. xliii–xliv.

77 See below pp. xlii–xliii and Cole MS, fos. 18–20, for more on Stisted.

78 For the unpopularity of Newcomen and Honifold, see pp. xxiv–xxv below.

refused to co-operate with a move to eject Chamberlin.[79] At any rate, he remained in Little Maplestead until in December 1646 he was successfully put forward for the vicarage of Bulmer, helped by testimonials from parishioners and clergy. Remarkably, two of the men who had deposed against him now confirmed that Chamberlin was 'a man of honest life and conversation and one that hath lived loveingly and peaceably amongst us dureing his abode with us … for the space of 15 or 16 yeares'. And Chamberlin's most effective sponsor for the Bulmer appointment was the godly minister Edmund Brewer, who went to some lengths to vouch for his soundness.[80] On appointment, Chamberlin signed the Essex Testimony in support of orthodox presbyterianism, and in 1650 he was found to be an able preaching minister.[81]

The purge gave parishioners of all stations a rare chance of getting rid of a minister they disliked, but it is usually impossible to be sure about the motives of individual deponents. Some had a history of conflict with the minister and may have been nursing a grudge.[82] Others no doubt were driven by a desire to ensure that in future the parish would be served by a competent and godly preaching minister. The purge was played out in the context of the personalities and the politics of the parish, varying from place to place, and influencing whether the minister was charged at all, and if so in what way and by whom.

The charges: absenteeism

In his instructions for the purge, Manchester had identified as targets any ministers who were non-resident, idle or lazy.[83] Eleven ministers were accused by their parishioners of not residing in their parish. Seven of them were pluralists who had chosen not to reside in the parish whose inhabitants were now seeking their sequestration. Four were sequestered from all the parish livings they held, while two were sequestered from one living but allowed to retain a second. Parliament was hostile to pluralism, and was successful in reducing the scale of it markedly by 1650; but it made sense to allow a pluralist to retain one living if he was thought able to give good service.[84] One of them, Edward Young, had organized his career in a responsible way to ensure that his parishes were well served.[85]

Four more ministers had simply been absent from their parish for a long period. Thomas Newcomen, minister of Holy Trinity and of St Runwald, Colchester, had

79 As explained at p. xlv below, the living was a donative, which under ecclesiastical law meant that the co-operation of the patron was required for the removal of the minister.

80 Parliamentary Archives, HL/PO/JO/10/1/219 (16 Dec. 1646).

81 *Lords Journal*, VIII, 615; Parliamentary Archives, HL/PO/JO/10/1/219 (16 Dec. 1646); Smith, *Ecclesiastical history of Essex*, pp. 108, 297. Chamberlin died in post in 1654: ERO, D/P 358/1/1.

82 Cliftlands, 'The "well-affected" and the "country"', pp. 231–2; Cole MS, fo. 45; Leicester MS 31, fos. 18, 19v (Margaret Wall).

83 Cole MS, fo. 8.

84 Harold Smith has a useful discussion of pluralism and non-residence at *Ecclesiastical history of Essex*, pp. 122–4. John Jarvis, Eliseus Burges, Walter Holmes and Thomas Wilson lost all their parish livings, while Joseph Long lost Fingringhoe but retained Great Clacton, and Edward Young lost Hadstock but retained Heydon: Cole MS, fos. 68–9 and 73–4; Leicester MS 31, fos. 10, 12v, 26v–27, 23, 30–31. William Jones of Ashen was apparently allowed to keep his living provided he appointed a curate chosen by the parish, an arrangement also applied to his Suffolk parish of Brantham: Smith, *Ecclesiastical history of Essex*, p. 302; Matthews, *Walker revised*, p. 156.

85 For Young's career, see Leicester MS 31, fo. 30 n. 87.

become notorious in the eyes of the godly for the part he had played in the 1630s in the prosecution of John Bastwick: he had also presented many parishioners for refusing to receive communion at the altar rails, including two local aldermen.[86] In August 1642, his activity as a minister in Colchester had come to an end when, acting as chaplain to Sir John Lucas, a local royalist, he played a prominent *rôle* in Lucas's plan to leave Colchester, taking with him men, arms and horses to support the king in the Civil War. A large group of parliamentary supporters thwarted this venture, in the process plundering Lucas's house and severely beating Newcomen. He was imprisoned by the town's authorities for his own protection and subsequently gaoled in London by parliament. He was released by order of the House of Commons on 24 December 1642, but presumably concluded that it was unsafe and unprofitable to try to resume his position in Colchester.[87]

Like Newcomen, Gabriel Honifold was a minister in Colchester who had become a hate figure in puritan circles. In 1642, his house was ransacked and he was forced to seek shelter in the town gaol. He decided to quit Colchester and leave his parish of St Mary Magdalen and its hospital of which he was Master in the hands of Samuel Cock, another local minister.[88] John Viccars, appointed rector of South Fambridge in 1640, was inclined to controversy throughout his interesting career. In December 1642, he took part in a protest aimed at persuading the common council of London to support a petition for peace, and was soon imprisoned by parliament. He remained in custody for several months, and parishioners complained that he never returned to the parish, supplying 'a knowne drunkard' as curate.[89] William Evett had been presented to the rectory of Little Yeldham in February 1643, on the death of the previous incumbent. The articles against him state that in the year or so since his presentation he had not taken up the service of the cure or appointed someone else to do so on his behalf, and claim that he had threatened parishioners who obeyed parliament. He was sequestrated.[90]

The charges: religious doctrine and practice

Many of the complaints made by parishioners were about their minister's churchmanship. Some Essex ministers were criticized on points of doctrine, rarely a ground of complaint in the neighbouring counties where the purge was also under way.[91] Thus, George Kindleton was said to teach that original sin is washed away in baptism, while Christopher Newstead was reported to have interrupted his own curate

86 *VCH Essex*, IX, 121–32; Smith, *Ecclesiastical history of Essex*, pp. 66–7, 413–16; Walter, *Understanding popular violence*, pp. 175–84.

87 Cole MS, fos. 71–2; Walter, *Understanding popular violence*, pp. 14, 152, 166. This was not the end of Newcomen's career as a minister: in November 1643, the earl of Salisbury, whose chaplain Newcomen had become, presented him to the living of Headbourne Worthy, Hampshire, and the appointment was approved by the House of Lords. Even more remarkably, in 1653, he was presented by Salisbury to the living of Clothall, Hertfordshire, and later approved by the triers: he held this living until his death in 1665: Webster, 'Matthew Newcomen', *ODNB*; *Lords Journal*, VI, 303.

88 Cole MS, fos. 66–7 and notes thereon.

89 G. J. Toomer, revised P. Auger, 'John Viccars (bap. 1604, d. 1653?)', *ODNB*; *Journals of the House of Commons*, III, 136; Leicester MS 31, fo. 11.

90 Cole MS, fo. 23; Leicester MS 31, fo. 15v.

91 For other counties, see *Suffolk scandalous ministers*, p. 19; *Cambridgeshire scandalous ministers*, p. 10; and McCall, *Baal's priests*, p. 88.

in mid-sermon when he preached that Christ's death was sufficient for all but not effectual to all: Newstead himself preached the next Sunday that Christ died for all, citing the catechism in the Book of Common Prayer.[92] Another common charge was that a minister favoured papists or their doctrines. George Crackenthorpe was said to preach that alms purge away sin and good works deliver from death. It was claimed that Newstead and Robert Guyon had said that papists might enter heaven, while John Jegon had allegedly preached that 'he saw little or no difference between the Papists and Us in Matters of Religion'.[93]

Ministers were also accused of decrying lay involvement in religious thought and debate, as when Jegon was alleged to have said that it was a pity that the bible had been translated into English, and Kindleton had taught that doctrine was the minister's business and that laymen should read the scriptures only so far as the creed, the Lord's prayer and the ten commandments. Gregory Holland allegedly preached that 'it was not fit for Farmers or Tradesmen to know the Mistery of their Salvation, but only for himself, and such as he was'.[94] Such remarks may or may not have reflected the considered opinion of the ministers who allegedly made them: but they certainly suggest a deep divide between some episcopalian clergy and a part of their parishioners – perhaps a small part, but a committed one – who were never going to accept the church's teaching without question. In attempting in the 1630s to silence such people and to force them to act against their conscience, Laud and his followers had stoked a fire which could not be put out. It is easy to understand the feelings of Robert Sida, a parishioner of Thomas Newcomen in Colchester, who complained in 1644 about Newcomen's response when Sida had asked him to omit the sign of the cross in baptizing his child. Newcomen had publicly ridiculed Sida's request, declaring 'We doe not receive this Child into the Congregation of Christ's Flock, neither doe [we] signe it with the Signe of the Crosse, in token that hereafter it shalbe ashamed to confesse the Faith of Christ crucified, and not manfully to fight against the World, the Flesh and the Divill, and not continue his faithfull Soldier.'[95]

The ceremonialist policies of Archbishop Laud had long been seen by the godly as popish and idolatrous and therefore a risk to the very survival of protestantism. Ceremonialism in the Laudian style was cited in the depositions against twenty-two of the thirty-nine Essex ministers charged in the Cole and Leicester manuscripts. The opening articles of the depositions against John Fenwick, rector of Chignal St James, list many such grievances:

1. Imprimis John Boosey and Edward Boosey of Chignall aforesaid yeomen sworne and examined depose that the saide Mr Fenwicke was very devout at all times to kneele at the Rales, and power [pour] out his devotion towards the East window of the church where was a picture of the Virgin Mary, and when he had soe done, he called up the Alehouse keeper to helpe him on with the surplice Tippett and Hood, then in the deske he reades in the service booke the Letany, and at the end of every Psalme he saith Glory be to the Father &c earnestly urging his people, both men and woemen and children to stand up, and answer him with a loud voyce (amen), saying he would have them answer him like a Thunder clapp, and used to bow at the name of Jesus.

92 Leicester MS 31, fo. 14; Cole MS, fo. 19.
93 Cole MS, fos. 14, 18, 25, 10.
94 Cole MS, fo. 10; Leicester MS 31, fo. 13v; Cole MS, fo. 65.
95 Cole MS, fo. 71.

2. John Empson and Sarah his wife depose that the said Mr Fenwicke did force his parishioners to come up to the raile to receive the sacrament saying he did not desire to leave a Puritan in his parish.[96]

The centrepiece of Laud's approach was the requirement that the communion table should be permanently placed at the east end of the chancel, 'altarwise' (that is, with the ends facing north and south), and enclosed by rails to protect it from intrusion by dogs or people who might profane it.[97] This policy was pressed on parishes in Essex from 1635, in the face of strong opposition from godly clergy and parishioners. Laud's foremost champion in Essex was Robert Aylett, who was both the official of the archdeacon of Colchester and the commissary of the bishop of London in Essex. By the end of 1635, Aylett had enforced the relocation and railing of altars in many parishes in the north of the county, where, for the most part, his jurisdiction lay. In 1636, he moved on to implement Laud's wish to ensure that all communicants received the sacrament kneeling at the rail: this was, as Fincham and Tyacke note, the most inflammatory and controversial policy of all.[98] It was pressed upon parishes and was generally implemented in the county, in some cases leading to parishioners being denied communion, and then excommunicated for not receiving, although Fincham and Tyacke incline to the view that Laud himself was willing to allow exceptions where the objector was motivated by genuine scruples.[99]

The opening of the Long Parliament brought rapid change. Laud's authority was undermined by his imprisonment and the king's speedy withdrawal of support; waves of iconoclasm, combined with pressure from parliament to reverse Laud's 'innovations' and the collapse of the ecclesiastical courts through which the church had enforced policy, ensured that by the end of 1643 few Essex parishes still had railed altars.[100] But memories of the disputes of the 1630s were still alive. Of the thirty-nine Essex ministers articled against in Manchester's purge, sixteen (41 per cent) were charged with having put pressure on parishioners to kneel at the rail for communion, usually by withholding the sacrament from those who refused to do so.[101] Similar proportions are found among the thirty Essex ministers listed by White in *First century*, and among the ministers of Cambridgeshire and Suffolk who were also victims of Manchester's purge.[102] I argue below (pp. xxxvi–xxxvii) that these charges in most, probably all, cases related to what the ministers had done in the 1630s; practice changed in the 1640s.

In Essex, as in other counties, ministers were accused of a range of ceremonial practices which were offensive to the godly, including bowing to the altar,[103] the

96 Leicester MS 31, fo. 1.

97 Fincham and Tyacke, *Altars restored*, especially chs. 4–6.

98 *Ibid.*, pp. 204, 210, 214.

99 *Ibid.*, p. 212.

100 For the rapid 'de-Laudianizing' of the church, see Milton, *Second reformation*, pp. 104–11; for the iconoclasm, see p. xxxvi below and n. 156.

101 Cole MS, fos. 9 (Jegon), 14 (Simpson), 15 (Lake), 17 (Clay), 25 (Guyon), 26 (Chamberlin), 31 (Frost), 35 (Fisher), 46 (Falconer), 65 (Holland), 71 (Newcomen), 73 (Cock); Leicester MS 31, fos. 1 (Fenwick), 14 (Kindleton), 23 (Long), 32 (Punter).

102 White, *First century*, pp. 2, 3, 5–6, 6, 7, 15, 19, 22, 30, 37, 45, 49, 49, that is thirteen ministers out of thirty (43 per cent); *Cambridgeshire scandalous ministers*, p. 11, where fifteen out of twenty-nine ministers are cited (52 per cent); *Suffolk scandalous ministers*, pp. 40, 42, 50, 57, 59–60, 64, 66, 68, 70, 71, 73, 74, 76, 81, 87, that is fifteen ministers out of thirty-eight (39 per cent).

103 Cole MS, fos. 12, 18, 60, 65, 70; Leicester MS 31, fos. 7, 8v, 13v. This controversial practice was not imposed by the church but was widely practised, and encouraged by Laud and his followers: Fincham and Tyacke, *Altars restored*, pp. 251–3.

reading of the communion service from the rails rather than the minister's desk[104] and the churching of women at or near the rails.[105] The godly also objected to the requirement, imposed on all by the canons of 1604, to bow at the name of Jesus, a charge levelled against seven ministers.[106]

Another frequent cause of complaint was the minister's record as a preacher, in the eyes of many puritan parishioners the most important aspect of his office. They wished to hear two sermons on Sundays, whereas the church regarded one as normal, and in 1629 royal instructions had ordered that afternoon sermons should be turned into catechizing by question and answer.[107] Five ministers were criticized for preaching only once a day. John Fenwick was said to have ordered his curate to preach but once a day, after people from a neighbouring parish had come to Fenwick's church to hear an afternoon sermon and had discouraged the local parishioners from observing the requirements to kneel and to stand at certain points in the service. Edward Strutt, on the other hand, having for years preached only once on Sundays, had apparently been persuaded to change his practice three months previously.[108]

Several ministers were said to be unprofitable preachers. Edward Shephard had 'a very bad Utterance' and a weak memory, and 'People delighted not to heare him, because he made no Application of his Doctrine and did not reprove Sin.' At Great Bardfield, Mary Wallis deposed that she could not 'edifie by Mr Mow', but when she went elsewhere to hear a better sermon, Mow punished her by the loss of her poor relief. Three ministers were accused of preaching against godly clergy. John Jegon was said to have preached against 'Professors in generall, terming them Spirit-mongers, Puritans, and People of phanaticall Spirits': in private, he had bitterly attacked by name the favourites of the godly, Stephen Marshall, Daniel Rogers, Edmund Brewer and Daniel Sutton. John Crosse of Gosfield was said to 'jeere and fleere' at godly ministers when they preached in his church and had tried to prevent a visiting preacher from praying extempore at the end of his sermon.[109] Some ministers were accused of hiring curates who were scandalous or who were poor preachers.[110]

Another cause for concern among the godly was observance of the Lord's day. In 1633, the king had issued a declaration which permitted recreational activities on Sundays after evening prayer. Some godly clergy had refused to promulgate this

104 Cole MS, fos. 17, 18, 26, 30. On those Sundays and holy days when communion was not celebrated, the first part of the communion service was read after morning prayer, and was commonly described as the 'second service'. Laudians insisted that the minister should read the second service standing by the communion table, as the prayer book required when communion was being celebrated. Puritans disagreed and wanted it read from the minister's desk, from where, they argued, it would be more easily heard: Fincham and Tyacke, *Altars restored*, p. 250.

105 Cole MS, fo. 18; Fincham and Tyacke, *Altars restored*, p. 251. For more information, including disputes at Saffron Walden about churching and its location, see *Cambridgeshire scandalous ministers*, pp. 36 and n. 36, 39 and n. 45, and 123 and n. 235.

106 Cole MS, fos. 9, 30, 70; Leicester MS 31, fos. 1, 7, 8v, 13v. Fincham and Tyacke suggest that the practice of bowing at the name of Jesus, though canonical, had been poorly observed and that it was Matthew Wren who, in a sermon before the king in 1628, set off a campaign to enforce its observance: *Altars restored*, p. 134.

107 Kenneth Fincham and Peter Lake, 'The ecclesiastical policies of James I and Charles I', in *The early Stuart church, 1603–1642*, ed. Kenneth Fincham (Basingstoke, 1993), pp. 38–41; *Visitation articles and injunctions of the early Stuart church*, II, ed. Kenneth Fincham (Church of England Record Society, V, 1998), pp. 37–8.

108 Leicester MS 31, fos. 1, 5, 17, 24, 26v.

109 Cole MS, fos. 12 and 22 (Shephard), fos. 62, 9, 31.

110 Cole MS, fos. 27, 37, 47; Leicester MS 31, fo. 5v.

'book of sports' (or sometimes 'book for liberty') to their parishioners, or had done so under protest. Ten years later, eight Essex ministers were charged with having read the book in church. John Crosse of Gosfield had read and commended the king's book, and when the parish's copy had been lost, he threatened the church-wardens with the High Commission because they had not bought a replacement. Five ministers were charged with either working on Sunday or tolerating the playing of games.[111]

The charges: politics

Thirty-five of the Essex ministers were charged with offences of a political nature, that is, of acting in a way which showed support for the king or, more often, opposition to parliament. Such people were, in parliament's terms, malignants. The most frequent accusation, made against twenty-four ministers, was that they had expressed such views, either from the pulpit or in conversation. Edward Strutt, rector of Faulkbourne, had enjoyed the hospitality of Sir Edward Bullock, lord of the manor, on new year's day 1643. Strutt had probably felt able to speak freely in Bullock's house of his rejection of parliament's actions, which, Strutt opined, made it 'as deepely guilty of Treason as the Earle of Strafford'.[112] John Mow, curate of Great Bardfield, was reported to have said that he had left his native Scotland in disgust at that nation's covenant of 1638, which could have required him to 'take upp Armes against my Prince which I ought not to doe, for [even] if he were not a religious King we ought not to take upp Armes, For the Weapons of the Church were Prayers and Teares'.[113] John Russell, rector of Chingford, was accused of constantly slighting parliament, and of having 'told the Under Collectors of his parish that if they obey such Ordinances of Parliament they were undone, askeing them if they did not see the kings proclamation to the contrary'. Russell also was said to have challenged the right of the earl of Manchester to discipline him; two other ministers, George Kindleton and Edward Strutt, had denied the legality of parliament's purge of the clergy.[114] Timothy Clay, rector of Wickham St Paul, asserted undying loyalty to the king, saying that 'he was sure that God made a king, but not a Parliament'.[115] Daniel Falconer, rector of Aldham, had apparently said that 'if ever the Tymes come to be as they have beene (as I hope they will) I will try a Suite with every one of those who are the Ceassers [assessors] and Collectors'. The deponent claimed that as a result 'some Persons have beene much discouraged in the Service to the Parliament'.[116] Edward Young, rector of Heydon, had preached that 'none ought to

[111] The charges concerning the book of sports and the observance of the sabbath, and the proportion of ministers so accused, are comparable to those found in Cambridgeshire and Suffolk. The Essex cases are at Cole MS, fos. 9–10 and 21 (Jegon), 15 (Simpson), 15 (Lake), 25 (Guyon), 27 (Jones), 30 (Crosse), 31 and 37 (Frost), 36 (Fisher), 45 (Falconer), 65 (Holland); Leicester MS 31, fos. 8v (Dove), 13v–14 (Kindleton). For the background, see Kenneth L. Parker, *The English sabbath: a study of doctrine and discipline from the Reformation to the Civil War* (Cambridge, 1988); and Alistair Dougall, *The devil's book: Charles I, the book of sports and puritanism in Tudor and early Stuart England* (Exeter, 2011).

[112] Cole MS, fo. 38. Bullock, unlike some of his guests, was a royalist: Llewellyn C. W. Bullock, *Memoirs of the Bullock family, A.D. 1166 to 1905* (Rugby, 1905), pp. 31–2.

[113] Cole MS, fo. 56.

[114] Leicester MS 31, fos. 6v–7, 14; Cole MS, fo. 40.

[115] Cole MS, fos. 17–18.

[116] Cole MS, fo. 46.

take up the sword, except he be commanded by the king'.[117] John Russell had objected strongly to paying taxes to parliament but he was not charged with actually refusing to pay them, unlike four other ministers.[118]

Further evidence of a minister's political allegiance could be based on his response to instructions given to him to read out in church orders from parliament or proclamations from the king. John Russell was adamant that he would not read parliament's ordinances in church, 'noe not he, he would curse them with bell, booke and candle'. Robert Fisher, vicar of Belchamp St Paul, was alleged to have 'published a Declaration that came from the King about a yeare since very audibly and distinctly; but at the same Time he read an Ordinance that came from the Parliament with a low Voyce, and read but Part of it'.[119]

Eleven ministers were accused of failing to observe in a proper manner the fast days which parliament had ordered for the last Wednesday of every month.[120] Stephen Nettles, minister of Lexden, was said to fail to give notice of fast days, while on the day itself he preached badly at the morning service, went home to dinner with guests and then went drinking in the tavern or in private houses.[121]

From early in its life, the Long Parliament had sought to engage the support of the people against the king by obtaining their assent to a series of oaths. The first step was the protestation, taken by parliament in May 1641 and widely taken in parishes in early 1642. This was followed in some counties, including Essex, by an attempt to bind individuals into an association (late 1642); by the vow and covenant of summer 1643; and by the solemn league and covenant in early 1644.[122] This sequence of oaths faced every parish minister with repeated tests of his attitude towards the parliamentary cause. The protestation was drafted in a way which enabled the great majority of ministers to subscribe, although many were no doubt suspicious of where it was leading. In particular, it bound the taker to support both king and parliament; some parliamentarians argued, and continued to claim even after the Civil War began, that the enemy was not the king but his evil counsellors. Among the Essex ministers in our manuscripts, only John Fenwick was reported to

117 Leicester MS 31, fo. 30v.

118 Leicester MS 31, fos. 6v–7 (Russell), 5 (Gouldman), 10 (Burges), 11v (Viccars); Cole MS, fo. 65 (Holland).

119 Leicester MS 31, fo. 6v; Cole MS, fo. 36. The king's practice of ordering some proclamations to be read in church is discussed in Lloyd Bowen, 'Royalism, print and clergy in Britain, 1639–1640 and 1642', *Historical Journal*, 56 (2013), 297–319.

120 Cole MS, fos. 11, 21, 25, 49; Leicester MS 31, fos. 1v, 3, 5v, 8v, 10, 23, 32. On the fast days ordered by parliament, all were required to attend church for special services and sermons, to refrain from secular work and recreation and to eat and drink in moderation: *Acts and ordinances*, pp. 22–4. The aim of these 'days of humiliation', called in times of national crisis, was to express repentance and to seek God's mercy. Regular fast days fell on the last Wednesday of every month, and additional days were designated from time to time, to mark special occurrences. Days of thanksgiving also involved church services, as well as secular celebrations: Christopher Durston, 'For the better humiliation of the people: public days of fasting and thanksgiving during the English revolution', *The Seventeenth Century*, 7 (1992), 129–49; *National prayers: special worship since the Reformation*, I: *Special prayers, fasts and thanksgivings in the British Isles, 1533–1688*, ed. Natalie Mears, Alasdair Raffe, Stephen Taylor and Philip Williamson (with Lucy Bates) (Church of England Record Society, 2013), especially pp. lv–lvi, lxxxv–lxxxvi.

121 Cole MS, fo. 49.

122 For detailed discussion of these oaths, see Edward Vallance, *Revolutionary England and the national covenant: state oaths, protestantism and the political nation* (Woodbridge, 2005), especially pp. 51–60 and 107–29; and John Walter, *Covenanting citizens: the protestation oath and popular political culture in the English revolution* (Oxford, 2017).

have expressed doubt about the protestation, and that was tongue-in-cheek, when he advised a puritan parishioner not to take the protestation because he would thereby be supporting ceremony in church.[123]

Soon after the outbreak of the Civil War, petitions for peace were being drawn up and canvassed. These were dismissed by the parliamentarians in Essex as a royalist device and insincere or 'pretended'. In London on 12 December 1642, a crowd of petitioners interrupted a meeting of the city's common council with demands for peace. John Viccars, rector of South Fambridge, was alleged to be a promoter of this 'mutinous' petition. He suffered imprisonment as a result.[124] A little later, a group of Essex gentry organized their own petition for peace for submission to parliament and to the king. Robert Fisher, John Mow and Edward Young were charged with having tried to persuade their parishioners to sign this petition.[125] It attracted considerable support from clergy in the county: the first subscribers listed were twelve doctors of divinity, including Edward Young. Other Essex ministers who signed the petition included Dr John Gauden, recently appointed rector and dean of Bocking, George Crackenthorpe of Bradwell by Coggeshall and Edward Strutt of Faulkbourne.[126] The laity also supported the petition, led by twenty baronets and knights and sixty-three esquires. This did not deter the earl of Warwick from dismissing the petition's subscribers as 'the slightest part of the country, and men of no religion or credit'.[127]

In December 1642, parliament ordered the counties of Essex, Hertfordshire, Cambridgeshire, Suffolk and Norfolk to form the Eastern Association for mutual defence against the king's forces.[128] To promote the Association, parliament ordered its county committees to convene meetings at which individuals would take an oath of association and contribute arms or money to the war against the king. There is little evidence as to how widely the oath was actually taken. In Essex, which was the county most forward in promoting the association, only two Essex ministers, Simon Lynch and Francis Gouldman, were accused of refusing to associate: in Cambridgeshire, four ministers were so accused, and in Suffolk seven.[129]

In June 1643, reacting to a royalist attempt to gain control of the city of London, parliament took 'a sacred vow and covenant' which it recommended should be subscribed throughout the nation. This committed the subscriber to supporting the parliamentary forces and omitted to reassert parliament's previous claims to be defending the king's honour and person.[130] There is considerable doubt about how widely the vow and covenant was taken throughout England. For Essex, there are

123 See Leicester MS 31, fo. 1v and n. 6 for Fenwick's argument.

124 See Leicester MS 31, fo. 11, and see above, p. xxv.

125 Holmes, *Eastern Association*, p. 42; Cole MS, fos. 37, 58; Leicester MS 31, fo. 31.

126 Parliamentary Archives, HL/PO/JO/10/1/141, fos. 22, 28. For Dr Gauden, see Bryan D. Spinks, 'John Gauden (1599/1600?–1662)', *ODNB*.

127 Holmes, *Eastern Association*, pp. 42–3; *Lords Journal*, V, 530.

128 Holmes, *Eastern Association*, pp. 62–8; *Acts and ordinances*, pp. 51–2; *Lords Journal*, V, 506–7; *Commons Journal*, II, 942. Huntingdonshire and Lincolnshire were added to the Association in 1643: *Acts and ordinances*, pp. 242–5, 291–8.

129 Holmes, *Eastern Association*, pp. 64–6; Vallance, *National covenant*, pp. 53–5; Leicester MS 31, fos. 3v and 5; *Cambridgeshire scandalous ministers*, pp. 57, 62, 67, 82; *Suffolk scandalous ministers*, pp. 20, 29, 36, 38, 41, 49, 72, 79.

130 S. R. Gardiner, *History of the Great Civil War 1642–1649* (4 vols., 1894), I, 149; Michael Braddick, *God's fury, England's fire* (2008), pp. 291–93; *Commons Journal*, III, 147; Vallance, *National covenant*, pp. 115–18.

extant returns showing that it was taken in eight parishes; our manuscripts show that in eleven more the minister was accused of refusing it or of trying to dissuade parishioners from taking it.[131] In most cases, their stated reason for refusal was that they had previously taken oaths of loyalty to the king (for example in the protestation) which the vow and covenant dishonoured and would thus, if they took it, make them forsworn. Raboshire Dove, the minister at Foulness, stated his position from the pulpit: 'the people might take it if they would, it was all one with the protestation, onely here was the difference, that was for the king and Parliament, this was for the Parliament against the king'. The result, in Foulness and many other parishes, was that it was not taken at all.[132] In the small parish of Middleton, William Frost argued strongly against the vow and covenant and it was only after the intervention of the parish's leading figure, Bartholomew Wall, that the oath was taken.[133] And where it was taken, some ministers expressed their reservations: for example, Edward Shephard, after once refusing to take it, later did so 'with these Limitations, so far as it was agreable to the Word of God, and not contrary to the former Protestation and Oath of Allegiance'.[134] On 25 July 1643, Sir Richard Everard wrote to Sir Thomas Barrington, noting that the oath was being widely refused 'in our parts'; it appears that the leading parliamentarians did not press the matter in parishes where there was resistance.[135]

Soon, however, driven by the need to agree a treaty with Scotland which delivered the support of a large Scottish army, parliament moved on and adopted the solemn league and covenant. It was taken by both houses in September 1643 and imposed nationally by an ordinance in February 1644. This covenant bound the parties to preserving the Scottish church in its presbyterian form and to reforming the Church of England 'according to the example of the best reformed churches'. This then was a commitment to abolish episcopacy, with all the hierarchy and disciplinary machinery of the Church of England. This new covenant also promised to preserve the rights and privileges of the parliaments of England, Scotland and Ireland, but also 'to preserve and defend the king's majesty's person and authority, in the preservation of the true religion and liberties of the kingdom'.[136] In early 1644, the pressure on the clergy of Essex to take the solemn league and covenant was intense. How they responded will be discussed below (pp. xxxvii–xxxviii).

131 J. Gibson and A. Dell, *The protestation returns 1641–42 and other contemporary listings* (Bury, 2004), p. 34; Cole MS, fos. 13 (Shephard), 14 (Crackenthorpe), 20 (Newstead), 28 (Jones), 39 (Strutt), 42 (Hull), 43–4 (Frost), 49 (Nettles), 57 (Mow); Leicester MS 31, fos. 9 (Dove), 31v (Punter). Clive Holmes noted that the evidence from Suffolk suggests that efforts were made to impose the vow and covenant there more widely than previously suspected, and that thirteen Suffolk ministers were charged with discouraging their parishioners from taking the oath: *Suffolk scandalous ministers*, p. 21.

132 Leicester MS 31, fo. 9.

133 Cole MS, fo. 43.

134 *Ibid.*, fo. 14.

135 Vallance, *National covenant*, p. 118; cf. Cole MS, fo. 39, where it is said that following the objections of influential clergy such as John Gauden and Samuel Collins, 'the said Vow and Covenant was called in againe'.

136 *The constitutional documents of the puritan revolution 1625–1660*, ed. S. R. Gardiner (Oxford, 1906), pp. 267–71; *Lords Journal*, VI, 411.

The charges: immorality

Nineteen of the Essex ministers faced charges related to drinking. In some cases, the charges were vague and did not allege that the minister himself drank to excess. It was enough that John Jarvis was a 'Man of very idle Conversation, being a great Frequenter of Ale-houses, and associates himself with Drunkards and prophane persons'. Some indeed found alehouses inherently wicked and they felt able to accuse John Jegon, who probably never went there, of being 'an Upholder of Alehouses in his Parish, reproving in his Sermon the Officers that would have suppressed them'. But the Essex committees also heard about some ministers who, if the deponents were telling the truth, did have a serious problem with drink. Timothy Clay was said to have 'layne out drinking 7 or 8 Dayes till he was distempered to Distraction': his doctor sent him word that he would be stark mad if he did not stop drinking sack. John Lake and William Frost had to be helped home by parishioners after becoming drunk during a night out at Braintree or Sudbury. Simon Lynch of Runwell was said to be a common haunter of alehouses, who kept company with common swearers and was often drunk. Edward Turner deposed that he witnessed Lynch and his clerical friend Mr Thorpe drinking and smoking in a ditch behind an alehouse in Runwell, with one captain Chester: they were drinking there because Chester had sworn not to enter the alehouse for a year. The south Essex committee noted that when Lynch appeared before them 'he was very farre in drinke and smelt soe that he was very offensive to some of us and being charged with it he confessed he had beene drinking and takeing Tobaccoe'.[137] Three-quarters of the ministers who were accused of drinking were also accused of swearing. The charge was usually that they had sworn 'by my faith and troth', an oath so mild that John Fenwick claimed it did not amount to swearing at all.[138] Some drinkers were also accused of keeping unsuitable company, with people of low status ('lewd') or with papists.

Four ministers were charged with gaming. Ambrose Foulsham deposed that Stephen Nettles frequented the house of Roger Warren, whose wife was a woman of easy virtue: Foulsham had seen eight or ten packs of cards at Warren's house, and people playing cards there.[139] Perhaps most shocking of all, Nettles and four other ministers were accused of sexual offences. Against Nettles and William Frost, the deponents included women victims of unwanted sexual advances and assaults who gave evidence at some length and in graphic detail.[140]

Finally, a number of charges were made claiming that the accused minister had behaved in ways which were unneighbourly or downright hostile towards parishioners. Disputes over tithes lay behind enmity between parishioners and John Mow, curate at Great Bardfield: he was also said to have withheld poor relief from a widow who gadded to other churches to hear sermons. Daniel Falconer had made

137 Cole MS, fos. 10 (Jegon), 11 (Steward), 13 and 28 (Crackenthorpe), 15–16 and 53–4 (Lake), 17 (Clay), 26 (Chamberlin), 31–2 and 45 (Frost), 33–5 and 63 (Bird), 41–2 (Hull), 47–8 (Falconer), 49–50 (Nettles), 66 (Holland), 68 and 74 (Jarvis); Leicester MS 31, fos. 1v (Fenwick), 3–3v (Lynch), 7 (Russell), 8v–9 (Dove), 23 (Long), 31v (Punter).

138 Leicester MS 31, fo. 1v.

139 The ministers accused of gaming were Steward (Cole MS, fo. 11), Nettles (*ibid.*, fo. 50), Honifold (*ibid.*, fo. 67) and Russell (Leicester MS 31, fo. 6v).

140 Charges of a sexual nature were made against Steward (Cole MS, fo. 12), Lake (*ibid.*, fo. 16), Clay (*ibid.*, fo. 17), Frost (*ibid.*, fos. 32, 37 and 43–4) and Nettles (*ibid.*, fos. 50–2).

free with other people's property and had refused to bury a godly young man who had gone to hear preaching at other places.[141]

The charges: evaluation

More than half of the ministers responded to the invitation to answer the charges.[142] These answers were considered by the county committee concerned and passed on to the earl of Manchester for consideration along with the depositions, but they were not included in the manuscripts which have come down to us. Some ministers may have conceded that they had conformed to the Laudian policies or that they had read a royal proclamation in church, but argued that they were obeying the instructions of legitimate authority and had no case to answer.[143] No doubt many responders also challenged the truth of the charges, which sometimes led the committee or Manchester to make further inquiries before reaching a decision.[144]

Without the ministers' responses, doubts inevitably arise since we have only one side of the evidence. Nevertheless, there is no doubt at all that very large numbers of the parish clergy in the 1630s had conformed to the bishop's instructions regarding, for example, the reading of the book of sports, the position and railing of the communion table, and reception there. But, as discussed below (at pp. xxxvi–xxxvii), it is probable that once the Long Parliament launched its attack on Laud and his programme, most ministers in Essex quickly gave up any attempt to keep it alive. In short, the charges made in 1644 relating to Laudian practices look plausible but usually related to events of the 1630s rather than to more recent practices. In contrast, the charges of malignancy (opposing parliament or supporting the king) must refer to what would have been more recent events, since the opening of the Long Parliament. Here, too, there is nothing implausible about accusations that many ministers opposed the policies being pursued by parliament, especially those aimed at destroying episcopacy. The charges of immorality may sometimes have been based on village gossip rather than first-hand evidence, and may say as much about the accuser as about the accused. Some deponents were ready to criticize any minister who entered an alehouse, even if there was no evidence of drunkenness. Some other charges are examples of the minor problems in personal relationships that commonly occur between neighbours. Nevertheless a small number of the accused ministers had a serious case to answer, mostly relating to drink and sexual misconduct. It is hard to believe that detailed and circumstantial evidence such as that against Simon Lynch of Runwell was fabricated.[145] And some of the accused ministers had previous form. William Frost of Middleton, now charged with

141 Cole MS, fos. 59, 47–8.

142 It is clear from statements in the two manuscripts that answers had been received from many ministers: see for example the entries at the top of the articles against Jegon and Steward at Cole MS fos. 9 and 11, and at the end of the articles against Fenwick and Lynch at Leicester MS 31, fos. 2 and 4.

143 There is no record in the Essex manuscripts of anyone actually replying in the manner of Samuel Lindsell, rector of Stratford St Mary, Suffolk, who appeared before the east Suffolk committee on 2 April 1644. Charged with ceremonialism and royalism (but not immorality), Lindsell 'confessed the articles to be true in the substance of them': *Suffolk scandalous ministers*, p. 38.

144 For example, Joseph Bird evidently challenged the evidence given against him by Elizabeth Coote and the committee subsequently heard that part at least of his defence was false: Cole MS, fos. 33 and 63.

145 Leicester MS 31, fo. 3.

drunkenness, adultery and pestering women with unwanted attention and assaults, had been charged in 1635 in the High Commission with drunkenness, incest with his wife's sister, Anne Howell (or Hovell) and adultery with two maidservants. The drink charge was proved. The other charges were not proved and Frost had purged himself with the support of eight compurgators, all of them clergy, five of whom had Essex parishes: one of them was John Lake of Great Saling.[146] Lake himself was charged in 1644 with being a drunkard and 'notoriously vile in attempting the Chastity of divers of his Mayds': four women accused Lake of attempting to persuade or force women to have sex with him. In 1637, Lake had been charged with a common fame of incontinency with Bridget Cante lately of Great Saling and Elizabeth Carter of Felsted, who were among the deponents against him in 1644. In the 1637 case, Lake appears to have escaped punishment, claiming in court that he had already been cleared of the charge at a previous hearing in which he had purged himself by oath.[147] In the church courts, it must have been difficult for aggrieved parishioners to obtain satisfaction against the word of their own parish minister, and it would not be surprising if a number of offenders escaped conviction until the 1640s when, for the time being, the tables were turned.[148]

The clergy

The thirty-nine ministers who were articled against in our two manuscripts represented some 10 per cent of the county's parish clergy. Almost all of them can be identified as graduates of either Oxford or Cambridge University. At least thirty-two held the degree of MA and eight had progressed to BD, DD or in one case DCL. Seven of the thirty-nine had been fellows of an Oxford or Cambridge college.[149] The great majority of the ministers were resident in their parishes: seven were pluralists who did not live in the parish which sought their sequestration.[150] Nearly all the ministers were between forty and sixty years of age, with only two in their thirties and six over sixty. The majority were married men, usually with children to support. The income of the thirty-six livings for which information is available ranged from two parishes at £25 a year to two at over £200 a year. The average income (median and mean) was a respectable £80 a year.[151] In these respects, the victims of Manchester's purge represented a fairly typical group of the county's clergy.

146 Cole MS, fos. 31–3, 37, 43–5, and Leicester MS 31, fos. 18–19v; TNA, SP 16/261, fos. 291v–292r; Smith, *Ecclesiastical history of Essex*, p. 48.

147 Cole MS, fos 15–16, 53–55; Smith, *Ecclesiastical history of Essex*, p. 48; ERO, D/ABA 8, fo. 142.

148 The objectivity of the court might be particularly questioned if the official presiding or the compurgators were fellow ministers of the accused, as in the case of Frost. For the system, see for example Martin Ingram, *Church courts, sex and marriage in England, 1570–1640* (Cambridge, 1987).

149 Twenty-nine ministers can be identified as Cambridge graduates, and seven as from Oxford. John Mow, curate of Great Bardfield, stated that he had recently migrated from Scotland and seems to have held the degree of MA from King's College Aberdeen. The remaining two ministers may also have been graduates but a definite attribution cannot be made. Six of the seven who had held fellowships had done so at Cambridge.

150 See p. xxiv and n. 84 above for more about these pluralists.

151 Christopher Hill estimated that the average income for Essex livings in 1650 was £85 a year for rectories and £50 for vicarages: Christopher Hill, *Economic problems of the church: from Archbishop Whitgift to the Long Parliament* (Oxford, 1956), p. 111.

On questions of religion and politics, however, the clergy of Essex were divided. A third or more of the county's parish clergy in 1640 were godly ministers who opposed the policies of Laud and the king.[152] Some of them had faced prosecution and the threat of deprivation in the preceding years and were eager for change. The majority of their fellow ministers were committed to the episcopal government of the church and had conformed to its orders, though some had surely been troubled by the challenge of implementing the Laudian policies against the sincere opposition of some of their parishioners. As Ian Green points out, the majority of the victims of the purge had completed their university education and the early years of their ministry before the Laudian policies were enforced, and for these men the innovations 'must have been as much of a deviation from the norm as they were for the laity'.[153] Whatever their views, the lives of these episcopalian ministers were to be profoundly affected by the actions of the Long Parliament and of local godly activists.[154]

An early issue for these clergy was whether they should continue to require their parishioners to kneel at the altar rail to receive communion.[155] In many parishes, the issue was pre-empted by unofficial action, as soldiers or local activists took matters into their own hands, taking down and destroying the altar rails. In the period leading up to the Civil War, nearly a hundred Essex churches may have been subject to this form of iconoclasm.[156] In the early months of the Long Parliament, clergy had little encouragement from their official leadership to stand up for the Laudian programme.[157] In September 1641, the House of Commons approved an order, subsequently rejected by the Lords, but nevertheless widely propagated, which required churchwardens to take down the rails and move the communion table from the east end of the church. This was acted on in many parishes, despite its doubtful legal status. By August 1643, when an ordinance of parliament was passed confirming the requirement, it is most unlikely that communion was being celebrated in the Laudian style in more than a few Essex parishes.[158] It is significant that in the sixteen cases recorded in our two manuscripts in which the minister is accused of having enforced reception of communion at the rail, no date for this action is specified. This also applies to the thirteen similar cases recorded in *First century*.[159] It is probable that all these charges refer to the minister's actions in the 1630s: certainly there is no suggestion in any of the texts of 1644 that the minister was still putting or had recently put pressure on parishioners to receive

152 Above, p. xv.

153 Green, 'Persecution', 529.

154 In describing these clergy as 'episcopalian', and in much else, I follow Fincham and Taylor, 'Episcopalian identity, 1640–1662'.

155 See p. xxvii above for the policy.

156 John Walter, 'Popular iconoclasm and the politics of the parish in eastern England, 1640–1642', *Historical Journal*, 47 (2004), 261–90, and especially 266–7. For the background, see Margaret Aston, *England's iconoclasts*, I: *Laws against images* (Oxford, 1988), and *Broken idols of the English Reformation* (Oxford, 2016); Julie Spraggon, *Puritan iconoclasm in the English Civil War* (Woodbridge, 2003); *The journal of William Dowsing: iconoclasm in East Anglia during the English Civil War*, ed. Trevor Cooper (Woodbridge, 2001).

157 Anthony Milton, 'Anglicanism and royalism in the 1640s', in *The English Civil War: conflicts and contexts, 1640–49*, ed. John Adamson (Basingstoke, 2009), pp. 63–5.

158 *Commons Journal*, II, 279 (1 Sept. 1641), and II, 283 (8 Sept. 1641); *Lords Journal*, IV, 295 (9 Sept. 1641); *Acts and ordinances*, pp. 265–6; Fincham and Tyacke, *Altars restored*, pp. 276–7; Milton, 'Anglicanism and royalism in the 1640s', p. 67.

159 See p. xxvii nn. 101 and 102 for these cases.

communion in the Laudian manner. If this had been the case, it would surely have been flagged: contrast the cases of John Russell and Raboshire Dove who were both accused in 1644 of *still* bowing towards the communion table and at the name of Jesus (small acts of defiance which did not involve any co-operation by parishioners); and of Simon Lynch who was reported to be *still* using the Book of Common Prayer.[160] Nor do the Essex texts contain any accusations that a minister had attempted to prevent the removal of altar rails following parliament's orders to that effect, or to protest against or reverse the act of removing the communion table from the east end of the chancel. Such charges were made against several ministers in Suffolk and Cambridgeshire.[161] While there were some ministers in the eastern counties who continued to fight for the Laudian style to be implemented in their parishes, few if any were still serving in Essex by 1644. Laudians of the stamp of Richard Drake of Radwinter had already been driven out.[162] Many of those who survived in office until 1644 had begun to adapt to the new regime: for example, George Kindleton of Magdalen Laver had ceased to insist that women wishing to be churched should be veiled, while Edward Strutt had begun to preach twice on Sundays.[163]

The Laudian 'innovations' quickly fell into abeyance but episcopalian clergy had much else to be concerned about. The very institution of episcopacy was now under threat. As the country descended into civil war, it took courage in Essex to speak out for bishops or for the king, let alone to organize and promote the petition for peace, or denounce the vow and covenant. The evidence discussed at pp. xxxi–xxxii above suggests that many Essex clergy did protest. But by the end of 1643, the penalty for doing so had become too high for most. The sequestration of royalist ministers by parliament had already become a common event, and it was clear that all who now refused to take the solemn league and covenant faced that outcome. At the outset of his purge, the earl of Manchester made it clear that members of the University of Cambridge who refused the oath would be ejected, and they were.[164] The ordinance which commissioned Manchester's purge also specifically empowered him and his committees to administer the oath. It seems probable that in their hearings of evidence the committees examined ministers' attitude to the covenant, as John White, chairman of the committee for plundered ministers, had done in determining the case against Daniel Whitby.[165] It is therefore interesting that only two of the ministers who appear in our manuscripts, George Kindleton and Edward Young, were accused of having refused to take the oath. A few others may have done so: Simon Lynch was accused of discouraging his parishioners from taking it, Raboshire Dove may have failed to take it at Chelmsford, and Samuel Cock of St Giles, Colchester, was said to have failed to provide his parish with information

160 Leicester MS 31, fos. 7, 8v, 3v.

161 The depositions against scandalous ministers in Cambridgeshire cite five cases, and in Suffolk six: *Cambridgeshire scandalous ministers*, pp. 67, 70, 71, 76, 94–6; *Suffolk scandalous ministers*, pp. 50, 64, 73, 79, 81, 87.

162 After protracted bitter conflict with his parishioners, Drake was forced out of his parish in January 1643: John Walter, '"Affronts and insolencies": the voices of Radwinter and popular opposition to Laudianism', *English Historical Review*, 122 (2007), 35–60.

163 Leicester MS 31, fo. 13v; Cole MS, fo. 39.

164 Twigg, *The University of Cambridge*, pp. 90–102, especially pp. 96–7. An early case of ejection for refusing the covenant is that of Stephen Hall, on 15 March 1644: Leicester MS 31, fo. A3v.

165 Cole MS, fos. 4–5; Matthews, *Walker revised*, p. 168, quoting Whitby's *Vindication*: BL, Thomason Tracts, E.40[34].

about it. But John Mow, who had been outspoken in his support for the king, had surely taken the solemn league and covenant by November 1644, when the articles against him were submitted: a failure to do so would certainly have been cited against him.[166] Comprehensive evidence about the taking of the oath is lacking, but the small number of ministers charged with refusing it suggests that many of the episcopalians who had thus far escaped sequestration decided to subscribe in the hope of continuing to hold their living.

Reluctant takers of the oath might well resort to evasive tactics, as many puritan clergy had done in the preceding decades when pressed to conform to the church's requirements. A common device was to qualify the commitment to carry out one's obligations under the oath by the formula 'as far as I lawfully may', or 'so far as it is agreeable to the word of God'.[167] A more elaborate approach may have been adopted by John Russell of Chingford. Two godly Essex ministers gave evidence against him to the south Essex committee for scandalous ministers. They had attended a meeting with Russell and other ministers at which they had taken the solemn league and covenant as a preliminary to administering the oath to their parishes. At the following dinner, Russell, an ardent episcopalian, was challenged over his having sworn the oath, which bound the taker to endeavour the extirpation of prelacy, clearly defined in parenthesis as 'Church government by Archbishops, Bishops, their Chancellors and Commissaries, Deans and Chapters, Archdeacons and all other ecclesiastical officers depending on that hierarchy'. Defending himself, Russell had said that he did not object to the hierarchy of the church, which he considered necessary, but only to its tyrannical behaviour, and he claimed that the parenthesis was not in the Latin text of the covenant which was the version 'according to which he had taken it'. This may have been a complete fiction, but the story suggests that some episcopalians had produced a Latin version of the oath which was both less objectionable to them and more obscure to prying eyes. In any event, despite having taken the covenant Russell was sequestered and ejected from his living, which he regained at the Restoration. He may have been troubled by his actions in 1644, for in 1660 he published a tract arguing that the covenant had been an undertaking to parliament which parliament could now renounce, so releasing those who had taken it from their obligations under it.[168]

In short, the evidence supplied by the Essex manuscripts suggests that over the period 1641–4 many episcopalian ministers modified their behaviour in order to reduce the risk of falling victim to sequestration. We cannot know whether this process was accompanied by a change in the beliefs and opinions of the individuals in question. What prudence dictated to many was to cease any attempt to practise the Laudian ceremonies; and while early in the life of the Long Parliament, some ministers did feel able to preach and campaign for the king or against parliament, by early 1644, anyone who wished to avoid the loss of his living had to face the acid test of taking the solemn league and covenant. Few refused to do so.

[166] Leicester MS 31, fos. 14, 31, 3v, 8v; Cole MS, fos. 73, 55–62.

[167] A ploy employed by Shephard and Crackenthorpe in respect of the vow and covenant: Cole MS, fos. 13, 14. See also Vallance, *National covenant*, pp. 124–9.

[168] Leicester MS 31, fo. 7–7v; John Russell, *The solemn league and covenant discharg'd* (BL, Thomason Tracts, E.1048[1]).

The conduct and outcome of the purge

Parliament's purges of the clergy had two aims: to silence opposition to its political and religious policies, and to install godly preachers in the nation's pulpits. Ejecting hostile parish clergy from their livings deprived them of a platform and intimidated many more, at the same time creating vacancies for godly preachers. Parliament proved able to achieve this outcome to a high degree in Essex and its neighbouring counties, all of which were effectively under the control of parliament from the outset of the Civil War.[169]

Two factors were particularly important in producing this outcome. First, the demand for change, fuelled by indignation at the religious policies of the king and the church under Laud, was felt strongly in parliament and very widely in parishes. The purge was not just another central initiative imposed on the localities, it was a policy for which there was a strong demand from many parts of the country, as the outbreaks of popular protest and of petitioning in the early years of the Long Parliament testify. Pressure was exerted in both directions and was mutually reinforcing. This is not to suggest that the active proponents of radical change, either in parliament or in the country at large, were more than a minority within the body politic. But they were remarkably successful in mobilizing action for their cause, both at Westminster and locally.[170]

Secondly, the purge was the more effective because parliament had succeeded in disabling the church as an institution.[171] Consequently, the purge was managed and its outcomes dictated by the laity: it was carried out not by the church hierarchy or under the authority of the king, but under the authority and direction of politicians at Westminster, by some of the gentry of the county, at the request of and on evidence provided by hundreds of parishioners, men and women of modest or low status. Puritan clergy were also involved. Manchester's chaplains, Simeon Ashe and William Good, were active in a support *rôle*, and a few ministers gave evidence against their colleagues.[172] Influential godly ministers such as Stephen Marshall and Edmund Brewer were consulted about individuals who were candidates for sequestration or for appointments.[173] But there is no sign that such clergy played more than a minor part in what was an exercise of lay power; moreover, that power was effective within the parish, a setting in which the minister, now the object of attack

169 According to Matthews' calculations, the numbers of parishes subjected to sequestration by parliament between 1643 and 1660 were as follows: Essex 152 (38% of the county's total), Hertfordshire 55 (43%), Cambridgeshire 62 (37%) and Suffolk 152 (36%). It is notable that Norfolk and Lincolnshire, both included in the Eastern Association, were less affected (132 or 20% and 80 or 13%): Matthews, *Walker revised*, pp. xiv–xv; McCall, *Baal's priests*, pp. 130–1.

170 Ian Green argued that similarities in the wording of articles, and the 'flood of articles' that greeted the opening of Manchester's purge strongly suggest that the deponents were subject to regimentation. So far as Essex (and Cambridgeshire) are concerned, this argument does not seem convincing. It underestimates the strength of feeling among puritan minorities who had only now been given a straightforward path to what they saw as justice and a better service from the church: Green 'Persecution', pp. 510, 519; *Cambridgeshire scandalous ministers*, pp. 14–16.

171 Milton, *Second reformation*, pp. 135–6, 149–52.

172 John Harrison at Cole MS, fo. 14, Theodore Herring and John Willis at Leicester MS 31, fo. 7, and (probably) Josaiah Church, *ibid.*, fo. 11.

173 Hugh Glover, Marshall's curate at Finchingfield, got the very well-paid rectory of Debden, on the ejection of Thomas Wilson; John Chamberlin would not have been appointed as vicar of Bulmer without the support of Edmund Brewer: Cole MS, fos. 69–70 and n. 147; Matthews, *Calamy revised*, p. 225; see p. xxiv above for Chamberlin.

and humiliation, was normally an important or even dominant figure. The disempowerment of the church's hierarchy and the suspension of the church courts had seriously altered the balance of power, making it difficult for the minister to enforce discipline or exact tithes.[174]

Manchester's instructions for the purge had underlined the *rôle* of the laity by requiring that any replacement for an ejected minister should be chosen by the parish, subject to approval by the Westminster Assembly. In assigning this *rôle* to parishioners, Manchester was affirming what was normal practice within presbyterian churches.[175] It was a serious move to empower the laity, even if the opportunity sometimes went unused, because the parish in question could not identify a suitable and willing candidate. The whole process, from the assumption of new powers by parliament, to the activities of some parishioners at local level, was revolutionary.[176]

It was, however, a revolution carried out within bounds: there were limits on what could be done. Of the twenty-eight ministers charged in the Cole MS, ten escaped sequestration and ejection, although in some cases conditions were imposed on their remaining in possession of the living.[177] This finding is surprising: such a high rate of survival is not apparent in the other areas where we have detailed records of Manchester's sequestrations.[178] The Cole MS is unique in providing what is a complete or almost complete set of the articles submitted to the north Essex committee, which can be compared to the record in Leicester MS 31 and elsewhere of the sequestrations that were actually made by Manchester.

Parishioners who wished to have their minister ejected could encounter difficulties. While it might be easy for a group of them to draw up a plausible case against their minister, the object of the exercise was to replace him with a better one, 'an able godly preaching minister', in the formula often used by the jurors in the parochial inquisition of 1650.[179] As mentioned above, Manchester's instructions envisaged that the new minister would be chosen by the parish, and by early 1644, people in Essex

174 In a letter of Sep. 1641 to Bishop Wren, William Alanson, vicar of Elm in the Isle of Ely, noted that 'moderate courses onely must be taken these times: for a pragmaticall Fellow, between Jeast and Earnest, asked mee: how I could recover my tyths if any denyed to pay them': Bodleian Library, MS Tanner 290, fo. 108.

175 Since the Reformation a few parishes within the Church of England had acquired the advowson of their living, and some lay patrons consulted parishioners over appointments, but these were rare instances of an approach of which, unsurprisingly, Laud disapproved: J. F. Merritt, 'Religion and the English parish', in *The Oxford history of anglicanism*, vol. I, ed. Anthony Milton (Oxford, 2017), p. 135. Bishop Juxon's articles for the London ministry of 1635 stated that 'the voice of the people is not required in the election of the minister': *Visitation articles*, p. 126; Webster, *Godly clergy*, p. 236.

176 Shaw, *History of the church 1640–1660*, II, 175–6.

177 See Appendix 2, p. liv below, for the identity of these ten ministers. Another minister, Edward Young, retained his living at Heydon, despite being articled against: his case was omitted from the Cole MS, because it was heard at Cambridge by a separate committee, as recorded in Leicester MS 31, fos. 30–31. In all therefore eleven north Essex ministers escaped sequestration, including four who while they retained the living, agreed to appoint a curate chosen by parishioners. As discussed below, these latter arrangements seem to have satisfied the complainants.

178 Only a small number of cases in which a minister had been articled against but not sequestrated can be identified in south Essex, in Suffolk and in Cambridgeshire: see pp. xlvi–xlvii below for further details.

179 The parochial inquisition was a survey, carried out in 1650 on the orders of parliament, to gather information about the income of parishes. It contains additional information for many parishes, including the opinion of the jurors on the abilities of the minister: the highest accolade was to be judged 'an able godly preaching minister'. The Essex returns are printed in Smith, *Ecclesiastical history of Essex*, pp. 233–321.

had had plenty of opportunity to observe the turbulent conditions in the market for such preachers. During the previous three years, parliament had already ejected at least sixty of the county's 400 parish clergy. The vacancies so created were additional to those resulting from death and resignation. The demand for ministers to fill these vacancies must have severely depleted the supply of suitable candidates for recruitment, while the numbers now graduating from Oxford and Cambridge had not increased.[180] Nor were vacancies caused by sequestration necessarily attractive. Some produced only a poor income.[181] Moreover, they were not secure. Manchester or the sequestrators appointed by him could choose someone to serve the cure in place of the sequestrated minister, but this newcomer (an 'intruder' in royalist eyes) had no freehold; in particular, his tenure ended when the sequestrated minister died or resigned, when it was for the patron to present to the living.[182] When patrons did so they often chose a new candidate, not the man who was acting as the minister at the time. In addition, many of the 'intruders' did not receive the normal income from the living. They might only be paid a modest stipend, and the system allowed parliament to require them to pay one fifth of the profits of the living to the family of the ejected minister. These conditions did not encourage ambitious ministers to seek appointment in a parish which was under sequestration. Only six of the thirty-nine parishes represented in our two MSS were able to nominate a candidate for the vacancy they wished to create, and only two or three of them were actually appointed.[183] In many parishes, the sequestrators had to make whatever arrangements they could to cover the vacancy, and this resulted in a succession of ministers who did not settle but quickly moved on.[184]

Moreover, the procedures laid down by Manchester allowed accused ministers

180 Green, 'Persecution', 526; Paul Seaver, *The puritan lectureships* (Stanford, 1970), pp. 274–5; Twigg, *The University of Cambridge*, pp. 291–2; Lawrence Stone, 'The size and composition of the Oxford student body 1580–1909', in Lawrence Stone (ed.), *The university in society*, I (Princeton, 1975), pp. 23, 94.

181 Two of the ministers who were articled against, Robert Fisher and William Hull, had livings producing only £30 a year. This may help to explain why neither was sequestrated: it would have been impossible to attract a good applicant on those terms.

182 These arrangemements are clearly set out and exemplified by Smith, *Ecclesiastical history of Essex*, pp. 157–62. Parliament implicitly recognized the concept of the advowson as a property which conferred the right of presentation to a benefice, although it often overrode advowsons in the ownership of the church hierarchy and delinquent royalists: Smith, *ibid.*, pp. 331–2; Shaw, *History of the church 1640–1660*, II, 187–9.

183 At Faulkbourne, Robert Chadsley, chosen by parishioners, was appointed, although he was forced out in 1647 when the sequestrated minister died and the patron presented someone else to succeed as rector: Cole MS, fo. 40, Leicester MS 31, fo. 17; *Lords Journal*, VIII, 644. At Debden, the parishioners procured the appointment of Hugh Glover, though he left in 1652 when the sequestrated minister died and the patron presented someone else: Cole MS, fo. 70; Smith, *Ecclesiastical history of Essex*, p. 161. It is unclear if 'Mr Benton', nominated by parishioners at Little Yeldham, was the 'Mr Bentham' who served there briefly: Leicester MS 31, fo. 15v; Matthews, *Walker revised*, p. 151. At Ashen, the parishioners did not secure the sequestration of William Jones and so were unable to attempt to recruit Richard Blackerby as their minister: Cole MS, fo. 28. At Chignal St James there is no evidence that 'Mr Sanders', probably Philip Sanders (for whom see Leicester MS 31, fo. 2 n. 8), ever served there. At Greenstead by Colchester parishioners asked for Nehemiah Long as minister, but by the time John Jarvis was sequestrated, Long had already been appointed to serve at Runwell: Cole MS, fo. 69; Matthews, *Walker revised*, pp. 156, 158.

184 Of the ministers first appointed to fill a vacancy created by Manchester's 28 sequestrations, only eight were still in place in 1650. Many parishes had two or three changes of minister in five years: Matthews, *Walker revised*; Smith, 'Sequence of Essex clergy, 1640–1664'; Smith, *Ecclesiastical history of Essex*, pp. 233–321.

some scope for mounting a defence, and it is clear that many did so, although none of their submissions to the north Essex committee has survived. Some of the ministers could rely on the support of a friendly patron, of influential parishioners or even of a puritan minister of repute. As will be clear from the discussion of individual cases below, the result of these defensive measures could be serious delays in reaching a conclusion, or a decision not to proceed to sequestration.

Given the difficulties which could beset an attempt to procure a sequestration and fill the resulting vacancy, in some parishes the parties were prepared to resort to compromise. In 1641, a group of parishioners at Radwinter had petitioned parliament against their rector, Richard Drake, a strong supporter of Laud's policies. They had already persuaded Sir Thomas Barrington and the House of Commons committee for scandalous ministers that Drake should be ejected, but finding that they now needed to obtain the agreement of the House of Lords, which might be refused, they offered to drop the case if Drake would allow them to choose a curate, whom he would pay £100 a year. Drake rejected this proposal.[185] Three years on, backs to the wall, three of the ministers caught up in Manchester's purge found a similar proposal acceptable. Deals were agreed under which Edward Shephard of Great Maplestead, William Jones of Ashen and Gregory Holland of West Bergholt all escaped sequestration by agreeing to allow parishioners to choose a curate, who would be well paid, to serve the parish.[186] It is probable that a similar plan was put in operation at Mount Bures.[187] These arrangements seem to have been satisfactory to the parishes concerned, causing no adverse comment at the parochial inquisition of 1650. For the incumbents, they were not far short of sequestration, with the curates taking the lion's share of the income, but some ministers found them preferable to outright sequestration.[188]

These arrangements represented a pragmatic way of resolving contested cases: practically speaking, the outcome was little different from what had been happening in the parish of Stisted over a long period. Richard Middleton, rector of Stisted, had been an absentee for twenty years until his death in 1641. The parish was served by a succession of five godly curates.[189] It is safe to assume that these men

185 The income of the living was about £135 a year. Despite his determination to remain, Drake was eventually forced to leave his parish: Smith, *Ecclesiastical history of Essex*, pp. 179–91 and 290; Walter, '"Affronts and insolencies"'.

186 There is no record that any of these three ministers was sequestrated, and the parochial inquisition of 1650 confirms they were not. At Great Maplestead, 'William Hicks supplies the cure by the choice of the parish': he was judged 'an able godly preacher'. The parish collected the tithes and paid Shephard £20 a year and Hicks £50 a year. Jones's parish of Ashen was served by Joseph Skynner, clerk, 'by the choice of the parish and the consent of Mr Jones', Jones paying Skynner £60 a year. Gregory Holland also remained in place but it was reported that he was aged and consented to the appointing of a curate by the parish 'for the better supply of the cure': Smith, *Ecclesiastical history of Essex*, pp. 296, 302, 309.

187 See Cole MS fo. 14 and n. 36 thereon.

188 Smith, *Ecclesiastical history of Essex*, pp. 296, 306, 309.

189 The curates are listed in the parish register, ERO, D/P 49/1/1. They were Jeremiah Burroughes (1623–7), who was deprived of his living in Norfolk by Wren in 1636 and fled to Holland; Samuel Stone (1627–30), who emigrated to New England with Thomas Hooker in 1633; Walter Atwood (1630–2), who was 'famous for conventicles and unconformity'; Mark Mott (1633–5), who declined to conform at the Restoration; and John Ludgater (1636–41), who held Great Birch and then Witham as intruder and was ejected in 1660: Tom Webster, 'Jeremiah Burroughes (1601?–1646)', *ODNB*; *idem*, 'Samuel Stone (1602?–1663)', *ODNB*; Smith, *Ecclesiastical history of Essex*, p. 39; Matthews, *Calamy revised*, pp. 358, 330.

were not foisted on an unwilling parish, but enjoyed the support of some at least of the influential parishioners. Indeed, it seems likely that parishioners played a part in choosing the curates, perhaps drawing on the advice of godly ministers in the area, and submitting the name to Middleton for his approval. This situation was remarkable in that Stisted was a peculiar of the archbishop of Canterbury, which was under the jurisdiction of the dean of Bocking, who acted as the archbishop's commissary. The dean in this period (1616–42) was Dr John Barkham. Under his unobservant eye, Stisted was clearly a broad church.[190] When Middleton died, after a protracted struggle Archbishop Laud managed to have Christopher Newstead appointed as rector, but the parish would not accept him. Parishioners took advantage of Manchester's purge to return to the case and Newstead was finally ejected in 1644.[191]

Seven of the ministers in north Essex who were articled against succeeded in remaining in full possession of their livings. John Jegon, rector of Sible Hedingham, fought a successful battle to keep his parish, which produced an income of £200 a year. He had been the rector since 1619, in succession to his father, Thomas Jegon. John was one of the parish's wealthiest residents. He also owned the advowson of his own living.[192] Some time before 1644, probably in the early months of 1643,[193] parishioners complained about him to parliament and the case was heard by the committee for plundered ministers: the details are obscure, but it is clear that he was not ejected. In 1644, some parishioners renewed the challenge, and at first succeeded. On the basis of the articles recorded in the Cole MS (folios 9–10), Manchester decided that Jegon should be sequestrated, but on being informed that Jegon had previously been cleared by the House of Commons he rescinded the sequestration and referred the matter back to parliament. The committee for plundered ministers confirmed that Jegon had been previously cleared and that the decision should stand.[194] This news provoked a series of protests at Sible Hedingham. Church services were disrupted, despite the efforts of Arthur Barnardiston, the local JP who had probably chaired the committee that had heard the charges against Jegon.[195] It is clear that some at least of

190 I am grateful to Professor Fincham for pointing out that Barkham was chaplain to both Archbishops Bancroft and Abbot, which may indicate that he favoured an inclusive conformity. His inclusiveness extended to employing Nathaniel Rogers, son of John Rogers, as his curate at Bocking. Cotton Mather commented that this was 'not without the wonder of many, how the son of the most noted puritan in England should become employed under an episcopal doctor, so gracious with Bishop Laud, but this Dr Barkham was a good preacher himself, and he was also willing to gratifie his parishioners, who were many of them religiously disposed'. It was only after some years that Barkham, attending a funeral in 1631, saw that Rogers, though officiating, was not wearing the surplice. 'Whereupon, though the doctor was so much a gentleman as to put no publick affront upon Mr Rogers, yet he gave him his private advice to provide for himself in some other place': Cotton Mather, *Magnalia Christi Americana* (2 vols., Hartford, 1853), I, 415–16.

191 Cole MS, fos. 18–20; Leicester MS 31, fos. 20v–21; Stephen Wright, 'Christopher Newstead (1597–1660x63), *ODNB*.

192 Jegon's father, Thomas, was master of Corpus Christi College, Cambridge, and brother of John Jegon, bishop of Norwich. The brothers were sons of a wealthy clothier of Coggleshall. Thomas established an important charity for the poor of Sible Hedingham. He also owned and bequeathed to his wife the advowson of the living, so ensuring that his son John would succeed him as rector and eventually come to own the advowson: Venn, *Alumni Cantabrigienses*, II, 466; J. Blatchly, 'John Jegon (1550–1618), bishop of Norwich', *ODNB*; TNA, PROB 11/131/460.

193 See Cole MS, fo. 21 and n. 61 thereon.

194 BL, Add. MS 15669, fos. 11v–12, 18v.

195 ERO, Q/SR 324/32; *ibid.*, Q/SR 324/109; *ibid.*, Q/SR 324/110. See Appendix 3, pp. lv–lvii, for more on Barnardiston.

the people who had tried to have Jegon ejected were radicals, probably separatists, who had little support in the parish.[196] Jegon's treatment by the committee for plundered ministers shows that he had some support from members, though their identity is unknown. Jegon survived at Sible Hedingham, continuing to serve there until his death in 1672. Although the articles against Jegon paint him as a strong opponent of puritanism, he clearly found ways of accommodating to the new regime. It may well be relevant that the curate he employed in 1640, Robert Abbott, was inclined to nonconformity.[197] Jegon may well have left many of the more difficult aspects of his dealings with parishioners to curates.

Another high-status survivor was Dr Edward Young. Rector of Heydon and of Hadstock, he was required by Manchester to give up Hadstock, where he had employed a curate who was also articled against, but he retained Heydon.[198] A close friend of Ralph Brownrigg, with connexions also to John Williams and to Richard Holdsworth, Young was probably a Calvinist and surely no Laudian: the articles against him do not tar him with that brush. Nor is there any criticism of his personal life and conduct. The only charge of weight was that he was a royalist who refused the solemn league and covenant.[199] Young also enjoyed the friendship of the Soame family, who owned the manor and the advowson of Heydon, and that family was well connected to the Barnardiston family.[200] Young was a firm episcopalian royalist who nevertheless by his personal qualities and his moderate views on ceremony may have earned the liking and respect of his parishioners at Heydon and of the local gentry and their godly relations. His prospects of keeping his living would, however, be much improved if he could refrain from public opposition to parliament. It is not clear whether he relented and actually took the solemn league and covenant, or whether he somehow evaded that hurdle, but in 1650 the parochial inquisition found him in place and judged him to be 'an able preacher'. He remained there until 1652, when he resigned and took up a new appointment at Anstey, Hertfordshire, where he continued to entertain the peripatetic Brownrigg.[201]

196 Six of the deponents against Jegon took part in the aggressive disruption of afternoon services at Sible Hedingham in 1645: see notes on Cole MS, fos. 9–10.

197 Abbott went on to be appointed vicar of Stansted Mountfichet in 1647, where the godly Timothy Middleton was patron, and was ejected from there in 1662 for nonconformity: Matthews, *Calamy revised*, p. 1: for Middleton, a member of the south Essex committee for scandalous ministers, see p. lxviii.

198 Leicester MS 31, fos. 30–32.

199 As a fellow of St John's College, Cambridge, Young was contemporary with Williams and Holdsworth in the college, and with Brownrigg who was at Pembroke Hall. In 1642, Young preached the sermon at Brownrigg's consecration as bishop of Exeter by Archbishop Williams. The next year Brownrigg made Young archdeacon of Exeter: Leicester MS 31, fos. 30–32v; Venn, *Alumni Cantabrigienses*, IV, 492; M. Wolffe, 'Ralph Brownrigg (1592–1659)', *ODNB*.

200 Sir Stephen Soame of Heydon (d. 1640) was the brother of Jane Soame, wife of Sir Nathaniel Barnardiston, and Nathaniel's stepmother, the formidable Lady Katherine, had previously been married to Bartholomew Soame of the same family. Peter Soame, whom Young had baptized in 1634, received a ring in Young's will of 1663. Dr Shipps considered that the ties between the Barnardiston and the Soame families formed part of a puritan alliance second in East Anglia only to that led by the Barringtons of Hatfield Broad Oak: Newcourt, *Repertorium*, II, 293; Alfred P. Beavan, *Aldermen of the city of London temp. Henry III – 1912* (1908), I, 209, II, 174; Janet Gyford, *Public spirit: dissent in Witham and Essex 1500–1700* (Witham, 1999), pp. 164–6; Greaves, 'Sir Nathaniel Barnardiston', *ODNB*; ERO, D/P 135/1/2; TNA, PROB 11/312/81; Shipps, 'Lay patronage', p. 80.

201 Smith, *Ecclesiastical history of Essex*, p. 285; Newcourt, *Repertorium*, II, 294; Venn, *Alumni Cantabrigienses*, IV, 492; Kenneth Fincham and Stephen Taylor, 'Vital statistics: episcopal ordination and ordinands in England, 1646–60', *English Historical Review*, 126 (2011), 335 n. 68; *The letters of*

Robert Fisher, vicar of Belchamp St Paul, also escaped sequestration despite charges of royalism.[202] In 1648, he signed the 'Essex Testimony' in support of a presbyterian settlement and was awarded augmentation of his income as vicar, and in 1650 the parochial inquisition found him an able godly preaching minister. He served through the 1650s and after subscribing in 1662 continued as vicar until his death in 1667.[203] It is not clear how Fisher eluded sequestration. His living was poorly paid at £30 a year, and no prize for a job hunter. It seems probable that he told the north Essex committee that he had taken the solemn league and covenant, and that he would abstain in future from speaking against parliament. Certainly his survival as vicar through a period of forty turbulent years suggests he was able to maintain relationships with the authorities of the time and with most if not all of his parishioners.

William Hull, vicar of Ulting, was another poorly paid minister: and according to his accusers, he drank too much, and his personal estate was 'little or nothing, for he spends it at the Ale-house so soone as he gets it'.[204] Apparently, the parish had no preferred candidate for the living. The committee may have decided that it would be better to leave Hull in place, anticipating a difficulty in recruiting a better minister to replace him. The verdict of the 1650 inquisition was lukewarm: 'he doth not neglect the cure, but is not a godly preaching minister'. Nevertheless Hull retained the living until his death in 1669.[205]

The charges made against John Chamberlin, the minister of Little Maplestead, were weak and as previously noted he had support within the parish and from Edmund Brewer, the influential puritan minister of Castle Hedingham, where Brewer's parishioners included Arthur Barnardiston.[206] Chamberlin's status as the curate of a donative living also raised a question as to whether he could be removed from the cure without action by the patron, who alone under ecclesiastical law had the right to appoint and dismiss the curate. The patron was Lady Wiseman, recently widowed by the death of Sir William Wiseman of Great Canfield, a noted royalist. Apparently, she took no action and Chamberlin remained in post until, nearly three years later, he moved to the vicarage of Bulmer, where, in 1650, he was reported to be an able preaching minister.[207]

Robert Guyon, minister at White Colne, was another curate who served a donative living: he also remained in post, although, as the articles against him suggest, he seems to have been in poor health and may often have been too sick to officiate.[208] It

George Davenport 1651–1677, ed. Brenda M. Pask with Margaret Harvey (Woodbridge, 2011), pp. 38, 43, 77. Young was appointed dean of Exeter in 1662, but died a year later: TNA, PROB 11/312/81.

202 Cole MS, fos. 35 37.

203 Smith, *Ecclesiastical history of Essex*, pp. 108, 209, 213, 300; ERO, D/P 408/1/1.

204 Cole MS, fo. 42.

205 Smith, *Ecclesiastical history of Essex*, p. 306; CCEd, Location ID 11489.

206 See pp. lv–lvii for Barnardiston.

207 Newcourt, *Repertorium*, II, 404–5; Sir Robert Phillimore *et al.*, *Ecclesiastical law of the Church of England* (2nd edn, 2 vols., 1895), I, 252–4; Morant, *History of Essex*, II, 283, 462; for the move to Bulmer, see p. xxiv above.

208 Cole MS, fos. 24–5; Newcourt, *Repertorium*, II, 186. No record has been found of Guyon's ejection from his appointment. The parochial inquisition of 1650 reported (incorrectly) that the parish was a vicarage presentative, and that there was 'no minister', which may mean that Guyon was temporarily absent or too ill to officiate. Guyon died in March 1657, not (as stated in *VCH Essex*, X, 137) 1667; Ralph Josselin, minister of Earls Colne, preached at his funeral and referred to Guyon as minister: *Josselin diary*, pp. 392–3.

appears that the patronage of the living in 1644 was in the Weston family but passed in 1645 into the hands of the staunch royalist and episcopalian, John Bramston junior. He may well have taken the view that the challenge to the appointee had no basis in law.[209]

John Mow, minister at Great Bardfield, was another curate who retained his position, despite extensive depositions alleging his support for the king. It is unclear how he survived: he may have been helped by the legal complexities of the position. The parish was a presentative living, to which John Packenham MA had been appointed in 1616; in 1639, he was given a dispensation to hold also the rectory of Stansfield, Suffolk, and soon thereafter he made an agreement with John Mow that Mow would serve the cure of Great Bardfield for twenty-one years.[210] Presumably Packenham resided at Stansfield: he was sequestered there in 1644, but appears to have left Mow undisturbed at Great Bardfield.[211]

The strength of the testimony against Mow may owe something to the fact that the parish was home to Sir Martin Lumley, the godly parliamentarian who had become MP for Essex early in 1641, and who doubtless enjoyed the support of the earl of Warwick, whose son he replaced in the Commons on the latter's elevation to the Lords.[212] But the advowson of Great Bardfield belonged to Edward Bendlowes, who also owned property in the parish and lived at Brent Hall, in neighbouring Finchingfield. Bendlowes is best known for his poetry: he was a royalist and possibly the only member of his family who was not a recusant. He was himself threatened with sequestration: in fighting his case he sought the help of Sir Thomas Barrington, commenting that he feared that 'these things arise from some personal differences between Sir M. Lumley and myself, wherein passion may overact'.[213]

This study of the detailed information which is provided by the Cole and Leicester manuscripts reveals that in north Essex over a third of the ministers who were articled against in 1644 escaped sequestration. This raises the question whether a similar outcome may have occurred elsewhere. In south Essex, ten ministers are recorded as having been sequestrated by Manchester,[214] but at least three more ministers in the south may have been articled against. Richard Hall, vicar of Barking, was not sequestered but he was ordered to employ a curate acceptable to the parish. This had not happened by April 1645 when Manchester's appointment ended, and on 2 May, the committee for plundered ministers appointed Peter Witham as curate at Hall's expense.[215] Andrew Harward was minister of Greenstead by Ongar and of Tring (Hertfordshire). He was probably articled against in both counties, though the articles are not extant. Manchester gave him the choice of retaining one or other of

209 *VCH Essex*, X, 136; Thomas M. Coakley, 'Sir John Bramston the younger (1611–1700)', *ODNB*.

210 The 1650 inquisition said, 'Mr John Packingham was presented to this viccarage, butt he doth not officiate himself butt hath putt in one Mr John Mow to whom he hath made a lease for one and twenty years, whereof ten are expired. What rent he hath reserved upon this lease we knowe not. Edward Benlowes Esq hath right of presentation.' But it seems clear from Newcourt and CCEd that Packenham's position was as rector, not vicar, with Benlowes owning the advowson: Newcourt, *Repertorium*, II, 28–30; CCEd, Person ID 28454 and 171388 (referring to the same man); Smith, *Ecclesiastical history of Essex*, p. 289.

211 Matthews, *Walker revised*, p. 340.

212 Andrew Barclay, 'Sir Martin Lumley', in *House of Commons 1640–1660*, VI, 827–31.

213 P. G. Stanwood, 'Edward Benlowes (1602–1676)', *ODNB*; Smith, *Ecclesiastical history of Essex*, p. 289; BL, MS Egerton 2647, fo. 312.

214 Appendix 1, li–lii below.

215 Smith, *Ecclesiastical history of Essex*, pp. 121–2; Matthews, *Walker revised*, p. 154.

his livings and ultimately he decided to resign from Greenstead.[216] Jeffrey Watts was another pluralist; earlier in the parliament, he had given up the living of Clavering with Langley, but was able to retain Great Leighs: if he was articled against there too, he succeeded in resisting the challenge.[217]

A few similar cases can be seen in other counties. In Cambridgeshire, William Rawley, rector of Landbeach, was a man of some distinction who was articled against by parishioners but escaped sequestration.[218] Thomas Elton, minister of Meldreth, retained his living but the parochial inquisition of 1650 records that the parish was served by Isaac Worrall with Elton's consent.[219] As in Essex, Manchester's purge in Cambridgeshire advanced the drive against pluralism. Two ministers were ejected from both of their livings in the county,[220] while two more were forced to give up one but allowed to retain the other.[221] In Suffolk, Clive Holmes noted three ministers who were articled against in Manchester's purge of that county but not sequestrated by him.[222] These cases illustrate how some ministers were able to delay and defeat attempts to remove them by argument, resort to lobbying influential people, and persistence. That harassed ministers in all counties were sometimes able to resist ejection is not surprising. The scale on which this happened in north Essex is, however, unexpected and suggests that, if better documentation were available, the small number of cases hitherto detected in south Essex and other counties purged by Manchester would be significantly increased.

Finally, the same conditions which made it possible for some ministers to escape sequestration enabled others, who were sequestrated, nevertheless to continue to find employment as a minister.[223] As we have seen, Edward Young lost one parish but retained the other, which he continued to serve for several years. Likewise, the absentee pluralist Joseph Long lost his living at Fingringhoe, but kept his second living of Great Clacton, where he was more welcome.[224] John Fenwick, ejected from Chignal St James in 1644, had regained possession by 1650. Two years later he resigned, eventually taking up a living in his native Northumberland.[225] In 1647,

216 Matthews, *Walker revised*, p. 199.

217 Smith, *Ecclesiastical history of Essex*, pp. 74–5; Matthews, *Walker revised*, p. 167.

218 Rawley was the assistant, editor and biographer of Francis Bacon. He was also well connected, not least as brother-in-law of Samuel Spalding, attorney, former mayor of Cambridge and influential member of the Cambridgeshire committee for scandalous ministers: Alan Stewart, 'William Rawley, c. 1588–1667', *ODNB*; Hart, 'Parish clergy of the diocese of Ely', pp. 200–4.

219 LPL, Comm. XIIa/3. 235.

220 Edmund Mapletoft (parishes of Downham and Hardwick) and Samuel Collins (parishes of Milton and Fen Ditton): Matthews, *Walker revised*, pp. 84, 78–9.

221 John Stanton (ejected Knapwell, retained Longstowe) and Thomas Whincop (retained Elsworth, ejected – or resigned – Lolworth): Matthews, *Walker revised*, p. 86; Hart, 'Parish clergy of the diocese of Ely', p. 233.

222 *Suffolk scandalous ministers*, pp. 95–119. In the preceding pages, Dr Holmes printed the articles submitted by the Suffolk committees to Manchester concerning thirty-eight ministers: these ministers were sequestrated by him. As is made clear at p. xiii above, the Suffolk and Cambridgeshire books are similar to Leicester MS 31 in containing only cases which the county committee had put forward to Manchester for sequestration.

223 Ian Green makes this point well, calculating that nearly 400 out of 2,120 ejected clergy were able to obtain a new living: 'Persecution', p. 525.

224 It was said that parishioners at Fingringhoe had pressed Long to reside there, but he had replied that 'there were such a companie of Puritans, he would not live amongst them': Leicester MS 31, fo. 23; Smith, *Ecclesiastical history of Essex*, p. 315.

225 Matthews, *Walker revised*, p. 152; Cambridge University Library, MS Mm. 1.42, 266; Venn, *Alumni Cantabrigienses*, II, 132.

Simon Lynch, ejected from Runwell, was appointed curate of Blackmore, where, to the annoyance of some in his new parish, he remained until his death in 1660.[226] George Crackenthorpe, ejected from Bradwell by Coggeshall, was appointed to Great Saling in 1647.[227] William Evett, ejected from Little Yeldham, returned to his native Worcestershire and took up the living of Grafton Flyford.[228] Thomas Newcomen, unable to return to his Colchester parishes, was appointed to good livings in other counties.[229] Perhaps the most resourceful of all, Thomas Punter, excluded from his position as curate of Hadstock as a result of Edward Young's sequestration, was soon appointed to Greenstead by Ongar, no doubt on the recommendation of Young, whose family owned the advowson of that living. Before long, Punter moved on to become the vicar of Linton, Cambridgeshire. There, in 1650, he was judged an orthodox godly divine, apparently well accepted in a parish where puritanism was strong. Forced out in 1660 by the return of a previous incumbent, he conformed to the Restoration Church and regained the living of Linton in 1663.[230]

Conclusions

The Long Parliament's ambition to reform the clergy, evident from its early days, was realized at differing speeds and to varying extents across England. In Essex, a county long known for the strength of puritanism among its clergy and laity, the response was vigorous. Godly gentry as landowners, employers and ecclesiastical patrons had ensured that a large number of like-minded ministers were already serving Essex parishes. The earl of Warwick and Sir Thomas Barrington, leading figures in the county, had also succeeded in promoting the election of godly men to all eight Essex seats in the Long Parliament. Barrington himself, as member of parliament for Colchester and chairman of parliament's committee for Essex, played a key *rôle* in linking the county and Westminster.

At Westminster, the Long Parliament launched a remarkably effective attack on the church's hierarchy, disempowering the bishops and neutralizing the disciplinary machinery of the church courts. It also assumed the power to summon individual ministers and to imprison them, and later to deprive them of their livings and to nominate their successors. It relied very heavily on the laity at local and county level to identify and provide evidence against the 'scandalous' and 'malignant' ministers who were the targets of the purge. Parliament's revolutionary approach broke the power of the church to regulate the clergy, transferring that power to the laity in parliament and to its supporters in the country.

Parishioners in Essex responded to parliament's willingness to act on complaints. By 1644, sixty or more of the county's clergy had been sequestrated, and Manchester's purge maintained the momentum. The evidence in the two manuscripts printed

226 The parochial inquisition of 1650 reported that Lynch 'was put out of Runwell for his scandalous life, and brought into this parish (Blackmore) without the consent of the well Affected Inhabitants'. But Lynch's son claimed that his father served Blackmore dutifully and refused a much more profitable appointment in Norfolk for honourable reasons: Harold Smith, 'Some Essex royalist clergy – and others', *The Essex Review*, 33 (1924), 82–3.

227 Smith, *Ecclesiastical history of Essex*, p. 295.

228 Matthews, *Walker revised*, p. 151.

229 See above, p. xxv n. 87.

230 Newcourt, *Repertorium*, II, 289; *VCH Cambridgeshire*, VI, 101.

in this volume suggests that the main cause of puritan discontent with episcopacy and those ministers who supported it was Archbishop Laud's policy of promoting certain ceremonies in church, especially those governing the position and railing of the communion table and the reception of the sacrament. In Essex, most ministers quickly abandoned the Laudian approach to worship in the face of serious disorder and widespread iconoclasm in the county's churches. The evidence in our two manuscripts does, however, show that some episcopalian ministers persisted in speaking out for the king, petitioning for peace in the early stages of the Civil War, an act dismissed by parliamentarians as a royalist manoeuvre, and resisting the vow and covenant. But by early 1644, parliament had reached an agreement with the Scots and imposed the solemn league and covenant, an oath which rejected episcopacy and endorsed a presbyterian settlement of the church. Any minister who obstructed it risked sequestration and ejection, and few of those still serving in Essex now refused it.

In the twelve months following March 1644, the earl of Manchester removed twenty-six Essex ministers from their livings. These ejections undoubtedly inflicted serious hardship on the victims and their families. Moreover, in many cases, they disrupted the service which the ministry normally gave to parishioners and left them, sometimes for years, without a satisfactory settled minister. But over time, progress towards parliament's aims was made. In 1650, when the parochial inquisition surveyed Essex, nineteen of the livings sequestrated by Manchester were now served by ministers who were judged favourably, for example as able or godly preachers. Moreover, Manchester had emphasized the need to reduce pluralism and non-residence, and notable progress had also been made in this direction.[231]

The outcome of the purge was not a clean sweep of all the ministers who had been targeted by their parishioners. Manchester and his committeemen had ample powers to carry out the purge, but they encountered obstacles. By no means all parishioners were dissatisfied with their minister, and many ministers escaped attention altogether, whether because they were seen as godly supporters of parliament or because, lacking that advantage, they kept a low profile and served in a parish in which there was little pressure for change. In parishes where change was demanded, parishioners might well aim to recruit a talented preacher but there was a shortage of good candidates and the process of filling a vacancy often proved lengthy and difficult. Where charges were brought against a minister, defence was possible. Some ministers under attack could call on the support of influential kin and friends. It could be difficult for a group of parishioners, perhaps not enjoying wide support in the parish, to dislodge a determined minister. In the end, compromise might well produce a better result than continued confrontation.

Thus, when the evidence of our two MSS and other sources is put together, it is clear that the process did not go forward smoothly in many places. In north Essex, eleven ministers who had been articled against managed to counter the attack

[231] The livings sequestrated by Manchester are listed in Appendix 1 below. The nineteen parishes stated to be well served were Runwell, South Ockendon, Canewdon, South Fambridge, Southchurch, Magdalen Laver, Little Yeldham, Stisted, Bradwell by Coggleshall, Wickham St Paul, Alphamstone, Debden, Wimbish, Gosfield, Hadstock, Belchamp Otten, Steeple, Springfield Richards and Arksden: Smith, *Ecclesiastical history of Essex*, pp. 244–304. See p. xxiv n. 84 above for the impact on pluralism.

and retain their position.[232] A minister under attack might try to retain his living by agreeing to stand back from serving the cure in favour of a curate, chosen by the parish and well paid at the expense of the minister. This device, used three or four times in Manchester's purge of Essex, could be attractive to any incumbent who could afford it: it was lawful, enabled the minister to remain in his home but distanced from his enemies in the parish, while he waited for times to change. It was not very different from the arrangements made in the past by ministers such as John Jegon in Sible Hedingham or Richard Middleton, absentee rector of Stisted.[233]

Another striking feature of the Essex purge is the evidence it provides that many of the ministers charged as Laudians and royalists were willing, if given the chance, to continue to serve in the church which was likely to be, at least in name, presbyterian and certainly without government by bishops. This was clearly the position of the eleven ministers who, as described above (pp. xlii–xlvi), were articled against but escaped sequestration and ejection. It was also the position of several more ministers, discussed at pp. xlvii–xlviii above, who were actually ejected by Manchester but were able, after an interval, to resume a living in the church without apparent difficulty. This evidence strongly supports Ian Green's conclusion that there was a high level of conformity to the parliamentary regime amongst the harassed clergy. It is also consistent with the finding of Kenneth Fincham and Stephen Taylor that a willingness to compromise and work with the powers that be has been a neglected feature of episcopalian mentalities in the interregnum. As Anthony Milton has concluded, 'The readiness to negotiate and cross boundaries was a key feature of the period, and the radicalizing of ideas could also help to make compromise possible.'[234] Even as the revolution was in progress, moderating influences were at work. Many episcopalian clergy were willing to continue to serve in the church despite the conditions now imposed by parliament. Whether a minister was fit to serve a parish was very much a matter of opinion, and minority opinion did not always carry the day, however powerfully expressed.

232 The eleven ministers are the ten listed at the end of Appendix 2 below, plus Edward Young, who was sequestrated from Hadstock but retained Heydon.

233 See above, p. xliv (Jegon) and pp. xlii–xliii (Middleton).

234 Green, 'Persecution', 525; Kenneth Fincham and Stephen Taylor, 'Episcopalian conformity and nonconformity 1646–60', in *Royalists and royalism during the interregnum*, ed. Jason McElligott and David L. Smith (Manchester, 2010), pp. 18–43; Milton, *England's second reformation*, p. 511.

Appendix 1

Essex ministers sequestrated and ejected by the earl of Manchester

During the 1640s and 1650s, parliament and its agents, including the earl of Manchester, sequestrated about 150 of the parish livings in Essex (37 per cent of the total).[1] In some of these cases, the timing is uncertain: what is recorded is not the date of sequestration, but the fact that a minister had been sequestrated in the past, noted in the course of subsequent action such as an appeal or the grant of one fifth of the living's income to the minister's wife. Despite uncertainty about the timing of some sequestrations, it is clear that Essex was in the forefront of parliament's drive to purge the clergy. Sixty or more parish livings had been sequestrated before Manchester began work in March 1644; twenty-eight more were sequestrated by him; and a further fifty or so by parliament during or after Manchester's purge.[2]

This appendix lists twenty-six ministers who suffered sequestration by the earl of Manchester. Thomas Wilson and Stephen Nettles were each ejected from two livings in the county, hence the total number of benefices sequestrated by Manchester was twenty-eight.

Sequestrations recorded in Leicester MS 31

John Fenwick (Chignal St James)
Simon Lynch (Runwell)
Francis Gouldman (South Ockendon)
John Russell (Chingford)
Raboshire Dove (Foulness)
Elizeus Burges (Canewdon)
John Viccars (South Fambridge)
Walter Holmes (Southchurch)
George Kindleton (Magdalen Laver)
William Evett (Little Yeldham)
Edward Strutt (Faulkbourne)
William Frost (Middleton)
Christopher Newstead (Stisted)
George Crackenthorpe (Bradwell by Coggeshall)
Joseph Long (Fingringhoe)

1 A. G. Matthews estimated the number of Essex benefices under sequestration between 1643 and 1660 as 152. There is room for debate about a small number of cases, but the total was certainly of that order: Matthews, *Walker revised*, p. xiv.

2 Essex accounted for the greatest number of cases recorded by John White in his *First century* of 1643 (30 of 100). Many more Essex cases in the period up to March 1644 are recorded in the parliamentary journals and other sources.

Timothy Clay (Wickham St Paul)
Rowland Steward (Alphamstone)
Thomas Wilson (Debden, Wimbish)[3]
John Crosse (Gosfield)
Edward Young (Hadstock)[4]

Additional sequestrations by Manchester

Joseph Bird (Belchamp Otten)[5]
Daniel Falconer (Aldham)[6]
Stephen Nettles (Lexden, Steeple)[7]
Robert Tourney (Springfield Richards)[8]
George Beardsall (Arksden)[9]
Thomas Eyres (Great Horkesley)[10]

3 Dr Wilson had three parishes, Debden and Wimbish (*sine cura*) in Essex, and Fulbourn St Vigor in Cambridgeshire, where he was resident. The entry in Leicester MS 31, fo. A30, sequestrates and ejects Wilson from all three.

4 Dr Young was also rector of Heydon, a living which he retained. At Hadstock, Young was sequestrated, and this led to the dismissal of Thomas Punter, Young's curate there.

5 Cole MS, fos. 33–5, 63, especially n. 91; BL, Add. MS 15669, fo. 239v; Smith, *Ecclesiastical history of Essex*, p. 302.

6 Cole MS, fos. 45–8 and especially n. 114; BL, Add. MS 15670, fos. 93, 113.

7 There is no record of the decision to sequestrate and eject Nettles from Lexden, but it is recorded that by 28 June 1645 Nettles had refused to hand over the parsonage and glebe of Lexden to Gabriel Wyersdale, the appointed intruder. The decision is more likely to have been taken by Manchester than by the committee for plundered ministers, though certainty is impossible: Cole MS, fos. 49–52; BL, Add. MS 15669, fos. 98v, 134v. Nettles was also vicar of Steeple, and by November 1645 Lemuel Tuke was complaining to parliament that parishioners there were opposing him as the minister. Clearly, Nettles had also been ejected from Steeple, probably by Manchester at the same time as from Lexden: BL, Add. MS 15669, fo. 207v.

8 BL, Add. MS 15569, fo. 130; Smith, *Ecclesiastical history of Essex*, pp. 119, 120, 123.

9 Articles against Beardsall were heard at Cambridge on 23 October 1644 by an *ad hoc* committee and he was sequestrated and ejected by Manchester on 16 January 1645. The case was recorded in the book for Cambridgeshire rather than the Essex book, presumably an error by the compiler of the record: BL, Add. MS 15672, fos. 42–3; *Cambridgeshire scandalous ministers*, pp. 87–9, 119.

10 Eyres, already minister at Mile End and at St Nicholas, Colchester, was appointed rector of Great Horkesley in 1642: CCEd, Location ID 11297. Within two or three years, the latter living was sequestrated: in February 1646, the committee for plundered ministers ordered that William Clopton should be paid for three months' service of the cure, which he had undertaken 'by order of the Earle of Manchester' after the latter's sequestration of the living: BL, Add. MS 15670, fo. 52; Bodleian Library, MS 324, fo. 136v.

Appendix 2

The outcome for the twenty-eight ministers articled against in the Cole MS

Sequestrated and ejected by earl of Manchester[1]

Rowland Steward (Alphamstone)
George Crackenthorpe (Bradwell by Coggeshall)
Timothy Clay (Wickham St Paul)
Christopher Newstead (Stisted)
William Evett (Little Yeldham)
John Crosse (Gosfield)
William Frost (Middleton)
Joseph Bird (Belchamp Otten)[2]
Edward Strutt (Faulkbourne)
Daniel Falconer (Aldham)[3]
Stephen Nettles (Lexden)[4]
Joseph Long (Fingringhoe)
Thomas Wilson (Debden)

Sequestrated and ejected by the committee for plundered ministers

John Jarvis (Greenstead by Colchester)[5]

Ceased to serve parish[6]

John Lake (Great Saling)[7]
Gabriel Honifold (Colchester St Mary Magdalen)[8]

1 Except where noted otherwise, the source for the sequestration decision is Leicester MS 31.
2 Not listed in Leicester MS 31, but see BL, Add. MS 15669, fo. 239v, and Smith, *Ecclesiastical history of Essex*, p. 302.
3 Not listed in Leicester MS 31, but see BL, Add. MS 15670, fos. 93, 113.
4 Not listed in Leicester MS 31, but see Appendix 1, n. 7, above.
5 Jarvis was minister of Greenstead and of North Fambridge. The charges relating to Greenstead (Cole MS, fos. 68–9 and 73–4) were not brought to a conclusion by Manchester. The committee for plundered ministers finally sequestrated and ejected Jarvis from both parishes on 28 April 1646: BL, Add. MS 15670, fo. 75v.
6 The parishes in question were vacated by the minister, but there is no evidence that this resulted from sequestration or ejection of the minister by Manchester or by parliament.
7 See Cole MS, fo. 15 and n. 40 for the outcome of the charges against Lake.
8 As Harold Smith noted, obscurity surrounds what happened as a result of the charges against three Colchester ministers, Gabriel Honifold, Thomas Newcomen and Samuel Cock. It is clear that they all

Thomas Newcomen (Colchester Holy Trinity)[9]
Samuel Cock (Colchester St Giles)[10]

Retained living on condition of appointment of an approved curate[11]

Edward Shephard (Great Maplestead)
William Jones (Ashen)
Gregory Holland (West Bergholt)
John Simpson (Mount Bures)

Retained living

John Jegon (Sible Hedingham)
Robert Guyon (White Colne)
John Chamberlin (Little Maplestead)
Robert Fisher (Belchamp St Paul)
William Hull (Ulting)
John Mow (Great Bardfield)

became unable to serve in their respective parishes, but there is no evidence that they were sequestrated by Manchester: Smith, *Ecclesiastical history of Essex*, p. 125; see the notes about these three ministers, at Cole MS, fos. 66, 71 and 72. It had been recognized as early as 1580 that the twelve urban parishes of Colchester needed restructuring. The parishes were small and in many cases had low incomes. For parliamentarians, another problem was that none of the livings was in the gift of a godly patron, which meant that the ministers appointed were often out of tune with the godly parishioners living there. It is possible that Henry Barrington, leader of the puritan group within Colchester council, persuaded his colleagues on the north Essex committee that there was no point in sequestration or any attempt to fill the resulting vacancies, pending the necessary restructuring. Certainly such a plan, to reduce the town parishes from twelve to four, was put forward in 1650 by the parochial inquisition, of which Barrington was a commissioner: P. Morant, *History and antiquities of Colchester* (in his *History of Essex*, I), p. 106; *VCH Essex*, IX, 129; ERO, D/B 5 GB4, fos. 174, 213, 218; *VCH Essex*, IX, 309–36; Smith, *Ecclesiastical history of Essex*, pp. 320, 308.

9 See n. 8 above.

10 See n. 8 above.

11 For more information on these cases see above, p. xlii and nn. 185 and 186.

Appendix 3

The membership of the Essex committees for scandalous ministers

The names of the twenty men appointed by the earl of Manchester to be members of the committees for Essex were listed in two commissions of 24 February 1644, as follows:

> To Sir Thomas Honeywood, Henry Mildmay Oliver Raymond Richard Harlackenden John Meade, Arthur Bernardestone Thomas Cooke, John Ellistone Robert Crome [*sic*] and Henry Barrington. The like commission to Sir Henry Holcroft, Sir Richard Everard, William Massam Timothie Middleton, John Wright Edward Birkhead, Cary Mildmay William Atwood Robert Calthorpe and Robert Maidstone.[1]

The first list corresponds to that given by Cole at BL, Add. MS 5829, folio 6, with 'Crane' for 'Crome'. Every case recorded in Cole's MS and therefore dealt with by the first committee concerned a parish in the north of the county. Unlike the Cole MS, Leicester MS 31 names the committee members who dealt with each individual case, and this confirms that the first committee handled cases from the north, while the second committee handled cases from the south.[2] The two Essex committees seem to have operated separately, communicating directly with the earl of Manchester, through his chaplains.

In addition to the twenty men named in Manchester's commissions, two more are known to have sat as committee members: Isaac Wincoll on the north committee and Sir William Martin on the south committee. The following biographical notes cover all twenty-two men.

North Essex committee

Arthur Barnardiston (*c.* 1590–1655)

Arthur was the second son of Sir Thomas Barnardiston (1563–1610) of Witham Place, Essex.[3] His elder brother Nathaniel (1588–1653) inherited the family's principal home at Kedington, Suffolk, and became a dominant figure in the religious and political

1 'Royalist clergy of Lincolnshire', p. 120.

2 Essex was divided for certain administrative and judicial purposes into six divisions. The three divisions in the north of the county covered the hundreds of Dunmow, Uttlesford, Freshwell and Clavering in the north-west; Hinckford; and Lexden, Winstree, Thurstable, Tendring and Witham in the north-east. To the south, three divisions covered the hundreds of Harlow, Waltham and Ongar in the west; Becontree, Havering, Chafford and Barstaple in the south-west; and Chelmsford, Dengie and Rochford in the east: Smith, *Ecclesiastical history of Essex*, pp. 3–4; B. W. Quintrell, 'The government of the county of Essex, 1603–1642', Ph.D. thesis, University of London, 1965, pp. 48–9.

3 *Visitations of Suffolk*, ed. Walter C. Metcalfe (Exeter, 1882), p. 113; Gyford, *Public spirit*, pp. 123, 166.

life of Suffolk from the late 1620s to 1648.[4] While Nathaniel and Arthur were still children, their mother died and in 1599, Sir Thomas married Katherine Soame, née Banks. Noted for her extensive godly network and her patronage of puritan ministers, Lady Katherine undoubtedly exercised a strong influence on the upbringing of her stepchildren.[5] Both of Arthur's marriages linked him to important godly families: his first wife was Ann Thornton, the widow of Sir Roger Thornton of Snailwell, née Hervey of Dagenham, died 1644: his second wife was Joan Mildmay, widow of Robert Mildmay, the godly lord and patron of Terling. Arthur himself must have been aware of the godly community at Terling in the 1620s, as Dame Katherine, his stepmother, had rejected the vicar of Witham and resorted to Terling to hear the preaching of Thomas Weld, the vicar, 1624–31.[6]

Arthur pursued a career as a lawyer, admitted to the Inner Temple in 1610 and called in 1620.[7] Though practising in London, he maintained his connexions with Essex, and became active in the county on behalf of parliament in the 1640s, serving as a member of commissions and as a JP from 1644.[8] His status as a lawyer and member of a prominent puritan family made him a natural choice for Manchester's committee on scandalous ministers, and it is evident that he played an important part in its work. Unlike any other commissioner, Barnardiston sat on all ten cases recorded in Leicester MS 31 as heard in north Essex, and in eight of them was named first in the list of commissioners. Moreover, it is surely no coincidence that the Cole MS, which recorded the proceedings of the north Essex committee, was given to Cole by Stephen Soame Esq., who 'had it as a Present from my Lady Bernardiston of Kedington': it seems probable that the book was either a record kept by Arthur during the committee's work or one kept by the secretariat of the committee and acquired by Arthur subsequently, and passed down by him within the family.[9]

Barnardiston lived at Castle Hedingham in the 1640s; he was taxed there in 1641, took the protestation there in 1642,[10] signed the Essex petition to the House of Commons there in January 1642[11] and was named as an elder for Castle Hedingham in the West Hinckford presbyterian classis.[12] Here was no lack of godly preaching: the minister, Edmund Brewer, was a nonconformist who attracted auditors from a distance, while the next parish, Gestingthorpe, supported a lectureship held during the 1630s and 1640s by the celebrated puritan preacher Richard Blackerby. Barnardiston must have known his godly neighbours in Gestingthorpe, the Ellistons

4 Greaves, 'Sir Nathaniel Barnardiston', *ODNB*.

5 Janet Gyford, 'Lady Katherine Barnardiston (née Banks), (d. 1633)', *ODNB*.

6 Gyford, *Public spirit*, p. 123

7 Inner Temple Archives (www. innertemplearchives.org.uk/detail.asp?id=11806).

8 *Acts and ordinances*, pp. 112, 292; ERO, Q/SR 322/132.

9 See above, p. xi and n. 13 there, and Cole MS, fo. 2.

10 TNA, E 179/112, 646, where he is listed, along with Isaac Wincoll, as liable for the subsidies; Parliamentary Archives, HL/PO/JO/10/1/91/19, where he is listed second, immediately below Edmund Brewer, the minister, and above Isaac Wincoll.

11 Parliamentary Archives, HL/PO/JO/10/1/112, where he heads the parish list, accompanied by Thomas and Nathaniel Bradshaw, Isaac Wincoll and Edmund Brewer the minister.

12 The name is printed in the original source as 'Arthur Barmston Esq': *The division of the county of Essex into severall classes: together with the names of the ministers and others fit to be of each classis. Certified by the standing committee of that county, etc.* (1648). 'Barn[ardi]ston' was clearly intended.

and the Sparrows.[13] At Castle Hedingham, Arthur was only ten miles distant from Kedington, where his brother Nathaniel lived and Samuel Fairclough, Blackerby's former pupil and now son-in-law, preached four times a week.[14]

After 1645, Barnardiston was a member of the parliamentary committee for Essex; taken prisoner with other members of that committee at Chelmsford and then imprisoned at Colchester during the siege of 1648, he was chosen by them as negotiator for their release.[15] He continued to act as a JP in Essex into the 1650s. He was also appointed Recorder of Colchester and a Master in Chancery. He died in 1655.[16]

Henry Barrington (1592–1660 or later)

Henry Barrington of Brick House, Colchester, was the son of a Colchester alderman, and not related closely, if at all, to the Barringtons of Hatfield Broad Oak. Henry was said to be a brewer. He was prominent in the government of Colchester from the 1620s to 1659, serving as mayor four times. In that town, he was, from 1642 to 1660, the leading figure on the side of parliament. He enjoyed the support of the earl of Warwick, the lord lieutenant, who appears to have appointed him governor of Colchester and a deputy lieutenant of the county in 1643. He was also appointed by parliament to a number of commissions.[17] Barrington appears to have played no part in the presbyterian system, which was poorly supported in Colchester: he is likely to have been a member of one of the numerous independent sects which flourished in the town in this period.[18]

As a member of the north Essex committee on scandalous ministers, Barrington sat on five occasions: at Colchester on 1 and 2 April, at Halstead on 20 March and 1 May and at Witham on 19 June.[19]

Thomas Cooke (d. 1682)

Thomas Cooke's family had been established at Pebmarsh for several generations; in his will of 1621, his grandfather described himself as yeoman.[20] Cooke was appointed a JP in 1639, possibly having made his mark through his involvement in the militia.[21] He was active as a sequestrator for parliament in ejecting the minister of Pebmarsh in 1643, and played a significant *rôle* for the Eastern Association committee at Cambridge.[22]

13 Webster, *Godly clergy*, pp. 242–4, 269; Samuel Clarke, *The lives of sundry eminent persons in this later age* (1683), pp. 58, 65; see also below, notes on John Elliston.

14 Clarke, *Lives*, p. 163.

15 BL, Thomason Tracts, E.589[4], sig A2; BL, Harley MS 6244, fo. 1r; *Josselin diary*, p. 352; Barbara Donagan, *War in England, 1642–1649* (Oxford, 2010), ch. 17, especially pp. 349–50, 356.

16 D. H. Allen, *Essex quarter sessions order book 1652–1661* (Chelmsford, 1974), p. xxxiii; Gyford, *Public spirit*, p. 123.

17 J. H. Round, 'Colchester during the Commonwealth', *English Historical Review*, 15 (1900), 642; Andrew Barclay, 'Barrington, Henry (1592 – after 1659)', in *House of Commons 1640–1660*, III, 320–3.

18 *VCH Essex*, IX, 128–9.

19 Leicester MS 31, fos. 23, 26v–27v, 20v–21, 18, 16v–17.

20 TNA, PROB 11/138/472.

21 TNA, C 231/5, 340; Andrew Barclay, 'Thomas Cooke', in *House of Commons 1640–1660*, IV, 293–5.

22 *Mercurius rusticus, or, the countries complaint of the barbarous outrages committed by the sectaries of this late flourishing kingdom* (1685), pp. 139–43; Holmes, *Eastern Association*, p. 126.

His aunt, Elizabeth Cooke, was married to the puritan divine and advocate of regicide, Hugh Peter; her daughter by an earlier marriage was the wife of John Winthrop junior.[23] Cooke was an elder of the presbyterian classis of East Hinckford and it is clear from Ralph Josselin's diary that he was counted among the godly.[24] He sat (usually at Halstead) on six of the ten cases heard by the north Essex committee.

In 1648, he acted with Sir Thomas Honywood to defeat the royalist uprising in Colchester and elsewhere and he went on to serve parliament in several *rôles* in the 1650s. He was elected MP for Essex in 1654. His political career ended at the Restoration; he lived until 1682, when his bequests included £11 to be distributed among poor ministers who were ejected from their livings for nonconformity.[25]

Robert Crane (d. 1658–9)

Crane was a wealthy grocer of Coggeshall.[26] Until the Civil War, he seems to have played no part in government of the county, but was well connected to godly circles in Essex and Suffolk. Around 1600, he had married Mary, daughter of Samuel Sparhawke of Dedham and elder sister of Edward Sparhawke, who was to be active in the 1630s as a 'fiery preacher'.[27] In 1620, their daughter Margaret married Nathaniel Rogers, son of the noted puritan preacher John Rogers; Nathaniel himself was a nonconforming minister, who as rector of Assington, Suffolk, in the 1630s sheltered under the protection of Brampton Gurdon before emigrating to New England.[28] In 1628, Mary Crane died and three years later Crane married Margaret Clopton, widow, the daughter of Robert Maidstone of Boxted and Great Horkesley. Margaret's sister Elizabeth (d. 1628) had been married to Nathaniel Bacon, and in his will Crane referred to Bacon as his brother-in-law. This relationship with the chairman of the Eastern Association's committee at Cambridge will have enhanced Crane's status.[29]

In 1635, Edward Sparhawke was suspended from his curacy and lectureship in London, and took refuge in Coggeshall. In 1637, the schoolmaster of Coggeshall denounced Robert Crane to the church authorities, along with Sparhawke and his brother John, John and Nehemiah Dod (the local vicar and his curate) and Edmund Brewer (minister of Castle Hedingham). They were accused of being involved in conventicles at Coggeshall.[30]

In 1643, Crane was appointed to commissions, for example as sequestrator of delinquents. He later served as an elder of the presbyterian classis for Lexden hundred.[31] By 1648, he was playing an active part in parliament's Essex county

23 Carla Gardina Pestana, 'Hugh Peter, (bap. 1598, d. 1660)', *ODNB*; Walter W. Woodward, 'John Winthrop, (1606–1676)', *ODNB*.

24 Shaw, *History of the church 1640–1660*, II, 387; *Josselin diary*, pp. 107, 110, 329.

25 Barclay, 'Thomas Cooke': TNA, PROB 11/371/418.

26 TNA, PROB 11/289/282; Hunt, *Puritan moment*, p. 272.

27 *Suffolk manorial families*, ed. J. J. Muskett (3 vols., Exeter, 1894–1914), II, 133–4; Matthews, *Calamy revised*, pp. 453–4; Webster, *Godly clergy*, p. 242.

28 Michael P. Winship, 'Nathaniel Rogers (1598–1655)', *ODNB*.

29 ERO, D/P 36/1/1; Lucy Lane Erwin, *Ancestry of William Clopton of York County, Virginia* (Rutland, VT, 1939), p. 68; *Fragmenta genealogica*, ed. F. A. Crisp (13 vols., 1889–1909), VIII, 31; Janelle Greenberg, 'Nathaniel Bacon (bap. 1593, d. 1660)', *ODNB*; Royal Commission on Historical Monuments, *An inventory of the historical monuments in Essex* (4 vols., 1916–23), III, 10 (recording Elizabeth Bacon's death); TNA, PROB 11/289/282.

30 Matthews, *Calamy revised*, pp. 453–4; *CSPD 1636–7*, pp. 513–14.

31 *Acts and ordinances*, p. 112; Shaw, *History of the church 1640–1660*, II, 388.

committee. In that year, he was, with other committee members, taken prisoner by royalist forces at Chelmsford and then imprisoned at Colchester during the siege.[32]

As a member of the north Essex committee for scandalous ministers he sat on seven cases.

John Elliston (*c.* 1599–1652)

John Elliston appears not to have held public office until 1643, when he was appointed to four commissions by parliament, including the Eastern Association committee at Cambridge.[33] He owned the manor of Overhall, Gestingthorpe, which his family had bought from John Sparrow and others for £3,600 in 1622.[34] About the same time, Elliston married John Sparrow's sister, Elizabeth; their first son, also John Elliston (*c.*1625–52) was to form an important relationship with his mother's nephew, also John Sparrow (1615–70). They both worked on translating and publishing the works of Jacob Boehme, the German mystic philosopher whose writings were to play a part in the development of Quakerism.[35]

Gestingthorpe's vicar in the 1630s and 1640s was John Tharby, judged in 1650 'an able godly preacher'.[36] The village was also the home of a flourishing lectureship, held by the celebrated puritan preacher Richard Blackerby for many years until his death in 1648.[37] It seems probable that Elliston and Sparrow played a part in funding this project. Elliston may well have favoured independency in religion. Unlike many of his colleagues in the committee for scandalous ministers, he was not named as an elder of the presbyterian classis in his area, and in 1647 he was one of the original investors in the Eleutherian plantation, a republic to be established in the Bahamas where religious freedom was to be practised. When he died in 1652, Elliston bequeathed his interest in the plantation to his grandsons.[38]

Kinship as well as godliness was no doubt a factor in Elliston's employment by parliament. His brother-in-law, John Sparrow, served as a colonel in the Eastern Association army in 1644. By this time, Elliston's wife had died and he had married Jane Clench, a widow, a sister of Richard Harlakenden of Earls Colne, described below.[39] Elliston played an important part in the committee for scandalous ministers, sitting on six cases, usually with Barnardiston, Crane, Cooke and Honywood.

John Elliston of Gestingthorpe is to be distinguished from John Elliston (d. 1658), clothier of Little Coggeshall. It is clear from the latter's will that he too was a man of property who supported independency, while his brother Matthew Elliston was intruded into the rectory of Stanford Rivers in 1643, and ejected from it in 1660.

32 BL, Thomason Tracts, E.589[4], sig. A2; BL, Harley MS 6244, fo. 1r; *Josselin diary*, p. 352; a Donagan, *War in England*, ch. 17, especially pp. 349–50, 356.

33 His name is variously given as 'Alliston' and 'Eliston of Gesthorp', that is Gestingthorpe, near Halstead: *Acts and ordinances*, pp. 169, 170, 243, 292; HMC, *7th Report, Part I* (1879), p. 550a.

34 Suffolk Archives, HA517/C15.

35 Thomas Wharton Jones, 'The pedigree of Alliston or Elliston of Essex and Kent', in *The herald and genealogist*, V, ed. John Gough Nicholls (1870), 24–6; Ariel Hessayon, *'Gold tried in the fire': the prophet TheaurauJohn Tany and the English revolution* (Aldershot, 2007), pp. 291–5; K. Grudzien Baston, 'John Sparrow (1615–70)', *ODNB*.

36 ERO, D/P 85/1/1; Smith, *Ecclesiastical history of Essex*, p. 298.

37 Clarke, *Lives*, pp. 58, 65; see also above, notes on Arthur Barnardiston.

38 Hessayon, *'Gold tried in the fire'*, p. 294; TNA, PROB 11/225/288.

39 R. R. A. Walker, 'John Elliston and John Sparrow', *Notes & Queries*, 167 (1934), 312; TNA, PROB 11/225/288; *Josselin diary*, facing p. 664.

This family of Ellistons were probably kin of John Elliston of Gestingthorpe; John of Little Coggeshall in his will of 1658 made four bequests of £5 each, to the poor of Little Coggeshall, Great Coggeshall, Gestingthorpe and 'the gathered church'.[40]

Richard Harlakenden (1606–77)

Richard Harlakenden was lord of the manor of Earls Colne, and a man of strong religious convictions. Educated at Emmanuel College, Cambridge and Gray's Inn, he succeeded his father in 1631: the latter had supported the preaching of the puritan Thomas Shepard in Earls Colne, until Bishop Laud forced Shepard to leave the parish.[41] In 1637, Sir Nathaniel Brent, Archbishop Laud's vicar-general, found that John Hawkesbey, vicar of Earl's Colne, had omitted the sign of the cross when baptizing children, although charges against Harlakenden for procuring such action were not upheld.[42] In 1641, Harlakenden arranged the appointment of a young puritan minister, Ralph Josselin, as vicar of Earls Colne, and Josselin's diary attests the strong support which the Harlakenden family gave to him and other godly ministers.[43]

Richard Harlakenden was a JP and a member of several parliamentary commissions, and in 1645–6 he served as high sheriff of Essex. He also became an elder of the Lexden presbyterian classis. Henry Mildmay of Graces, Little Baddow (1619–92) was Richard's brother-in-law; Alice (d. 1631), Henry's sister, was Richard's first wife.[44] As noted above, John Elliston of Gestingthorpe was another brother-in-law, being the husband of Richard's sister Jane. Richard's cousin, William Harlakenden, played a prominent part in the Eastern Association, as commissary-general of the army and latterly as the earl of Manchester's 'indispensable personal assistant'.[45]

As a member of the north Essex committee, Richard Harlakenden sat on six cases.

Sir Thomas Honywood (1587–1666)

Honywood's father, Robert Honywood of Charing (Kent) acquired an estate at Markshall, between Colchester and Braintree, in 1605. Thomas inherited the property in 1631, and was knighted in 1632. He played no part in the government of the county in the 1630s. In the 1640s, he took on a variety of *rôles* in which he proved a loyal and energetic supporter of parliament. He was appointed JP and to many parliamentary commissions. He was also active as a deputy lieutenant and a colonel in the militia. He was a committed puritan, as is clear from the many references to him in the diary of Ralph Josselin, the like-minded vicar of Earls Colne, and was listed as an elder in the Lexden presbyterian classis.[46] He played a full part in the north Essex committee on scandalous ministers, sitting on seven cases.

40 Jones, 'Pedigree of Alliston or Elliston', pp. 24–6; TNA, PROB 11/283/306; Matthews, *Calamy revised*, p. 183 (Matthew Elliston).

41 Venn, *Alumni Cantabrigienses*, IV, 60: Michael Jinkins, 'Thomas Shepard (1605–49)', *ODNB*; Webster, *Godly clergy*, pp. 38–9, 169–70.

42 Smith, *Ecclesiastical history of Essex*, pp. 51–2.

43 John Walter, 'Ralph Josselin (1617–83)', *ODNB*; *Josselin diary*, *passim*.

44 ERO, Q/SR 321/129; *Acts and ordinances*, pp. 91, 112, 147, 243, 292; Shaw, *History of the church 1640–1660*, II, 388; H. R. French and R. W. Hoyle, *The character of English rural society: Earls Colne, 1550–1750* (Manchester, 2007), pp. 97–8.

45 Holmes, *Eastern Association*, pp. 128–9.

46 Bill Cliftlands, 'Sir Thomas Honywood, (1587–1666)', *ODNB*.

In 1648, Honywood, with Thomas Cooke, played a leading *rôle* in defeating royalist forces at Colchester, and in 1651 he commanded a regiment of foot at the battle of Worcester. Elected member of parliament for the county in 1654 and 1656, he was appointed to the upper house in 1657. He retired from public life at the Restoration and died six years later.[47]

John Meade (d. 1656)

John Meade of Finchingfield is not recorded as having heard any of the cases against scandalous ministers: he may have given evidence in the case of Thomas Wilson (see p. xxii above). Meade's father, also John (d. 1629), was a member of Lincoln's Inn.[48] Meade himself, having been a fellow commoner at Emmanuel College, Cambridge from 1629, was admitted to Lincoln's Inn in 1632 but was not called to the bar.[49] It appears that he played no part in county government until the Civil War. In 1643, he was appointed a sequestrator and a member of the Eastern Association committee, and by 1645, he had become a JP.[50] He was listed as an elder of the presbyterian classis of West Hinckford, together with the senior layman resident in Finchingfield, Sir Robert Kemp, and the minister, Stephen Marshall.[51] Meade continued to serve as a magistrate and occasionally as a commissioner in the 1650s, for example on the Essex commission for ejecting scandalous ministers. He was buried at Finchingfield on 23 September 1656.[52]

Henry Mildmay of Graces, Little Baddow (1619–92)

Henry Mildmay sat only once to hear cases against Essex ministers, unlike his relatives who were very active in their areas. His cousin Carew Hervey Mildmay sat on the south Essex committee and his grandfather and his uncle, both Brampton Gurdon, sat on the west Suffolk committee for scandalous ministers.[53] Henry was probably fully engaged elsewhere. Only twenty-five years old, he was already a deputy lieutenant of the county and a member of parliamentary commissions. The earl of Manchester chose him as a member of the small committee of the Eastern Association which sat in Cambridge, and promoted him to colonel in parliament's army. In March 1644, he was carrying messages between the committee of both kingdoms and the earl of Manchester.[54] He was appointed governor of Cambridge Castle in 1644 and an elder of Chelmsford presbyterian classis in 1646. He continued to serve parliament during the interregnum, being elected as one of the MPs for Essex in 1654 and 1656.[55] He

47 *Ibid.*; Andrew Barclay, 'Sir Thomas Honywood', in *House of Commons 1640–1660*, VI, 10–14.

48 *The records of Lincoln's Inn, the black books*, ed. W. P. Baildon *et al.* (6 vols., 1897–2001), II, 31, 243, 254.

49 Venn, *Alumni Cantabrigienses*, III, 170; *The records of Lincoln's Inn, admissions*, ed. W. P. Baildon (2 vols., 1896), I, 216.

50 *Acts and ordinances*, pp. 112, 292; ERO, Q/SR 325/117.

51 Shaw, *History of the church 1640–1660*, II, 386.

52 Allen, *Essex quarter sessions*, p. xxxvii; *Acts and ordinances*, p. 971; Smith, *Ecclesiastical history of Essex*, pp. 336–8; ERO, D/P 14/1/1.

53 See below for Carew; for Brampton Gurdon, father and son, of Assington, see *Suffolk scandalous ministers*, p. 25.

54 Holmes, *Eastern Association*, p. 125; *CSPD 1644*, p. 66.

55 *CSPD 1645–7*, pp. 45, 74; Shaw, *History of the church 1640–1660*, II, 377; Andrew Barclay, 'Henry Mildmay', in *House of Commons 1640–1660*, VII, 107–9.

dropped out of public life at the Restoration, but came to prominence later as leader of the exclusion party in Essex. He served as MP for Essex in the parliaments of 1679 and 1681, and again in those of 1689 and 1690. He died in 1692.[56]

Oliver Raymond (d. 1679)

Oliver Raymond of Belchamp Walter was appointed to the north Essex committee but there is no record that he ever sat to hear a case. Raymond's mother was a member of the Sparrow family of Gestingthorpe, for which see above, p. lix.[57] Educated at Cambridge and Lincoln's Inn, Raymond was appointed a JP in 1641. His commitment to the parliamentary cause was ambiguous at first: in July 1642, he had joined with twenty-four other Essex justices in signing a petition pledging support for the king.[58] By 1644, however, he had been appointed to important parliamentary commissions. He was an elder of the presbyterian classis of West Hinckford, and his public career continued into the 1650s, when he was elected as MP for Essex in 1654 and 1656, and beyond.[59]

Isaac Wincoll (1594–1650)

Wincoll was not named in Manchester's commission, but was brought in as an additional member to hear five cases.[60] Wincoll's father, Isaac Wincoll of Little Waldingfield, Suffolk, was a wealthy gentleman who had a new house built at Twinstead. Isaac junior inherited the property, although in 1641 he was living at Castle Hedingham, where he was a neighbour of Arthur Barnardiston.[61] Like his father, Isaac was educated at Cambridge. His marriage to Mary Waldegrave connected him to two important local godly families, while his sister married a puritan minister.[62] Like several other commissioners, he does not seem to have been active in county government before the Civil War, but he was appointed by parliament as a sequestrator of delinquents in June 1643 and became a JP in 1644.[63]

In 1645, Wincoll was employing as his family chaplain John Collinges, recently graduated from Emmanuel College, who was to become a noted controversialist and preacher.[64] In the same year, Wincoll was probably instrumental in getting Collinges

[56] Barclay, 'Henry Mildmay'.

[57] *Visitations of Essex*, ed. Walter C. Metcalfe (2 vols., 1878–9), II, 696.

[58] Holmes, *Eastern Association*, p. 41 and p. 248 n. 39.

[59] Andrew Barclay, 'Oliver Raymond', in *House of Commons 1640–1660*, VIII, 45–6; Shaw, *History of the church 1640–1660*, II, 386.

[60] Leicester MS 31, fos. 15v, 16v (though not listed at the end of this case, fo. 17), 18, 19v, 24, 25v.

[61] L. C. Sier, 'The Wyncoll family', *Transactions of the Essex Archaeological Society*, 12 (1913), part 1, 1–13. Wincoll inherited property in many parishes, and his presence in Castle Hedingham, as a neighbour of Arthur Barnardiston, is well attested: see Appendix 3 n. 10 above; ERO, Q/SR 313/74 and /100; and Parliamentary Archives, HL/PO/JO/10/1/91/22, where he is listed as a churchwarden for the parish in 1641/2.

[62] Venn, *Alumni Cantabrigienses*, IV, 435. Wincoll's wife Mary was the daughter of Thomas Waldegrave of Bures and Elizabeth Gurdon of Assington. His sister Judith was married to John Harrison, the puritan preacher of Sudbury. Wincoll's nephews John and Isaac Harrison were both appointed to livings in 1643 (Little Waltham and Hadleigh, Suffolk, respectively) which they lost at the Restoration: Sier, 'The Wyncoll family'; Matthews, *Calamy revised*, p. 249.

[63] *Acts and ordinances*, p. 169; TNA, C231/6, fo. 8.

[64] Stephen Wright, 'John Collinges (1623/4–1691)', *ODNB*; Matthews, *Calamy revised*, p. 128.

appointed to the living of Alphamstone, following the ejection of Rowland Steward, in which Wincoll had been involved both as witness and as committee member.[65] Wincoll seems to have been an elder of the presbyterian classis of East Hinckford.[66]

South Essex committee

William Atwood (1596–1647)

William Atwood was the eldest son of John Atwood Esq., of Littlebury, Stanford Rivers, in the hundred of Ongar (d. 1623).[67] William entered Queens' College, Cambridge in 1614, as did John Wright of Wrightsbridge.[68] William was admitted to the Middle Temple in 1616, where his father was a longstanding member of the bar.[69] William was married to a niece of Sir Thomas Cheke, member of parliament for Harwich in the Long Parliament, and a prominent puritan.[70] William's younger brother John (1599–1672) was steward of the manor of Burnells in the service of Carew Hervey Mildmay, for whom see below, and was appointed a magistrate in or before 1644.[71] Their brother Walter Atwood was licensed as curate of Wethersfield in 1632; in that year, Dr Robert Aylett, commissary of the bishop of London, reported to Bishop Laud that Walter Atwood was 'a great unconformist' who had formerly been at Stisted, where 'he was famous for conventicles and unconformity'.[72]

William Atwood was thus well connected and from early in the Long Parliament began to be appointed to serve it. In 1642, he was a commissioner for raising money and plate, and in 1643 a commissioner for sequestration and a member of the county committee.[73] On the south Essex committee for scandalous ministers he heard five cases. In 1646, he supported a petition for the appointment of the puritan Matthew Elliston to the rectory of Stanford Rivers; see p. lix above for the Ellistons. Atwood was also listed as an elder of the presbyterian classis of Ongar. He died in 1647.[74]

65 Cole MS, fos. 11–12; Leicester MS 31, fo. 25.

66 Shaw, *History of the church 1640–1660*, II, 387, where, under Twinstead, it is noted that a later hand has added the name 'Mr Isack', albeit as minister.

67 *VCH Essex*, IV, 215; ERO, D/P 140/1/1.

68 Venn, *Alumni Cantabrigienses*, I, 55. For Wright, see pp. lxix–lxx below. In his will of 1644, Wright bequeathed his black breeding mare to 'my brother Mr William Atwood'; the two men were married to sisters, two nieces of Sir Thomas Cheke, MP for Harwich, and brother-in-law of the earl of Warwick. Moreover, Atwood is recorded as living at Noak Hill, and was thus also a neighbour of Wright: ERO, D/AEW 21/186; B. W. Quintrell, 'The divisional committee for southern Essex during the Civil Wars and its part in local administration', MA dissertation, University of Manchester, 1962, p. 160.

69 Venn, *Alumni Cantabrigienses*, I, 55; *Middle Temple Records*, ed. Charles Henry Hopwood (4 vols., 1904–5), II, 603, 683.

70 See n. 68 above, and Andrew Thrush, 'Sir Thomas Cheke', in *The history of parliament: the House of Commons, 1604–1629*, ed. Andrew Thrush and John P. Ferris (6 vols., Cambridge, 2010), III, 500–5.

71 ERO, D/DAV 56; *ibid.*, Q/SR 321/129, Q/SR 325/117, Q/SR 329/158; Allen, *Essex quarter sessions*, p. xxxiii.

72 Venn, *Alumni Cantabrigienses*, I, 55; CCEd, Location ID 11511; Smith, *Ecclesiastical history of Essex*, p. 39.

73 *Lords Journal*, V, 203; *Acts and ordinances*, pp. 112, 292; ERO, D/Y 2/7/4, D/Y 2/7/5.

74 Leicester MS 31, fos. 1–2, 3–4, 5–5v, 6v–7v, 13v–14; Parliamentary Archives, HL/PO/JO/10/1/211, 6 Aug. 1646; Shaw, *History of the church 1640–1660*, II, 381; ERO, D/P 140/1/1A.

Edward Birkhead (d. 1662)

In the 1630s, Edward Birkhead held minor positions at court; in December 1637, he was made one of the king's sergeants-at-arms. By the early 1640s, he had acquired property at Romford, and in 1641 he acted as collector of the poll tax in Havering, and as a subsidy commissioner.[75] In 1643, called 'Edward Berkhead of Rumford, Esquire', he was appointed by parliament as treasurer of the funds to be raised for an Essex force of 1,000 dragoons. Holding the rank of lieutenant-colonel, Birkhead worked under the direction of Sir Thomas Barrington to finance and equip this force.[76] By 1644, he was also a JP, a position he held into the 1650s.[77]

As a member of the south Essex committee for scandalous ministers Birkhead heard only one case, that against Francis Gouldman at Ongar on 9 April 1644.[78] From 1645, Birkhead's activities in Essex tailed off, probably on account of his appointment as sergeant-at-arms to the House of Commons. He continued to hold this appointment, despite declining health, until 1660. He died in 1662.[79]

Robert Calthorp (d. 1665)

Calthorp was a gentleman of Great Dunmow. He acted for Dame Joan Barrington in leasing a property and as the steward of the manors of Newton Hall, Great Dunmow and Little Dunmow.[80] In 1643, he was appointed by parliament in three *rôles*.[81] In 1644, he was acting as 'treasurer of the moneys receyved upon the sequestrations' in the divisions of Dunmow, Hinckford and Lexden.[82] He was certainly appointed a member of the south Essex committee for scandalous ministers, but there is no evidence of his activity as such. Later, he was appointed an elder in the presbyterian classis of Dunmow and Freshwell.[83] His will of 1663, proved on his death in 1665, suggests he was of modest means.[84]

Sir Richard Everard Bt (*c.* 1600–79)

Everard of Langleys, Great Waltham, was of a long-established Essex family. In 1621, following studies at Cambridge and Lincoln's Inn, Everard married Joan Barrington, daughter of Sir Francis of Hatfield Broad Oak. The marriage connected Everard to men who would be among the county's leading figures for parliament in the 1640s; to his brother-in-law Sir Thomas Barrington, and through that family to Sir Gilbert Gerard and Sir William Masham. Thus, Everard was connected to the circle around the earl of Warwick, and it was the first earl who procured him his baronetcy in 1629. From 1642, Everard played a full part in the government of Essex, serving on many

75 Quintrell, 'Committee for southern Essex', p. 161.
76 *Acts and ordinances*, p. 245; Nuttall, 'Sir Thomas Barrington and the puritan revolution', pp. 73–5.
77 ERO, Q/SR 321/129; Allen, *Essex quarter sessions*, p. xxxiv.
78 Leicester MS 31, fo. 5.
79 *Commons Journal*, IV, 417; *ibid.*, VIII, 1; H. D. W. Sitwell, 'Royal sergeants-at-arms and the royal maces', *Archaeologia*, 102 (1969), 213–14; TNA, PROB 11/309/328.
80 ERO, D/DBa E14, D/DU 293/103, D/DU 472/18.
81 *Acts and ordinances*, pp. 112 (sequestration), 229 (raising of money), 292 (county committee).
82 BL, Add. MS 5494, fo. 101.
83 Shaw, *History of the church 1640–1660*, II, 383.
84 ERO, D/AMW 6/252; *ibid.*, D/P 11/1/2.

commissions, appointed a JP, deputy lieutenant and as high sheriff for 1645. He was also very active in the county committee.[85]

Everard was no doubt a godly man. He was assiduous in attending the south Essex committee for scandalous ministers; along with Holcroft, Martin and Mildmay, he attended all its recorded sittings and was usually listed first. He was appointed an elder in the presbyterian classis of Chelmsford.[86] In 1654 and 1656, he was elected to parliament as a member for Essex. After the Restoration, he was allowed to remain a JP for some years and he continued in local offices until his death in 1679.[87]

Sir Henry Holcroft (*c.* 1586–1650)

In 1616, Holcroft's career took off when he was appointed secretary by his stepfather, Sir Oliver St John, the new lord deputy of Ireland. On his return to England in 1621, Holcroft held the post of remembrancer for Irish affairs 1621–9; he was knighted in 1622 and had two brief spells as a member of the parliaments of 1624 and 1628. Having settled at East Ham, he became an Essex JP in 1639.[88] In the 1640s, he was a strong supporter of parliament, acting as a deputy lieutenant and playing a leading *rôle* in the county committee which met at Chelmsford.[89] Evidently trusted by Sir Thomas Barrington, he was a natural choice for and frequent member of the south Essex committee for scandalous ministers, hearing all nine cases recorded.[90] In the following years, he was an elder in the Becontree, Havering and Chafford presbyterian classis. His son Francis rose to prominence after the Restoration as the leading figure in the vigorous Congregational movement which developed in Cambridgeshire.[91]

Robert Maidstone (1615–84)

The Maidstones were gentry of modest wealth and status, but well connected to important godly families in Essex and Suffolk. Robert and his older brother John (1606–67) were brought up in Boxted, a parish much influenced by the preaching of John Rogers at nearby Dedham. They were nephews of John Winthrop of Groton; in 1629, at the age of twenty-three, John wrote to his uncle to recommend that he should take the minister of Boxted, George Phillips, with him to New England.[92] When Phillips left for America, he was replaced at Boxted by Edward Collins (or Collinges), another godly minister close to Rogers.[93] In 1633, John Maidstone became the impropriator of Boxted rectory in succession to his father, and in 1637 he refused to co-operate with the installation of a rail before the communion table in the chancel; he threatened to sue anyone who entered the chancel to set it up.[94] His objections were evidently set

85 Andrew Barclay, 'Sir Richard Everard', in *House of Commons 1640–1660*, IV, 967–9; BL, Stowe MS 189, fos. 5–38.

86 Leicester MS 31, fos. 1–14, Shaw, *History of the church 1640–1660*, II, 377.

87 Barclay, 'Sir Richard Everard'.

88 Virginia C. D. Moseley and Rosemary Sgroi, 'Sir Henry Holcroft (c. 1586–1650)', in *House of Commons, 1604–1629*, IV, 748–9.

89 Quintrell, 'Committee for southern Essex', pp. 18–19; BL, Stowe MS 189, fos. 5–38.

90 Leicester MS 31, fos. 1–14.

91 Shaw, *History of the church 1640–1660*, II, 374; Matthews, *Calamy revised*, pp. 271–2.

92 *Visitations of Essex*, I, 447; ERO, D/P 155/1/1; Webster, *Godly clergy*, pp. 46–7, 206, 295; Massachusetts Historical Society, *Winthrop papers* (6 vols., Boston, MA, 1863–92), II, 164–5.

93 Webster, *Godly clergy*, pp. 47, 206.

94 *VCH Essex*, X, 62 and n. 59; ERO, D/ACA 52, fos. 137, 165v.

aside, and in 1638 and 1639 Robert, along with his father, mother and two sisters, was presented for failing to receive communion at Easter, probably because they declined to kneel at the rail.[95]

The Maidstone brothers were also related to Nathaniel Bacon, grandson of Lord Keeper Sir Nicholas Bacon. Nathaniel was married to their cousin Elizabeth Maidstone (d. 1628); he was also a neighbour, living in the next parish of Langham. In the 1640s, Bacon played a leading *rôle* for parliament, serving as chairman of the Eastern Association's committee at Cambridge and as recruiter MP for Cambridge University from 1645.[96] Margaret Maidstone, another cousin of the brothers, was married to Robert Crane, the wealthy grocer of Coggeshall who was also was a commissioner for scandalous ministers (see p. lviii above); he was an important figure in the godly community of north-east Essex.

There is no record that any of the Maidstone family held public office before the Long Parliament, but in the 1640s, both Robert and his brother John served parliament. By 1650, John was lieutenant-colonel in a regiment commanded by Thomas Cooke of Pebmarsh (see above pp. lvii–lviii), and he soon became a JP. From 1653, he played an important *rôle* in Cromwell's household as steward. He was elected member of parliament for Colchester in 1654 and 1656.[97]

Robert's career was less successful, but in the 1640s, he served as a member of the Eastern Association committee, and as a commissioner for assessment.[98] He was also a safe choice to sit in judgment on scandalous ministers; he was appointed to the committee dealing with cases in the south of the county, and sat for three days in March and April 1644 at Chelmsford and at Maldon, hearing six cases.[99] He was commissioned as a captain of dragoons in the militia in 1650, was appointed a member of the ejectors commission in 1654 and went on to hold a minor government appointment as clerk of endorsement for alienations from 1656, a position which he probably owed to the influence of Nathaniel Bacon.[100]

The brothers persisted in their religious nonconformity after the Restoration. Following a dispute between the Maidstones and the vicar of Boxted, Edmund Hickeringill, the latter had the brothers indicted for failing to attend any services at the parish church for a period of eleven months before Easter 1664.[101] In May 1664, Hickeringill brought proceedings in the archdeacon's court against Robert, along with other dissenters, resulting in his excommunication.[102] In 1672, the house of Robert Maidstone at Boxted was licensed as a Congregational meeting place.[103]

95 ERO, D/ACA 52, fos. 234, 246v; D/ACA 53, fo. 203; D/ACA 54, fos. 12, 26v.

96 Greenberg, 'Nathaniel Bacon', *ODNB*; Andrew Barclay, 'Nathaniel Bacon', in *House of Commons 1640–1660*, III, 219–28; Royal Commission on Historical Monuments, *Inventory of the historical monuments in Essex*, III, 10.

97 Andrew Barclay, 'John Maidstone', in *House of Commons 1640–1660*, VI, 855–9.

98 *Acts and ordinances*, pp. 292, 537.

99 Leicester MS 31, fos. 1–4 and 8v–12v.

100 *CSPD 1650*, p. 508; *Acts and ordinances*, p. 971; BL, Add. MS 4184, fo. 255; *CSPD 1660–1*, p. 102; *CSPD* Addenda 1660–85, p. 6; *A calendar of the docquets of Lord Keeper Coventry 1625–1640*, ed. Jan Broadway, Richard Cust and Stephen K. Roberts (4 vols., List and Index Society, 2004), p. 533.

101 ERO, Q/SR 400/30.

102 ERO, D/ACA 55, fos. 35–40; Justin Champion and Lee McNulty, 'Making orthodoxy in late Restoration England: the trials of Edmund Hickeringell, 1662–1710', in *Negotiating power in early modern society*, ed. Michael J. Braddick and John Walter (Cambridge, 2001), pp. 233–6.

103 *Original records of early nonconformity under persecution and indulgence*, ed. G. Lyon Turner (3 vols., 1911–14), II, 937.

Sir William Martin (d. 1679)

The son of Cuthbert Martin, an alderman of the city of London who was Master of the Skinners' Company in 1612, William obtained a grant of arms in 1615 and was knighted two years later.[104] In 1618, described as of Woodford, he bought the manor of Netteswell in the hundred of Harlow, where he lived until his death in 1679.[105]

In the early 1640s, Martin became very active for parliament, being appointed a JP and deputy lieutenant, and serving on commissions for the raising of taxes and for sequestration, and on the committee of the Eastern Association.[106] He was an active member of parliament's Essex county committee, which Sir Thomas Barrington chaired.[107] He was not included in Manchester's list of members of the south Essex committee for scandalous ministers, but he was brought in as an additional member and sat on all nine south Essex cases recorded in Leicester MS 31.[108] There is little evidence concerning Martin's religious views: it is probably significant that he sent his eldest son to Emmanuel College, Cambridge, but he is not recorded as a presbyterian elder in 1647, whether through dislike of the system or for some other reason.[109] In the later 1640s, he seems to have withdrawn from public life, while his position under the Protectorate is unclear.[110]

William Masham (*c.* 1616 – by 1655)

William Masham's short career in public office, from 1643 to his death in 1654 or 1655, owed much to his father, Sir William Masham Bt, of Otes, High Laver. Sir William was a prominent figure in the county, and closely aligned to the Barrington family: his marriage to Elizabeth, the daughter of Sir Francis Barrington of Hatfield Broad Oak, made him, like Everard, Sir Thomas's brother-in-law. Sir William Masham represented Essex constituencies in parliament in the 1620s and in the Short and Long Parliaments, in which he was a strong supporter of religious reform and the war against the king.[111]

From early in the Civil War, young William was appointed to many commissions by parliament, and by 1644, he was a JP.[112] He was an active member of the south Essex committee for scandalous ministers, sitting in seven cases.[113] He and his father were both appointed elders of the presbyterian classis of Ongar.[114] In 1646, he

104 *Visitations of Essex*, I, 445; J. F. Wadmore, *Some account of the worshipful Company of Skinners of London* (1902), p. 192; *The knights of England*, ed. W. A. Shaw (2 vols., 1906), II, 160.
105 *VCH Essex*, VIII, 208; ERO, D/P 33/1/1.
106 Quintrell, 'Committee for southern Essex', p. 167; *Acts and ordinances*, pp. 91, 112, 229, 292.
107 BL, Stowe MS 189, fos. 5–38.
108 Leicester MS 31, fos. 1–14.
109 William Martin junior was admitted to Emmanuel as a fellow commoner in 1640: Venn, *Alumni Cantabrigienses*, III, 153.
110 Martin was apparently appointed high sheriff of Essex by parliament on 10 November 1653 (*Commons Journal*, VII, 348), although Morant notes that other unnamed sources stated that the office was held by Cuthbert Martin (Sir William's son): Morant, *History of Essex*, I, ix. Martin is also listed as assessed at £20 for the decimation tax of 1655, which was levied against royalists, although he was not included in the second and third tranches of the tax, raising the possibility that he appealed successfully: 'The Cromwellian decimation tax of 1655, the decimation lists', ed. J. T. Cliffe, in *Camden Miscellany XXXIII* (Cambridge, 1996), 436–7.
111 Andrew Thrush, 'Sir William Masham Bt (1591–1656)', in *House of Commons, 1604–1629*, V, 276–80.
112 *Acts and ordinances*, pp. 91, 112, 229, 292, 536, etc.; ERO, Q/SR 321/129.
113 Leicester MS 31, fos. 5v, 7v, 9, 10, 11v, 12v, 14.
114 Shaw, *History of the church 1640–1660*, II, 380.

entered parliament as a member for Shrewsbury, and was elected, with his father, as one of the thirteen MPs for Essex in 1654. He died in 1654 or early 1655, before his father.[115]

Timothy Middleton (1590–1655)

Middleton was the younger son of Sir Thomas Middleton, a successful merchant who was lord mayor of London in 1613 and who entered parliament for Merioneth in his native Wales in 1597 and again, now for the city of London, in 1624, 1625 and 1626. In 1615, Sir Thomas bought the manor of Stansted Mountfichet, which Timothy inherited, along with other property in Essex, on his father's death in 1631.[116]

Timothy was educated at The Queen's College, Oxford and Gray's Inn, following the same path as his elder half-brother, Thomas, later Sir Thomas Middleton.[117] Thomas inherited his father's extensive property in Wales and was MP for Denbigh in the Long Parliament. In Civil War Essex, Timothy was active for parliament, serving on numerous commissions and as a JP.[118] Along with Arthur Barnardiston and Robert Crane, he was among the members of parliament's Committee for Essex who were held prisoner in Colchester in 1648.[119] In religion, he was an elder of the presbyterian classis of Clavering and Uttlesford.[120]

Middleton continued to serve as a JP until his death in 1655.[121] His record as a godly supporter of parliament made him a suitable member of the committee for scandalous ministers, but there is no evidence that he ever sat to hear cases. He may have simply been too busy, given his other commitments including as high sheriff of Essex in 1644.[122]

Carew Hervey alias Mildmay (1596–1676)

Carew was a member of the prolific Mildmay family, one of the most prominent gentry families in the county. He was the son of William Mildmay of Moulsham. Educated at Emmanuel College, Cambridge, where he became friendly with Stephen Marshall, Carew was admitted to the Inner Temple in 1617.[123] In 1626, he married Dorothy, daughter of Sir Gilbert Gerard, and in 1627 he inherited property in and around Dagenham from his uncle, Sir Gawen Hervey. After that, he lived at Marks Hall, Dagenham, and took the name Carew Hervey alias Mildmay. Henry Mildmay, nominated as a member of the north Essex committee for scandalous ministers, was Carew's first cousin.[124]

115 Andrew Barclay, 'William Masham', in *House of Commons 1640–1660*, VII, 8–10.

116 Charles Welch, 'Sir Thomas Myddelton [Middleton], (1549x56–1631)', *ODNB*; Simon Healy, 'Sir Thomas Myddelton I (c. 1556–1631)', in *House of Commons, 1604–1629*, V, 465–9.

117 Foster, *Alumni Oxonienses*, III, 1011; *The register of admissions to Gray's Inn, 1521–1889*, ed. J. Foster (1889), pp. 114, 115.

118 *Acts and ordinances*, pp. 91, 112, 147, 229, 243, 292, 536; ERO, Q/SR 324/26.

119 See notes on Barnardiston, above.

120 Shaw, *History of the church 1640–1660*, II, 385.

121 Allen, *Essex quarter sessions*, p. xxxviii; ERO, D/P109/1/1, fo. 97.

122 ERO, Q/SR 321/1.

123 *Visitations of Essex*, I, 453–4; Venn, *Alumni Cantabrigienses*, III, 187; Inner Temple admissions database (www.innertemplearchives.org.uk). A letter of 1619 from Marshall shows him offering spiritual support to Carew: ERO, D/DMS C2.

124 Andrew Barclay, 'Carew Hervey alias Mildmay', in *House of Commons 1640–1660*, VII, 749–52.

Carew held a series of minor public offices in the 1630s. During the Civil War, he was an active supporter of parliament, appointed to many commissions and serving as a JP.[125] He played a full part in the county's divisional committee for south Essex, attending its meetings at Romford ten times in the first half of 1644.[126] During March and April of that year, he sat to hear all nine cases against scandalous ministers.[127] Carew was also a colonel in the militia, playing an important *rôle* in parliament's defeat of the royalist attack on Essex during the second Civil War.

He was appointed an elder of the presbyterian classis of Becontree, Havering and Chafford. He represented Essex in the parliaments of 1654 and 1656.[128]

John Wright (c. 1598–1644)

The Wright family had held the manor of Wrightsbridge, Noak Hill, in the liberty of Havering since at least 1550.[129] John Wright's father, also John Wright (1569–1632), had studied at Emmanuel College, Cambridge and Gray's Inn, where he became a bencher and treasurer.[130] In 1612, he was appointed clerk of the House of Commons, a position he held during the subsequent parliaments until 1629. He also held appointments in Essex, as recorder of Maldon and as a JP. A godly man who was said to have shown favour to the king's opponents, he enjoyed the friendship of Robert Rich, 2nd earl of Warwick.[131] His wife, Martha Castell of East Hatley, Cambridgeshire, came from another godly family: her brother's children included Robert Castell, a colonel in parliament's forces during the Civil Wars, and Elizabeth, the wife of Stephen Marshall, the presbyterian preacher and minister of Finchingfield.[132]

John Wright the younger, born around 1598, was admitted to Queens' College, Cambridge in 1614 and to Gray's Inn two years later, and called to the bar in 1628.[133] His marriage brought useful connexions. He married Mary Mole, whose mother was a sister of Sir Thomas Cheke, member of parliament for Harwich in the Long Parliament, and a prominent puritan. As noted above, p. lxiii, William Atwood, a neighbour of John Wright, was married to another niece of Cheke.[134]

Wright was employed by his father as deputy clerk of the House of Commons, an appointment which lapsed in 1629.[135] He may have practised law in the 1630s, but there is no evidence that he held public appointments in that decade. He was off the mark soon after the beginning of the Civil War, being appointed to every Essex commission named by parliament in 1643 and named as a JP early in 1644.[136]

125 For example, he served on commissions for raising money and plate, for sequestration and for the raising of money: *Lords Journal*, V, 203; *Acts and ordinances*, pp. 170, 229. And as JP: ERO, Q/SR 321/129; 325/117; 329/158; 334/84.

126 BL, Add. MS 37491, fos. 3v–5v, 7, 8v, 9v.

127 Leicester MS 31, fos. 1–14.

128 BL, Add. MS 37491, fo. 81; Shaw, *History of the church 1640–1660*, II, 375; Barclay, 'Carew Hervey alias Mildmay'.

129 *VCH Essex*, VII, 72; *Visitations of Essex*, I, 533–4.

130 Venn, *Alumni Cantabrigienses*, IV, 474; *The pension book of Gray's Inn 1569–1669*, ed. Reginald J. Fletcher (1901), pp. 289, 299, 308.

131 *House of Commons, 1604–1629*, I, 231–43.

132 Cambridgeshire Archives, P 87/1/1; *VCH Cambridgeshire*, VIII, 44; G. J. Toomer, 'Edmund Castell, (bap. 1606, d. 1686)', *ODNB*.

133 Venn, *Alumni Cantabrigienses*, IV, 474; *Pension book*, p. 283.

134 *Visitations of Essex*, I, 534, 338.

135 *House of Commons, 1604–1629*, I, 242.

136 *Acts and ordinances*, pp. 91, 112, 147, 229, 243; ERO, D/Dmy 15M50/233.

But his promising career was cut short. In April 1644, he made his will and he died in August of that year.[137] He may well have been in poor health even as he was appointed a member of the south Essex committee for scandalous ministers; for whatever reason, he is not recorded as having heard any of the cases dealt with by the committee.

137 ERO, D/AEW 21/186; ERO, D/P 128/1/2.

Editorial conventions

In the transcripts, the original spelling and capitalization are retained. I have extended contractions and added punctuation where needed for clarity. Both manuscripts use old-style dating, in which the year began on 25 March rather than 1 January. This has been retained in the transcripts, but dates quoted in the Introduction and footnotes are adjusted to reflect modern practice: thus the old-style date 20 March 1643 at Cole MS, folio 9, is restated in the footnote as 20 March 1644.

BL, Add. MS 5829, folios 1–74 (the Cole MS), is a copy made by William Cole of an original manuscript given to him by Stephen Soame. Cole supplemented his copy of Soame's manuscript with numerous comments and notes of his own. In the following text, Cole's additions have been printed in italics to distinguish them from the original text.

At folios 8 and 9 of his manuscript, Cole notes that the original is written and interlined in various hands, and that he has indicated where a change occurs by placing the words in question in crotchets (square brackets) or adding a cross or other symbol. These indicators have been reproduced in this transcript.

Leicester MS 31 was written from both ends, with many blank pages between the two sections. The articles against Essex ministers are at folios 1–32v, printed at pp. 55–9 below. They are preceded by four unnumbered folios, one of which contains an incomplete entry relating to Fen Drayton (Cambridgeshire), as follows:

> Wheras the Parish of Fendrayton being destitute of an able Minister for executing that Cure the which Incumbent Mr Huxley being   a man of scandalous life and conversation and of unsound Doctrine, These are therefore to prohibite the said Mr Huxley that from henceforth he presume not medle with that Cure, and I doe.[1]

The material about the purge of the University of Cambridge and warrants for the sequestration and ejection of the Essex ministers are written at the other end of the book and are foliated A3 – A32. They are printed at pp. 89–100 below.

In the Introduction and editor's notes, the place of publication is London unless otherwise stated. The county of all parishes named is Essex, unless otherwise stated.

[1] This is a stray entry, discontinued in mid-sentence, about the parish of Fen Drayton in Cambridgeshire: see Introduction above p. xiii for other examples of stray entries in related manuscripts. The rectory of Fen Drayton was owned by Christ's College, Cambridge, which appointed curates to serve the cure there. In 1644, the curate was Thomas Huxley, a fellow of the college. Huxley was ejected from the fellowship. Some parishioners evidently considered him unfit to serve at Fen Drayton, and because he did not hold the benefice, sequestration was not required: the college could simply appoint a successor. It appears that an order was prepared for Manchester to approve, requiring Huxley to cease any involvement in the cure: *A history of the county of Cambridgeshire and the Isle of Ely* (10 vols., Victoria County History, 1938–2002), IX, 300–1; *Biographical register of Christ's College, 1505–1905*, ed. J. Peile (2 vols., Cambridge 1910–13), I, 438; Matthews, *Walker revised*, p. 290.

British Library, Additional MS 5829, folios 1–74 (Cole MS)

fo. 1

Wm. Cole Cantabr Maij 24 1757

Vol: 28

Extraneous from Cambridgeshire[1]

fo. 1v

See this sneaking Earl's Visitation of the University of Cambridge, in my vol. 51. p. 430 to 434.[2]

fo. 2

Blecheley May 14 1757

Acts of Committee against scandalous Ministers in Essex

The following MS original of the villainous and iniquitous Actings of the Commissioners, appointed by the Parliament of 1643, against such as they were pleased to call scandalous Ministers, was given to me by Stephen Soame of Thurlow in Suffolk Esquire in 1752. He had it as a Present from my Lady Bernardiston of Kedington in the same County, with 2 other MSS of Pedigrees of the Suffolk Families; all in 4to.[3] *This Committee's Acts is a thin 4to of about 40 Leaves, in different Persons Hands: before it is placed the Copy of the Earl of Manchester's Commission to these Persons to act by: and to the whole is sewed the printed Ordinance of Parliament empowering the said Earl to commit these Devastations. It is remarkable, that the said Earl of Manchester, who had so great and principal a Part in the base Practices of those Times, lived long enough under them to be heartily tired of such dirty Work; and, at the Restoration, was the Person pitched upon to restore, in the University of Cambridge and elsewhere, where he had very unjustly deprived Numbers of very honest Men of their Free-holds and Substance, such as were by him turned out of their Preferments, as were then alive and to disposess all such as had succeeded illegally: which, methinks, must have been a very mortifying Service, whether he approved of his former Actings or not.*[4] *I shall*

1 The greater part of Cole's collections related to Cambridgeshire. Fortunately, he sometimes recorded other material of interest to him. For more on Cole see the Introduction, p. x.

2 This refers to what is now BL, Add. MS 5852, fos. 193v–195v. There, Cole recounts that he was copying from a manuscript written by the late Dr Richardson, master of Emmanuel College, and lent to him in October 1780. That material, relating to the earl of Manchester's purge of Cambridge University, appears to have been copied by Richardson from one of three transcripts made by Thomas Baker of the material in Leicester MS 31, printed at pp. 89–94 below. See Introduction, p. xii n. 20 for Baker's copies.

3 See Introduction, p. xi n. 13 above.

4 The earl of Manchester was chancellor of the university 1649–51 and again from May 1660 until his death in 1671. At the Restoration, he was involved in the process of restoring senior members of the

transcribe the said Ordinance and Commission, to the End that the wicked and ensnaring Purposes of those puritannical Hipocrites may be descried and detected; who under a Veil and Mask of Religion, treacherously called upon all Sorts of People, and those of the lowest and basest Sort in each Parish, to come and inform against their respective Ministers: of how wicked a Tendency such a Proceeding must be at that Time when Peoples Spirits were heated by religious Disputes, may easily be discerned when we reflect what the Consequence of such Encouragement would be

fo. 3

for Informers even at this Time. Every one who has had it in his Power to make Observations on the Nature of Country People must be convinced how easily they are to be influenced, particularly against their Superiors; and more especially when their Interest coincides with Encouragement: many Reasons may be given why the very best of a Country Parish want no Hallooings to quarrel with their Minister: the great Article of taking the Tenth is more than sufficient to have each individual, who contributes toward it, though they have no Right to it themselves, a secret Enemy to the Parson of the Parish: not to mention the Business of Vestries, Poor Rates and many other Affairs of the like small Import, which, if the Clergy-man will resolutely do his Duty, and insist that others do theirs, will be a never-failing Fund of Contention between him and his Parish. From what has been said, I suppose it may easily be conjectured that Informations are no hard Things to be got from a country Parish, where a nice and constant Attention to every little Art to get Money is no where more assiduously put into Practice, and where a more determined Dislike to their Superiours and especially of the Clergy, for some of the abovesaid Reasons, is more inherently fixed and settled. But I shall now copy the printed Ordinance.

Die Lunae, 22 Jan: 1643[5]

Ordinance for regulating the University of Cambridge, and for removing of scandalous Ministers in the 7 associated Counties

Whereas many Complaints are made by the well-affected Inhabitants of the associated Counties of Essex, Norfolk, Suffolk, Hartford, Cambridge, Huntington and Lincolne, That the Service of the Parliament is retarded, the Enemy strengthened, the Peoples Souls starved, and their Minds diverted from any Care of God's Cause, by their idle, ill-affected, and scandalous Clergy of the University of Cambridge, and the associa-

fo. 4

ted Counties; And that many that would give Evidence against such scandalous Ministers, are not able to travel to London, nor beare the Charges of such a Journey: it is ordained by the Lords and Commons assembled in Parliament, That the Earle of Manchester shall appoint one or more Committees in every County, consisting of such as have been nominated Deputy Lieutenants or Committees by any former Ordinance of Parliament, in any of the said associated Counties, every Committee to

university who had been ejected by him in 1644: Twigg, *The University of Cambridge*, pp. 99, 238, 263, 289.

5 The text of the ordinance was printed by order of parliament in *Two ordinances of the Lords and Commons assembled in parliament* (1644): BL, Thomason Tracts, E.30[4]. It is also printed in *Acts and ordinances*, pp. 371–2. Under modern practice, the date of the ordinance is 22 January 1644.

consist of ten, whereof any 5 or more of them, to sit in any Place or Places within any the said associated Counties where the said Earle shall appoynt, with Power to put in Execution these Instructions following, and in pursuance thereof, to give Assistance to the said Committees.

First, They shall have Power to call before them, all Provosts, Masters, and Fellowes of Colledges, all Students and Members of the University, and all Ministers in any County of the Association, and all Schoole-masters that are scandalous in their Lives, or ill-affected to the Parliament, or Fomentors of this unnaturall Warre, or that shall wilfully refuse Obedience to the Ordinances of Parliament, or that have deserted their ordinary Places of Residence, not being imployed in the Service of the King and Parliament. And they shall have Power to send for any Witnesses and examine any Complaint or Testimony against them, upon Oathes of such Persons as shall and may be produced to give Evidence against them, and shall certifie their Names with the Charge and Proofes against them, to the said Earle of Manchester, and he shall have Power to eject such as he shall judge unfit for their Places, and to sequester their Estates, Meanes and Revenues, and to dispose of them as he shall think fitting, and to place other fitting Persons in their Roome, such as shall be approved of by the Assembly of Divines sitting at Westminster.

The Earle of Manchester, or the said Committee or Committees shall have

fo. 5

Power to administer the late Covenant taken and to be taken of all the 3 Kingdoms of England, Scotland, and Ireland, to all Persons in any of the said associated Counties, and the Isle of Ely, upon such Penalties as are or shall be assigned by the Parliament in this Behalfe.

And be it ordained, That the said Earle of Manchester shall have Power to dispose of a fifth Part of all such Estates as they shall sequester, for the Benefits of the Wives and Children of any of the aforesaid Persons.

The said Committee or Committees shall imploy a Clerke for the registering of all Warrants, Orders, Summons, and Ejectments made by them: And that they choose some convenient Place for the preserving of the Writings of this Committee.

That the said Earle of Manchester shall have Power to examine and inhibite all such as doe obstruct the Reformation now endeavoured by the Parliament and Assembly of Divines.

And be it further declared, That all such as shall doe anything in Execution of this Ordinance shall be kept indempnified by the Authority and Power of both Houses of Parliament.

And further be it ordeined, That the Earle of Manchester shall have Power to appoint a convenient Number, consisting of one or more out every Countie, one out of the Citie of Norwich and one out of the Countie and Citie of Lincolne: Provided, that 3 of these be Deputie-Lieutenants to sit at Cambridge, for the better ordering of all Businesses of the Association, according to Ordinances and Orders of Parliament, and according to his Commission granted by his Excellencie the Earle of Essex; And that the present Committee for the Association sitting at Cambridge shall cease, when the Earle of Manchester shall have appointed another under his Hand and Seale.

John Browne Cler. Parliament

Finis

Then follows the Commission of Inquisition, for surely it can deserve no other Name, granted by the Earle of Manchester; being indeed the first Page of the Manuscript.

fo. 6

The Coppy of the Commission given to us by the Earle of Manchester with others to be a Committee to heare and take the Articles and Depositions of any that shall be exhibited against scandalous Ministers and Schoole-masters within the County of Essex.[6]

By Vertue of an Ordinance of Lords and Commons in Parliament assembled to mee directed, entituled An Ordinance for regulating the University of Cambridge and for removing scandalous Ministers in the 7 associated Counties, I doe authorize, constitute and appointe you Sir Thomas Honywood, Henry Mildemay, Oliver Raymond, Richard Herlackenden, John Meade, Arthur Barnardiston, Thomas Coke, John Elleston, Robert Crane and Henery Barrington Esquires, or any fyve of you, to calle before you all Ministers and Schoole-masters within the County of Essex that are scandalous in their Lives, or ill-affected to the Parliament, or Promoters[7] of this unnaturall Warre, or that shall wilfully refuse Obedience to the Ordinances of Parliament, or that have deserted their ordinary Places of Residence, not being imployed in the Service of the King and Parliament, with full Power and Liberty to sende for any Witnesses, and to examine any Complaints in Testimony [against] such Ministers upon the [Oaths] of such Persons as shall and may be produced to give Evidence against them. And also to certefy the Names of such Ministers with the Chardge and Proofes against them to mee. And I doe further hereby authorize and appointe you to administer the late Covenant taken or to be taken of all the 3 Kingdoms of England, Scotland and Ireland to all Persons within the said County; and to performe and execute all other Things directed by the said Ordinance within the said County.[8] And whatsoever you or any 5 of you shall doe in the Premisses, this shall be your Warrant. Given under my Hande and Seale the 26 day of February 1643.

Manchester

Instructions to the Commissioners for removing scandalous Ministers within the County of Essex.

1. You are with all Diligence to apply yourselves to the speedy and effectuall executing this Ordinance, and for that End you are to divide yourselves into severall Committees (5 of you being a Committee) and to appoint certaine Daies for your sitting at severall Places within the

[6] Manchester's commission to the committees, and the accompanying instructions, survive in much the same form, except for the names of the commissioners, for Lincolnshire and east Suffolk. Unlike the Cole MS, these other sources also contain a copy of a letter which Manchester sent with the commission, urging the committees to act vigorously and warning them that 'if a generall reformacion follow not within your Countye, assuredly the blame will be laid upon you, and you must expect to be called to accompt for it, both here and hereafter'. It seems likely that a similar letter was sent to the Essex committees: 'Royalist clergy of Lincolnshire', pp. 116–19; *Suffolk and the great rebellion 1640–1660*, ed. Alan Everitt (Suffolk Records Society, 1960), pp. 62–5.

[7] The other commissions cited above have 'fomentors of this unnatural warre'.

[8] For the covenant, see the Introduction, p. xxxii and pp. xxxvii–xxxviii above.

fo. 7

County, that so all Parties by the Easines of Accesse may be encouraged to address themselves to you with their Complaints.
2. When any Complaints are made unto you and Articles preferred against any Minister, you are to send out your Warrants to the Witnesses, and also to the Minister, to appeare before you at the Time and Place by you appointed.
3. I thinke it not fit that the Party accused should be present at the takeing of the Depositions, because of discountenancing the Witnesses and disturbing the Service: but when the Depositions are taken upon Oath, you are then to let the Party accused have a copy of them, if he will, if he will pay for it; and to give him Day to returne his Answer in Writing, and to make his Defence at another Meeting appointed within 14 Dayes or thereabouts.
4. You are to returne both the Accusation and the Defence under your Hands sealed up to Mr Good and Mr Ash, whom I have appointed to receive the same, and to acquaint me with the Particulars, who thereupon shall receive such further Directions as shall be thought fit.[9]
5. If the Party accused will not appeare nor make his Defence, you are to certifie the Cause of his Absence or Neglect herein; for if he be non-resident, or in Armes against the Parliament, or the like, I shall proceed against him notwithstanding.
6. And because it is found by sad Experience that Parishioners are not forward to complaine of their Ministers, although they be very scandalous, but haveing this [10] and Power in their handes, yet want Hearts to make use thereof, too many being Enemies to that blessed Reformation so much desired by the Parliament and loath to come under a powerfull Ministry, and some spareing their Ministers, because such Ministers to gaine the good Opinion of their People, for the present doe spare them in their Tythes, and thereupon are esteemed quiett Men or the like: you are there-

fo. 8

fore willed to call unto you some well-affected Men within every Hundred, who having no private Enagagements but intending to further the publique Reformation may be required and encouraged by you to enquire after the Doctrines, Lives and Conversations of all Ministers and Schoolemasters, and to give you Information both what can be deposed, and who can depose the same.
7. And for better Encouragement both of the Commissioners and Prosecutors of this Service, every Commissioner shalbe allowed 5^s per Diem that sits to execute this Ordinance to be paid by   the Sequestrators of the said County, who are hereby required to pay it upon Demand, and who shalbe allowed it upon Account:[11] out of which Money it is desired that the Clarke may receive some Pay; that soe the said

[9] Simeon Ashe and William Good were Manchester's chaplains. It seems likely that they played an important part in managing the process of the purge, not only as the points of contact between Manchester and the county committees, but also as advisers to Manchester. Ashe has an entry in the *ODNB*, and both men are described by Ann Laurence: Ann Hughes, 'Simeon Ashe (d. 1662)', *ODNB*; Ann Laurence, *Parliamentary army chaplains 1642–51* (Woodbridge, 1990), pp. 92–3, 129–30.

[10] Cole leaves a blank: the missing word is printed by Everitt in the Suffolk papers as 'prise' and by Hill in the Lincolnshire manuscript as 'price'. The better reading seems to be prise, meaning a lever, or leverage: *OED*, under 'prise, n. 3'.

[11] The members of the committee appear to have been paid at the end of the purge: see Introduction, p. xvii n. 43.

Clark may not discourage the Prosecutors or Informers by demanding Fees either for Warrants or Copies of the proceedings, unles the Writing be very large, and the Parties will not voluntarily give him something.[12]

8. You are to proceede against all Ministers and Schoolemasters that are scandalous in their Doctrines, or Lives, non-residents, Ignorants or unable for the Service, idle, lazy, and all that are any waies ill-affected to the Parliament or to the proceedings thereof, expressed either by their Speeches or Actions.

9. You are to require the Parishioners to make Choise of a fit and able Minister to succeed, who must bring unto mee a very good Testimoniall from the best-affected Gentry and Ministry of the County of his Sufficiency, as also of his Life and Conversation; and you are to take a speciall Care that no Anabaptists or Antinomians be nominated, but only such as are very orthodox in their Opinions, and such as the Assembly of Divines now assembled at Westminster will accept of.

10. You are to enquire out the true Value of everie Living that shalbe questioned before you, and to certifie the same to me, as also the Estate and Livelyhood of the Party questioned, that so I may know what Allowance to make to the Partie upon the Sequestration to maintaine his Wife and Children according to the Ordinance of Parliament.

11. You are required to use all other Waies and Means according to your Discretion for the speeding this Service.

Then follows the Examination of Witnesses and their Depositions wrote and interlined in various Hands; which shows it to have been the Original Draft.

fo. 9

Committee against scandalous Ministers in Essex

[+ Depositions to which the Answer is come in]

+ *These marked in this Manner are in a different Hand from the Rest of the MS. or in Crochets thus [ ] throughout the whole Transcript.*

1. Witnesses examined against John Jegon Parson of Sibble-Hedingham[13] at Halsted, March 20. 1643.[14]

1. That the said John Jegon was very active in setting up the Rayles, indevorring to compell his People to come up to the same, by courteing them: there professeing, if these factious Fellows were not punisht, he would lay downe his Ministry: and to persuade them to go to it he coated Math: 15.12.15* and Jer: 15.29.* denying to publish Absolution, whereupon divers lefte the Towne.[15]

[12] The Lincolnshire and Suffolk versions omit 'not': 'and the parties will voluntarily give him something'.

[13] John Jegon (1596–1672) was the son of Thomas Jegon, master of Corpus Christi College, Cambridge and rector of Sible Hedingham (d. 1618). John graduated BA (1614) and MA (1618) from Corpus, and was appointed rector of Sible Hedingham in 1619: Venn, *Alumni Cantabrigienses*, II, 466; Newport, *Repertorium*, II, 324; CCEd, Location ID 11287. See also Introduction, pp. xliii–xliv above, for more about Jegon.

[14] This hearing on 20 March 1644 is the first recorded session of the committee: Jegon's opponents had previously tried to have him ejected by parliament and were eager to try again. They added further charges on 8 April 1644 (fo. 21 below). The session on 20 March was at Halstead, and also heard charges against Christopher Newstead. That case (and probably that against Jegon) was heard by a group of five members, including and probably chaired by Arthur Barnardiston: Leicester MS 31, fos. 20v–21.

[15] Parishioners of Saffron Walden similarly claimed that godly people had been forced to move away from that town by the vicar, Edward Grey, who prosecuted them in the church courts: *Cambridgeshire scandalous ministers*, pp. 35–6.

Sydrack Smyth, Ralphe Gilbert, William Butcher, John Cooper.[16]
* *These Quotations must be wrong put down in the MS, I having consulted the Passages referred to during my transcribing them and find nothing alluding to the Subject in either Place: indeed the 15 Ch: of Jeremiah has only 21 Verses.*
2. That he was negligent in preching untill this Parlament and when he did, he pressed Bowing at the Name of Jesus, coating for it Isa: 45. 23 and from thence inferred, that the Refusors made God forsworne and deliverd other dangerous Pointes of Doctrin: his Curats being most of them also scandalous.[17]
Sydrack Smyth, Ralphe Gilbert, William Butcher, John Cooper.
3. That he hath often bitterly inveighed against godly Ministers in private, nameing Marshall, Rogers, Brewer and Sutton.[18]
Sidrack Smith.
4. And ordinarily in his Sermons railed against Professors in generall, terming them Spirit-mongers, Puritans, and People of phanaticall Spirits.
Ralphe Gilbert, John Cooper, William Butcher senior.
5. That he delivered in a Sermon, that God had Mercy on Judas, in that he sent him not to Hell but to his owne Place.
John Browne, John Cooper, William Butcher senior, Ralph Gilbert.
6. That he ordinarily sweares by his Faith and Troth.
Andrew Bridge, Joane Dennis [who were his Servants].*
* *What is included in Crochets is wrote in a different Hand.*
7. He is a Prophaner of the Lord's Day, sending his Servants usually on Errands: and one Day left his Wife and Servants to bag Hops, when himself went to Eve-

fo. 10

ning Prayer, and threatened to cudgell his Man to it, because he argued the Unlawfulnes of it: and those Hops were the same Day wayed and carted towards Bury.
Andrew Bridge, George Butcher.
8. He is an Upholder of Alehouses in his Parish, reproving in his Sermon the Officers that would have suppressed them.
Ralph Gilbert, Sidrack Smith, William Butcher senior.
9. That in his Sermon he said, he saw little or no Difference between the Papists and Us in Matters of Religion.

16 A year later, six of the deponents were charged with interrupting church services in protest against the failure of the attempt to eject Jegon. They were Ralph Gilbert, William Butcher, John Cooper, George Deeks, Nicholas Brag and George Finch. See Introduction, pp. xliii–xliv above.

17 Isaiah xlv. 23: 'I have sworn by myself, the word has gone out of my mouth in righteousness, and shall not return, That unto me every knee shall bow, every tongue shall swear.' It seems likely that Jegon employed a succession of curates to carry out some of his duties in the parish, though their identity is often unknown. One who surely did not deserve the accusation of scandal was Robert Abbott, curate in 1640. In 1647, he was appointed vicar of Stansted Mountfichet on the nomination of Timothy Middleton (for whom see Appendix 3, p. lxviii above), and in 1662 he was ejected for nonconformity: CCEd, Person ID 58863; Matthews, *Calamy revised*, p. 1.

18 The godly ministers referred to were Stephen Marshall, vicar of Finchingfield; probably Daniel Rogers, preacher of Wethersfield; Edmund Brewer, vicar of Castle Hedingham; and Daniel Sutton, curate at Wethersfield: Tom Webster, 'Stephen Marshall (1594/5?–1655)', *ODNB*; Yiannikkou, 'Daniel Rogers', *ODNB*; Smith, *Ecclesiastical history of Essex*, pp. 53, 56, 297; and Matthews, *Calamy revised*, pp. 71–2, for Brewer; Smith, *Ecclesiastical history of Essex*, p. 54; and Matthews, *Calamy revised*, p. 470, for Sutton.

William Burst, George Deekes, Nicholas Greene.
10. He blamed the Parliament for raising Armes, and the County of Essex for their forward Contribution.
Nicholas Brag, William Burst.
11. He hoped that Bishops would rise to a greater Power than they had before; and then he would plague his Parishioners more than ever.
William Burst.
12. About 2 Weekes since, he said in his Sermon out of Romans the 13, that the Professors in these Times are the Cheife in making the Combustion in the Kingdome.[19]
William Butcher senior, George Finch.
13. The same Day the Railes were pulled up, he said it was Pitty the Bible was ever translated into English.
Andrew Bridge.
14. That he did very seldome pray in his Familie or reade the Scriptures to them.
Andrew Bridge, Joane Dennis.
Ex: See more taken since, foliis 9 and 10 against him.[20]

Vide p. 20.

By this first Specimen the Villainy of those iniquitous Inquisitors may easily be discerned, when even Servants were encouraged to come and give Evidence against their Masters and to disclose the private Concerns of a Family.
No Notice is taken of this John Jegon's persecution either by Newcourt or Walker in his Sufferings of the Clergy.[21]

fo. 11

[Alpheston. Depositions. The Answer is retorned]
2. Depositions against Rowland Steward Parson of Alpheston in the county of Essex, taken at Halsted the 22 of March 1643.[22] *Vide p. 86.*[23]

[19] Romans xiii advocates obedience to the higher powers which are ordained of God. To preach in March 1644 ('2 weeks since') in the sense alleged was courageous.

[20] Here, and at other points in the Cole MS (fos. 22, 31, 33 and 37), 'Ex' is a contraction of 'Examinatur', signifying that the entry has been checked by the clerk of the committee: see also Leicester MS 31, fo. 25v n. 81. The user is then referred to later evidence against Jegon at fos. 9 and 10 of the original manuscript. These further depositions are at fos. 21–22 below. (The folio numbers added to the book in modern times differ slightly from Cole's original foliation, hence his '*Vide p. 20*'.)

[21] As explained in the Introduction, pp. xliii–xliv above, Jegon was not sequestrated by Manchester and therefore does not appear in Leicester MS 31. There is no sign that either Newcourt or Walker, who published in 1710 and 1714 respectively, had access to the present manuscript, which appears to have been in private hands until given to Cole later in the century.

[22] See Leicester MS 31, fos. 25 and A29 (pp. 80–1 and 99 below) for the final version of these articles and the warrants for Steward's sequestration and ejection. Steward graduated BA (1608), MA (1612) from St Catherine's College, Cambridge. He was appointed rector of Alphamstone, a parish lying on the county boundary with Suffolk, in 1614. His parish income was estimated at £70 a year and he had a wife and ten children. He did not petition for restoration in 1660, and may well have died before then: Venn, *Alumni Cantabrigienses*, IV, 162; Newcourt, *Repertorium*, II, 8; Leicester MS 31, fo. 25v.

[23] This is a reference to fo. 87 of the present manuscript, BL, Add. MS 5829 (fo. 86 in Cole's foliation). This part of the manuscript, not reproduced in this edition, contains copies by Cole of various notes made by Zachary Grey, in this case summarizing the charges against Steward. See Introduction, p. xii n. 20 above. Grey's notes clearly derived from his study of Leicester MS 31, and add nothing to the information in that manuscript.

1. He is a common Swearer of deepe Oathes, as by God.
Isaack Wincoll Esq,[24] William More, Solomon Clarke.
2. He is a Disc [25] the Service of the Parliament, (as appeares by his preaching at the Time of the Propositions coming forth) about Almes: he said, there is a Giving; now I doe not like that; for that makes the Breach the bigger;[26] And also by his Neglect to pray for the Army, and his blaming one of his Neighbours for letting his Sonne goe a Voluntier; And when some of them were killed, he said to one of his Neighbours, I told you what would come of it.[27]
Robert Harison, Robert Moyce, John Clarke, William More.
3. He hath neglected and slited the keepeing of the Fast.
William More, Robert Moice.
4. He is a common Frequenter of the Company of Papists, and of other lewd Persons, at Innes, their Houses and also his owne.
William More, Robert Moice, John Clark, Solomon Clark.
5. He hath bin a notorious common Gamester at Dice and Cards.
William More, John Clarke, Solomon Clark, John Clark.
6. He hath bin an excessive Drinker, urging others thereto by drinking Healths and that on his Knees, boasting that he had bin drunke 20 Times in one House.
William More, John Clarke, Henry Leffingwell.
7. He hath playd at Cat and trap with Boyes of his Parish on the Saboth Day, and a constant Looker on them that played thereat, teaching his Children therein that Day.[28]
William More, John Clark.

fo. 12

8. He hath brag'd, he hath had the Use of divers Women besides his Wife: and this he hath spoken before his Wife.
William More, John Clarke.
9. He hath bin alwaies negligent in his Function.
William More, Robert Harison, John Clark.
Neither Newcourt or Walker take Notice of this Roland Steward's Persecution.

---

[24] It was unusual for a member of a committee hearing a case to be cited as a witness for that case. Wincoll lived in a neighbouring parish and no doubt knew of Steward's reputation. Steward's subsequent ejection from Alphamstone had the happy outcome for Wincoll that the vacancy was filled by John Collinges, a young Emmanuel graduate who was also employed as Wincoll's chaplain and who married his daughter: Wright, 'John Collinges', *ODNB*.

[25] The missing words are 'discourager of', as shown by Leicester MS 31, fo. 25.

[26] In June 1642, parliament promulgated its propositions for money and plate, a scheme for financing the parliamentary militia by voluntary contributions. It was well supported in Essex, despite some opposition from the pulpit: Fletcher, *Outbreak*, pp. 336–8; Holmes, *Eastern Association*, p. 35 and n. 15, where several instances of opposition by clergy are quoted.

[27] See Leicester MS 31, fo. 25: that later version concludes with 'affirming the contrary forces to be the stronger', emphasizing Steward's hostility to parliament.

[28] The boys were apparently playing some version or variant of the games of tipcat and/or trap-ball, for which see *OED* and Iona and Peter Opie, *Children's games with things* (Oxford, 1997), pp. 316–21, 325–8.

[Depositions to which the Answer is returned.]
3. Depositions against Edward Shephard Vicar of Maplested Magna taken at Halsted the 22 of March 1643.[29]
1. That whilst the Railes stood, at his first Entrance into the Church, he ordinarily prayd at it, with his Face towards the East, bowing towards it, before he came at it.
James Fuller, John French, Sextons.
2. He is a Man not fitted for the Ministry, having a very bad Utterance, and, as they conceive, a weake memory.
Mary Laverick, Joane Fosset.
3. He said it was never merry World since there was so much preaching; for now all Hospitality and good-fellowship was laid a Bed; further saying, that Mr Brewer (a very diligent Preacher upon all Occasions) was a railing and preach that which was false.[30]
John French, Daniell Chandler.
4. That catechising the youth before the Sacrament, he taught them there was 7 Sacraments, as 1. Marriage; 2. Churching of Women; 3. Penance; 4. Burialls; 5. Taking up of Lands

fo. 13

by a Clover with a white Rod stuck in it.[31]
Marmaduke Twier, Alice , Fleetwood Wentford.
5. And further said, that Soules went to 3 Places; some to Heaven, some to Hell, and some to a middle Place from which they might be resolved by Prayer.
Fleetwood Wentford, Alice , Marmaduke Twier.
6. When he read the Vow and Covenant on the Saboth (as they remember) he tooke it not then; but on a Weeke Day he tooke it with some of his Parish, with these Limitations, so far as it was agreable to the Word of God, and not contrary to the former Protestation and Oath of Allegiance.
William Harington Gent, Thomas Male Gent.
7. That on the Saboth afore William Laverick, offering to take the Vow and Covenant, after the reading of it, and desiring the Minister to subscribe his Name, he would not suffer it to be done.
William Laverick.
This Man's Sufferings is not mentioned by Walker or Newcourt. See more p. 21.[32]

---

[29] According to Venn, Shephard was a graduate of Jesus College, Cambridge (BA 1610–11, MA 1614). His early career is obscure: in 1639, he was appointed vicar of Great Maplestead, on the presentation of Thomas Shepheard, presumably a relative, who had purchased the patronage *pro hac vice*: Venn, *Alumni Cantabrigienses*, IV, 59 (under Sheppard, Edward); Newcourt, *Repertorium*, II, 404. There are gaps and obscurities in the articles that cannot be clarified by reference to Leicester MS 31, which does not include this case because Shephard was not sequestrated. See Introduction, pp. xxi–xxii above for further evidence relevant to the case and p. xlii and n. 186 above for its outcome.

[30] The sense of this passage was, presumably, that Edmund Brewer, minister of Castle Hedingham, was abusive and used false arguments in his preaching.

[31] It is not clear what has gone wrong with this article: perhaps the original manuscript had lost some words at the junction of fos. 12 and 13. The reference to a clover with a white rod stuck in it is obscure: see also the charges against Shephard by Elizabeth Spurgeon that he beat himself with white rods, at Introduction, pp. xxi–xxii above, quoting ERO, Q/Sba 2/57.

[32] The further depositions against Shephard are at fo. 22 below (21 in Cole's numbering).

[Depositions, the Answer is returned]
4. Depositions against George Crackingthorpe Viccar of Bradwell taken at the 21 of March 1643.[33]
1. He usually by Faith and Troth.
Thomas Collens, John Raven.
2. He is a common Tipler, and often drunk, as at Braintree a Quarter of a Yeare since, where he could not come Home without reeling into the Hedges; and this is usuall with him: and about Yeare since he was so distempered with drinking that he fell a whooping and hallowing till he lay downe and slept.
John Emery, John Barnard.

fo. 14

3. That he refused to take the Vow and Covenant in the Expressions thereof, but alterd it and so read it: And in the Afternoone refused to take it, and bad them often take Heed what they did, saying he would not take it otherwise then he had framed it, though he lost his Living.[34]
Anthony Blackborne, Robert Franck, [Joshua Raven].
4. He hath preached about yeare since, that Almes purge away Sin, and good Workes deliver from Death.
Thomas Collins.
His Benefice is worth about 60^{li} per Annum. He hath a Wife and 8 Children.
See more fol: XIIII and XV.
Mr Newcourt takes no Notice of his Persecutions. See also more concerning him p. 27 and 28.[35]

[Depositions the Answer is retorned]
5. Depositions against John Simpson Viccar of Mount Bewers taken the 21 of March 1643 at .[36]
1. That he would not come out of the Railes to administer the Sacrament; but rather sufferd his People to be molested in the Courts.

[33] George Crackenthorpe graduated BA from The Queen's College, Oxford in 1608. In 1617, he was appointed vicar of Great Saling by the patronage of Sir Henry Maxey. In 1623, he left to take up the rectory of Great Barton, Suffolk, but returned to Essex in 1639 when Sir William Maxey presented him to the rectory of Bradwell-juxta-Coggeshall. Sir William's memorial in Bradwell church, marking his death in 1645, asserted that he died a good servant of King Charles and no rebel, and that he was a man of Joshua's resolution that he and his house should serve the Lord. His practice was to call his children at five in the morning for prayer and bible reading: Foster, *Alumni Oxonienses*, I, 345; Newcourt, *Repertorium*, II, 514, 83; ERO, T/Z 151/113. The case against Crackenthorpe was referred to Manchester, who agreed that he should be ejected. The articles as submitted to Manchester are at Leicester MS 31, fo. 22. Cole evidently had difficulty in reading his manuscript and left several blank spaces in his transcript. They can be supplied from MS 31, as follows: the hearing took place at Halstead; in article 1, 'swears'; in articles 2 and 4, the action took place 'about a year since'. Leicester MS 31 also terms Crackenthorpe 'parson' of Bradwell (he was the rector, not the vicar as stated in the Cole MS) and gives the date of the hearing as 22 March 1643/4.

[34] For the vow and covenant, see Introduction above, pp. xxxi–xxxii.

[35] These further depositions against Crackenthorpe are at fos. 28–9 below.

[36] John Simpson was educated at Queens' College, Cambridge (MA 1606), and in 1616 he was presented to the rectory of Mount Bures, an Essex parish on the border with Suffolk. These articles were certainly submitted to the north Essex committee, but there is no evidence that Simpson was sequestered or ejected. His case is not included in Leicester MS 31, or in the records of the committee

John Harison Minister,[37] Samford, John Brett.
2. He often sweares by his Faith and Troth.
John Harison Minister, Henry Samford, John Upchar.
3. He is so lazy in his Function, that for many yeares he preched the same Sermons over and over againe.
Henry Samford, Richard Siday.
4. He hath and doth employ ill-affected and scandalous Ministers, as Cooper, Layfield and one

fo. 15

Simpson his Kinsman,[38] that preached finall falling from Grace, and that in his Presence.
Henry Samford, Richard Siday, Winifred Lay, Gabriel Wheeler.
5. He hath formerly suffred the youth of his Parish to use Sports on the Lord's Day, as Scales, Foot-balls, not reproving them for the same when he saw it.[39]
John Upcher.
6. He said, he tooke the Archbishopp to be a wise holy Man, wishing himself as godly a Man as he.
Richard Siday.
7. He prayed not for the Parliament till of late.
Richard Siday.
[He is worth 100^{li}] [His Benefice worth 80^{li} per Annum. He hath neither a Wife nor Child].
No notice is taken of this Vicar's Persecution either by Newcourt or Walker. From every Article brought against this Person the deplorable Iniquity of those hypocritical Times may be discovered; and rather make for than against him.

---

for plundered ministers. When Simpson died in 1648, the parish register recorded that 'John Simson senior clerke minister of the parish of Bures at the Mount by the space of 32 yeares was buried the 3rd of December'. His will was proved later that month, his nephew John Simpson acting as executor. He was succeeded as rector by his nephew, who had been ordained in 1639 and who was doubtless the kinsman mentioned in the articles as one of the curates employed by Simpson senior. It is probable that Simpson senior negotiated an agreement that he might retain the living but would delegate the service of it to his nephew, who would comply with the presbyterian regime required by parliament. The John Simpson who signed the petition of Suffolk and Essex presbyterian ministers in 1646 was probably the younger Simpson: Venn, *Alumni Cantabrigienses*, IV, 79; CCEd, Location ID 11173; ERO, D/P 281/1/1; TNA, PROB 11/206/442; Smith, *Ecclesiastical history of Essex*, pp. 199–200; BL, Thomason Tracts, E.339[11].

37 John Harrison, curate of St Peter's Sudbury (Suffolk), had been a well-known puritan preacher in the local area: his wife Judith was a sister of Isaac Wincoll, for whom see Appendix 3, pp. lxii–lxiii above. Harrison died in 1641, so the minister who deposed was probably John Harrison's son John, appointed minister of Little Waltham in 1643: *Suffolk manorial families*, II, 135; W. W. Hodson and C. F. D. Sperling, *A short history of the borough of Sudbury in the county of Suffolk* (Sudbury, 1896), p. 119; Matthews, *Calamy revised*, p. 249.

38 See n. 36 above for Simpson's nephew, who seems to have upset some parishioners by preaching that the elect might fall from grace. He may have fallen silent on the topic later.

39 F. G. Emmison quotes rare Essex sources as including 'scales' in a list of games and suggests that it was 'probably for cales or ninepins'. The *OED* defines 'kayles' as ninepins or skittles, and quotes 'skailes' as a variant from 1598: F. G. Emmison, *Elizabethan life*, I: *Disorder* (Chelmsford, 1970), pp. 224, 230; *OED*, under 'kayles'.

[Depositions the Answer is retorned]
6. Depositions against John Lake Parson of Saling magna taken the 22 of March 1643.[40]
1. He published the Booke for Liberty on the Lord's Day.[41]
Henry Smith, William Dixton, Richard Rumsy.
2. He denied the Sacrament to those that would not come to the Raile, but within this halfe yeare gave it to a wandring Pedlar that railed against Round-heads.
Henry Smith, Richard Rumzy, William Sorrell, Thomas Powter.
3. He is a very common Tipler, often drunke, so that sometimes he is not able to goe Home

fo. 16

without leading; and that he hath not forborne tipling on Saterday Night till next Day it rung to Church, and then he went Home and preached.
William Sorrell, Thomas Powter, William Smith.
4. He is an ordinary Swearer, and in his Passion not forbearing the Name of God.
Richard Rumsy, William Sorrell, Thomas Powter.
5. He is notoriously vile in attempting the Chastity of divers of his Mayds, by often Allurements, and sometimes by Violences, not forbearing the same on the Lord's Day when his Mayd was helping him on with his Gowne to go to Church, telling one of them when she was sure of her Husband, you know your Husband, you need not now care, not ceasing his Solicitations since Marriage: and following another on to a Hay-goffe[42] when she went to give his Cattle Meat, forcing her to skip downe to escape; and using another of about 16 yeares of Age with such Violence, that by her striving she was brought into a dangerous Sicknes and other Inconveniences.[43]
Elizabeth Smith, Joane Osborne, Elizabeth Carter, Bridget Cant.
The value of his Living is betweene 50 and 60^{li} per Annum. And hath 6^{li} per Annum of his owne and hath a Wife and a Daughter unmarried.
Vide more p. 52.[44] *Notwithstanding this vehement Article he found Means to keep his Living, dying possessed of it in 1646 as appears in Newcourt's Repertorium vol 2, p. 514.*

---

[40] Lake's origins and career are poorly documented. He was probably the man ordained deacon and priest by the bishop of Oxford in 1615, but there is no record of his graduation. In 1623, he was appointed vicar of Great Saling by Sir Henry Maxey (on whom see n. 33 above). Though articled against in 1644, there is no evidence that Lake was sequestrated or ejected. It is clear from Cole MS, fos. 53–5 that he resisted ejection and was still in possession in October 1644. The Maxey family, patrons of the living, were no friends of parliament and may have supported Lake, who in any event soon died: his death is recorded in 1646 as the reason for the appointment of his successor, Thomas Stubble, on 1 Oct.: CCEd, Person ID 13700; CCEd, Person ID 43070 (record of George Crack-enthorpe, Lake's predecessor at Great Saling); Newcourt, *Repertorium*, II, 514.

[41] The 'book for liberty' refers to the king's declaration of 1633, the 'book of sports': see Introduction, pp. xxviii–xxix and n. 111 above.

[42] The *OED* defines hay-goaf, or golph, or gulfe as 'hay-mow', that is a stack of hay.

[43] See Introduction, p. xxxv above, for the previous accusations against Lake.

[44] Further depositions against Lake are at fos. 53–5 below.

[Depositions to which his Answer is by way of a Letter retorned]
7. Depositions against Timothy Clay[45] Parson of Wickham taken the 21 of March 1643 at *Vide p. 86.*[46]
1. He used to preach but once a Day, nor any other for him; and then railing against painfull

fo. 17

and godly Ministers; and said it was not lawfull to call the People from their Worke on the weeke Day to heare a Sermon, abusing the 4th Commandment to prove it.
Richard White, Elizabeth Granger.
2. He deferred a Sacrament by him appoynted and provision made till the Raile was set up; and when it was up, read the 2nd Service at it, threatning them with the High-Commission that would not receive it there.[47]
John Perry, Richard Golding.
3. He hath layne out drinking 7 or 8 Dayes till he was distemperd to Distraction, that Mr Ady (his Physitian) sent him Word that if he would not leave his drinking Sack he would be starke mad; and in his drinking Fit, he, with another Parson, now gone to Oxford, kept a noted Whore with them sometimes in private the most part of 2 Daies and 2 Nights, to the Expence of above 5li to their Parts[48] from Munday to Friday-night in these Disorders.
Richard White, John Perry, Richard Golding, John Strut, Thomas Hedgeman.
4. That he is a prophane Swearer.
Robert Digby, William Elliston, William Sayward.
5. He said he was sure God had made a King, but not a Parliament.
Samuell King.
6. He dranke a Health to Prince Rupert saying the Queene and Prince Rupert were right for us, but the King would come to the Parliament if he could, and said, but now we have gott him we will keepe him, and that there never were merry Daies since the Bishops went downe, and that he would venter his Life for

45 Timothy Clay, a graduate of Christ's College, Cambridge (BA 1614, MA 1617), was ordained priest in 1617. In or before 1637, he was appointed rector of Wickham St Paul by the dean and chapter of St Paul's, the patron of the living. (The relevant records of St Paul's were destroyed in the fire of 1666, but Clay was certainly serving the cure in 1637, when he signed the parish register.) The north Essex committee heard the depositions against Clay in March 1644, and Manchester's warrants for his sequestration and ejection were approved on 5 February 1645, which suggests some further inquiries or negotiations were needed before a decision was reached. Clay's wife was awarded one fifth of the living's income by parliament on 18 September 1646. It is not clear whether Clay returned to his living at Wickham in 1660, but in 1663 the dean and chapter of St Paul's appointed him vicar of High Easter, where he remained until his death in 1671: Venn, *Alumni Cantabrigienses*, I, 350; ERO, D/P 213/1/1; Leicester MS 31, fos. 24 and A28; BL, Add. MS 15670, fo. 218: CCEd, Location ID 11239.

46 No venue is stated for this hearing, but Cole refers to p. 86 (fo. 87 of BL, Add. MS 5829) where the venue is given as Halstead, in a note by Grey based on Leicester MS 31, fo. 24.

47 See Introduction, pp. xxvii–xxviii and n. 104, for the Laudian approach to communion and to the 'second service'.

48 Leicester MS 31, fo. 24 has 'for their Partes'.

fo. 18

the King, and goe to him if he could, but would die in the Roome[49] rather then yeild to the Parliament.
John Cannam.
His Living is worth above 60[li] per Annum.
[He hath a Wife and Children.]
He was probably ejected: tho' his Name occurs not in Walker and Mr Newcourt mentions no Rector of Wickham St Paul's from 1451 till the Restoration, at which Time This Timothy Clay was presented to the Vicarage of Easter Alta in Essex by the Dean and Chapter of St Paul's.

[Stisested, his Answer is in part retorned]
8. Depositions taken upon oath against Christopher Newsted Parson of Stiested 20 of March 1643 at Halsted.[50]
1. He hath bin a greate promoter of the late Innovations, as bowing to the Altar toward the East, reading the second Service and churching Women there, prosecuting tender Consciences that durst not observe those Innovations, affirming it to be Treason not to obey the same.
John Dawes, Richard Norton by Information from Abington.[51]
2. He preached that the Sin of Ignorance is but a small Sin, and that a Papist may be saved as well as a Puritan, but that (he said) a Papist must goe a little further about: And that that Sin which makes some Men infamous, made Mary Magdalen famous.

[49] This word is spelled 'rome' in Leicester MS 31, fo. 24. The *OED* gives many variant spellings under 'room'. The meaning seems to be 'position' (sc. of loyalty to the king).

[50] See also Leicester MS 31, fos. 20–21, for this case. Stisted was a peculiar of the archbishop of Canterbury, within the jurisdiction of the deanery of Bocking. In 1641, the rector of Stisted died, and parishioners, supported by the earl of Warwick, promoted the claims of John Clarke and then Edward Sparhawke, the two most recent in a long line of puritan curates there (see Introduction, pp. xlii–xliii above). Archbishop Laud had, however, promised the living to Christopher Newstead, who had been put forward by Sir Thomas Roe. Unable himself to appoint Newstead without the agreement of the House of Lords, Laud contrived to have Newstead appointed by the crown in June 1642. Some parishioners continued to oppose Newstead's appointment, but in May 1643 the House of Lords confirmed it. Violent protests ensued and the Lords ordered the parishioners to comply. Soon Manchester's purge gave parishioners the opportunity to try again, and finally to succeed in overturning Newstead's appointment. But the parish could not agree on who should be appointed to serve. Ralph Josselin, vicar of Earl's Colne, was invited to mediate, noting 'the towne was divided and would not condiscend, one to another: oh wofull, sad divisions'. Newstead's subsequent attempts to obtain a living were obstructed until 1660, when he regained possession of Stisted, but by 1663, he was dead: Wright, 'Christopher Newstead', *ODNB*; CCEd, Person ID 81111; *Lords Journal*, VI, 59, 97; Parliamentary Archives, HL/PO/JO/10/1/150, /151, /153; *Josselin diary*, pp. 23–4; John Walter, 'Confessional politics in pre-Civil War Essex: prayer books, profanations and petitions', *Historical Journal*, 44 (2001), 677–701, especially 680.

[51] This refers to Abingdon (Berkshire). In 1629, Newstead had been appointed vicar of St Helen's and of St Nicholas' church, Abingdon, following the ejection of Edward Rood, a godly minister, by the High Commission. In 1640, Rood sought restoration and Newstead, perhaps recognizing the strength of support for Rood in parliament and amongst parishioners, agreed to resign. Rood was accordingly restored. The parishioners of Stisted had little experience of Newstead, but they obtained testimony against him from Abingdon. It is not clear whether the deponents Norton and Dawes were from Abingdon or were men of Essex who were deposing on the strength of statements made by residents of Abingdon: Wright, 'Christopher Newstead'; Arthur E. Preston, *The church and parish of St Nicholas, Abingdon* (Oxford, 1935), p. 219; Manfred Brod, *Abingdon in context: small-town politics in early modern England, 1547–1688* (Peterborough, 2010), pp. 64–7.

William Drake, John Browne, John Dawes, Richard Norton, These 2 last Witnesses by Information from Abington.
3. He hath buried many dead Corpses with Crosses on their Brests: and, there being in his Church at Abbington the Pictures of God the

fo. 19

Father, and of Purgatory, he caused to be raced out some Scriptures which were upon the Walle, shewing the Unlawfulnes of them: and others to be putt up falsely quoted and aplied to justifie and maintaine them, as 1 Peter 3. 19.[52] And affirmed that Lent was observed for more then politicke Ends; and being told, there was an Act of Parliament shewing that it was but for politique Ends, he said, what care I for an Act of Parliament.[53]
John Dawes, Richard Norton, by Information from Abington.
4. He is no waies gifted or fitly qualified for the Ministery, and negligent to prepare his People for the Sacrament by not preaching concerning that Ordinance.[54]
John Dawes, Richard Norton, John Browne.
5. His Curate in Catechising shewing that Christ's Death was sufficient for all, but not effectuall to all, he interrupted him, commanding him to goe noe further: And next Lord's Day preached that Christ died for all, proving it by the Catechisme in the Common Prayer Booke, vizt. Christ died for me and all Mankind.
John Dawes, Richard Norton, by Information from Abington.
6. He hath declared his Malignancy against the Parliament, and in particular against my Lord Say, saying, he was no good Subject.[55]
John Dawes, Richard Norton, by Information from Abington.
7. His Conversation hath bin most familiarly with Malignants and ill-affected Persons, choosing those of the most base and lewd Life for his Church-Wardens.
John Dawes, Richard Norton, by Information from Abington.
8. When Mr Rood (Minister of Abington before him) was imprisoned by the High-Com-

[52] It appears that there were paintings in St Helen's church depicting God and purgatory, and that texts condemning idolatry and superstition had also been installed. The deponents claimed that Newstead had had the texts erased and others substituted, including 1 Peter iii. 19, 'By which also he [Jesus Christ] went and preached unto the spirits in prison.' This obscure text has been interpreted as meaning that Christ preached to souls in purgatory, thus confirming the existence of purgatory: if Newstead did indeed believe in purgatory, it was in defiance of the thirty-nine articles of religion, which condemned it as a 'Romish Doctrine … repugnant to the word of God'.

[53] Newstead evidently supported the traditional practice of fasting during Lent, pointing out that it had a spiritual value for the individual, regardless of the various attempts by government to enforce it for reasons of public policy, such as the promotion of the fishing industry. For fasting, see also Introduction, p. xxx n. 120, and Chris R. Kyle, '"A dog, a butcher and a puritan": the politics of Lent in early modern England', in *Connecting centre and locality: political communications in early modern England*, ed. Chris R. Kyle and Jason Peacey (Manchester, 2020), pp. 22–43.

[54] Presumably the ordinance in question was that of 26 August 1643, 'for the utter demolishing removing and taking away of all monuments of superstition or idolatry'. Its orderly implementation in this parish would have benefited from support from Newstead, which was not given: *Acts and ordinances*, pp. 265–6. See also Leicester MS 31, fo. 20v n. 72, for the omission of 'not'.

[55] Lord Saye and Sele was indeed a leading opponent of Charles I: David L. Smith, 'William Fiennes, first viscount Saye and Sele (1582–1662)', *ODNB*.

fo. 20

mission unjustly, he the said Newsted, in the Absence of Mistris Rood, threw their Goods out of the House, and also their Children, exposing them to the [Extremity of the] Cold barefoot.[56]

John Dawes, Richard Norton, by Information from Abington.

9. At his taking Possession of Stiested Living last Summer,[57] he said, he must goe to his Master the King.

William Drake.

~~10. He made an Oath to the House of Lords against some of his Neighbours (vizt) that they brake the Peace, when he went to take Possession of Stiestead Church.~~

William Drake.

~~11. This Oath was false, for the Peace was kept, the Constable to that Purpose charging divers Persons.~~[58]

William Woodley, Robert Wood, John Rashbrooke, Robert Dyar, George Hurrell, Arthur Owers, Clement Davis.

12. He behaved himself so ill at Abington, that his Parishioners were about to exhibite a Bill against him, which he having Notice of, resigned his Living to prevent them, and did bind some of his Parishioners not to sue him.[59]

John Dawes, Richard Norton, by Information from Abington.

13. He preached that God had spareing Mercies for the Damned in Hell.

Arthur Owers, Marian George.

14. He would not take the Vow and Covenant; being asked if he would not take that himselfe which he would give to others, he said ye must not doe as I doe, but as I say: so that it was never taken in his Parish.[60]

Robert Dier, Robert Wood, Barnaby Warren.

Mr Newcourt has omitted Christopher Newsted

fo. 21

among the Rectors of Stistead: though he mentions him as obtaining the Prebend of Cadington Minor in the Church of St Paul at London on the Restoration and dying in 1662. Walker also has some Account of him p. 318 of his Sufferings of the Clergy.

---

56 Cole's brackets indicate that those words have been added in a different hand, surely in an attempt to emphasize the cruelty of Newstead's actions. The words are included in the text of Leicester MS 31, fo. 20v.

57 See Leicester MS 31, fo. 21 and n. 73 for a correction to this article.

58 Articles 10 and 11 are struck through in Cole's transcript, indicating that they had been struck through in the original manuscript. They are omitted from Leicester MS 31, with the subsequent articles 12, 13 and 14 below renumbered 10, 11 and 12. The omission suggests that the committee dismissed the deponents' contention that Newstead had given false evidence to the House of Lords.

59 As noted above (n. 51), it is true that Newstead resigned the living of Abingdon in 1640 or 1641, enabling Rood to be restored. It seems that he was the target of puritans who objected to his churchmanship, but also to his having replaced Rood in 1629, and his sponsorship by Laud. But a pamphlet of 1641, written by a supporter of Rood, clearly states that Newstead had 'behaved himselfe very honestly, and like a gentleman, all the time of his abode in Abingdon': Giles Gulter, *The archbishops crueltie, made knowne in a true story of one Mr. Edward Rood, who was minister at Saint Helens in Abingdon, and dismissed of his meanes and ministery by him* (BL, Thomason Tracts, E.166[4]).

60 See Introduction, pp. xxxi–xxxii, for the vow and covenant.

Vide p. 8

Additions to the Charge of Mr Jegon deposed unto, since and besides the Depositions against him fol: 1. viz: 8th April 1644 at ....

[Thomas Coartman deposed that]

Mr Jegon sent ~~2 or 3 daies before~~* the last Aprill-Fast for ~~one~~ Thomas Courtman this Deponent, and on the Fast-Day-morning; who that Morning went to him to his House; and Mr Jegon being then in his Chamber, sent for him to come thither to him; and being come, he said, Tom, I find myselfe not well, I would have thee copy out my Depositions, which he read to me the Deponent and I wrote out these most Part of that Day and the next.[61]

* *The words scratched out here are so in the original.*

Thomas Courtman.

2. Last September 3 yeares, Mr Jegon commanded this Deponent and his Brother, who wrought with him, to bag his Hops on the Lord's Day Afternoone, presently after Dinner; and about Sun-downe the same Day he caused them to be carried to the Rode, where a Cart was to take them up.

Thomas Gall.

3. Mr Jegon's Sonne said his Fathers Hops were a bagging at the Time they went to Church in the Afternoone (being the Time the said Deponent Gall speakes of). And that the said Hops were at Sturbridge Faire.[62]

George Deekes.

4. Susan Kent deposed that he said twas Pitty that ever the Bible was translated into English; for

fo. 22

now every Woman and beggarly Fellow thinke themselves able to dispute with reverend Divines.

Susan Kent.

5. This Deponent passing by Mr Jegon's Stable-Dore heard him sweare by God.

Martin Newman. Ex

Vide p. 11.

Additions to the Charge of Mr Shepard Vicar of Maplested magna deposed unto besides and since the Depositions against him fol: 3. vizt the 8th Aprill 1644.

1. This Deponent being Church-Warden, Mr Shepard would have him present his Parish because they went to other Churches, which this Deponent refused to doe, telling him, his People delighted not to heare him, because he made no Application[63] of his

[61] The complaint here is that by engaging Courtman in writing documents Jegon was failing to observe parliament's policy that no work should be done on its public fast days. The day in question will have been, as usual, the last Wednesday in the month, namely 26 April 1643. The 'depositions' were probably copies of Jegon's evidence to the committee for plundered ministers, which was considering a petition from parishioners to eject him: see Introduction, p. xliii.

[62] Hops were an important crop in the Hedinghams in the seventeenth century; they were usually sold at Stourbridge fair, outside Cambridge, in September: D. C. D. Pocock, 'Some former hop growing centres', *Agricultural History Review*, 13 (1965), 17–22.

[63] It was claimed that Shepard's preaching failed to bring the benefits of redemption to bear on the heart of the hearer: *OED*.

Doctrine and did not reprove Sin: Mr Shepard answered, he knew no Whoremasters, Drunkards, nor such like in his Parish: and what should he doe rayling in the Pulpit.
Daniell Chandler.
2. Upon the Parliament's first taking up Armes, Mr Shepard divers Saboths in preaching diswaded Men from going in the Parliament's Service, saying he knew not whether they or the King were for the Truth.
John French, John Eastland.
3. Being after asked why he discouraged the Youth from Parliament's Service, his Answer was, shall I stand for the Parliament when they stand not for mee?
John Folkes.
4. He told this Deponent in private, he knew not whether the King or Parliament were for the Truth: And at another Time, why should he stand for the Parliament when they stood not for him.
Edward Britton.

fo. 23

5. 16 Women of his Parish, some of good Sort, came to the Committee to desire a godly Minister, affirming Mr Shepard altogether unfit to be a Minister.

[Depositions. Noe Answer but the Living is sequestered]
Depositions against William Evet pretended Parson of Yeldham magna taken the 9 of Aprill 1644.[64]
1. Notwithstanding a pretended Presentation to the Rectory of that Parish yet he hath never either by himselfe or any for him officiated there: so as for the Space of above 12 Moneths last past the Parish hath bin wholly destitute of any Meanes for their Soules, except what they procured by their private Uses.
2. It appeares by a Letter under his Hand, dated the 29 of July 1643 that he contemned the Power of the Parliament: threatening the Parishioners for their Obedience thereto, because of the King's Proclamation.[65]
The Benefice is worth 60^{li} per Annum.
Vide p. 85.[66]

64 The parish in question here was Yeldham Parva (Little Yeldham): the error was corrected in Leicester MS 31, fo. 15v. William Evett, a graduate of Balliol College, Oxford (BA1633, MA 1635), was presented to the rectory there in February 1643 on the death of the previous rector. The articles state that Evett had never attended the parish or appointed anyone as curate, and that in July 1643, he had written to the parish in a way that indicated hostility to parliament. As the entries in Leicester MS 31 show, Evett was sequestrated and ejected by Manchester. He evidently settled in his native Worcestershire, where he was instituted to the living of Grafton Flyford on 28 March 1645: Foster, *Alumni Oxonienses*, II, 475; Leicester MS 31, fos. 15v and A22; CCEd, Location ID 16554.

65 It seems likely that Evett's letter had been prompted by a wish to remind his parishioners that they should notify him of the harvest so that his tithe could be collected. In doing so, he apparently quoted the royal proclamation of 15 May 1643, *A proclamation against the oppression of the clergy by the intrusion of factions and schismaticall persons into their cures, and inverting and detaining their tithes and possessions by orders of one or both houses of parliament, contrary to all law and justice*: printed in *Stuart royal proclamations*, ed. J. F. Larkin and P. L. Hughes (2 vols., Oxford, 1973–83), II, 896–9. Perhaps the parishioners set aside the tithe and sold it to fund the appointment of a curate recruited by them, hence the statement at the beginning of these articles, 'the living is sequestered'.

66 Cole here refers to what is now fo. 86 of BL, Add. MS 5829. He then adds a note which summarizes Zachary Grey's note, which in turn is a summary of the contents of the entry relating to Evett in

No Mention of this Man's Persecution either in Walker or Newcourt. But in a MS formerly lent me by my worthy good Friend Dr Zachary Grey at Cambridge, containing some Extracts from the Committee Book of Essex, belonging to Dr Philip Williams of St John's College, and which came to Dr Williams from his Relation Mr Nalson, there is a short Account of his Case as before, with this Addition, that the Parishioners desire Mr Benton may be their Minister. Names of the Committee, J. Barnardiston,[67] *Thomas Honywood, Richard Harlackenden, Isaac Wincoll, John Elliston.*
It is also said in my Extract that he was non-resident for

fo. 24

12 Yeares, but this is a Mistake, as appears both from my original MS as above, as also from the Date of his Institution in Newcourt, vol 2, p. 690, where we find it 20 February 1642. Perhaps I might make the Mistake in transcribing Dr Grey's Copy, and put down Years for Months.

[Depositions. His Answer retorned]
Depositions against Robert Gyon Vicar of White Colne taken the 9th Aprill 1644.[68]
1. As is conceived, he is sometimes in the Yeare distempered in his Braine, as appeares by these following Expressions in the Pulpit at severall Times, as first That the best Sport is played at Night when the Candle is out.
John Munt, Henry Ricard.
2. Being to baptize a Child, he read a great Part of the Matrimony and after baptized it.
Nathanael Wilshire, John Potter.
3. He said of all Sports Blind Hol is the best, laughing at his owne Expressions: And when the Maids laughed in the Church, he called them .
William , Henry Ricard.
4. He rayling at another time on his People, which some not enduring, departed: whereupon he said it was enough for a Company of Clowns.
Jeofrey Potter, John Parmiter.
5. On Easter Day, instead of the Confession, he read the Prayers before the Sacrament

fo. 25

and then went into the Pulpit and chose the Officers; then bad Master Cooper set a Psalme. One William Bridge asking .[69]
John Parmiter, William Bridge.

Leicester MS 31, fo. 15v. Whether Grey or Cole was responsible for the error, the fact is that Evett had been absent for twelve months or so, not twelve years.

67 'J. Barnardiston' is an understandable misreading of 'A. Barnardiston': see Leicester MS 31, fo. 15v n. 63.

68 Robert Guyon, a member of a family of prosperous clothiers of Coggeshall, was a scholar of Emmanuel College, Cambridge, and graduated BA 1618 and MA 1621. It is unclear when he was appointed minister of White Colne, a donative living, but his name appears in the parish register in 1627 and Newcourt records him as 'licensed' (presumably by the bishop) on 5 September 1634: Venn, *Alumni Cantabrigienses*, II, 277; ERO, D/P 243/1/1; Newcourt, *Repertorium*, II, 186. As explained in the Introduction, p. xlv n. 208, there is no record of his ejection from the parish before his death in 1657.

69 William Bridge was a man of some standing in the parish, assessed to pay £2 13s in ship money in 1637. The article lacks some words, perhaps indicating that Bridge intervened to ask Guyon why he had strayed from the process laid down in the prayer book.

6. He hath preached divers erroneous Doctrines, as that a Man may live and die a Papiste and yet goe to Heaven.
John Munt, John Parmiter.
That Solomon was damned.
Thomas Lefferwell.
He hath bin an Innovator, refusing to give the Sacrament to those that would not come to the Rayle, though he might have reached to them.
William Cowell, George Potter.
He hath divers Times neglected keeping the Fast and in August last preached his Farewell Sermon, and never preached there since, nor provided for any other.
William Bridge, George Potter, Jeffrey Potter.
3 or 4 severall Lord's Dayes he set his Maid to keep his Catle in other Mens Grounds, and that in Sermon Time.
Christian Midleton.
His Benefice is worth 25li and his temporall Estate 60li per Annum and his Wives.
He hath a Wife and one Child.
No Mention of this Man's Persecution in either Newcourt or Walker.

---

fo. 26

[Depositions to which his Answer retorned]
Depositions against John Chamberlin Minister of Maplestead parva taken Aprill the 9 1644.[70]
1. It was deposed upon Oath at the Coroner's Inquest that Mr Chamberlyn was in an Alehouse from 2 in the Afternoone till halfe an Howre afore Day next Morning.
Robert Harington.
2. He is a common Frequenter of the Alehouse in his Parish. and six Daies in one Weeke, and that the very next Weeke after the Officers had reproved him when they tooke him there.
Martha Clark.
3. The Officers finding him in the Alehouse, and telling him they were sory to see him in that Place, he replied, doe the best you can, and then called the Church-warden Knave.
Thomas Rainer. Edmond Clark told Mr Cooke the same before his Death.
4. He would not give the Sacrament to any of his Parish at Church unles they would come up to the Railes.
Robert Harington, Edward Harington, Martha Clark.
5. Because his Parish refused to pay for his License, he refused to preach and did onely read them Homilies, and the later Service at the Raile, with his Face to the East.[71]

[70] John Chamberlin's early life and education are obscure. In 1646, it was stated that he had served as curate of Little Maplestead for fifteen or sixteen years: there is a record of him there in 1637. The living was a donative, in the gift of Lady Wiseman, whose husband, Sir William of Great Canfield, had died in 1643. As discussed in the Introduction, pp. xxiv and xlv above, Chamberlin was not sequestrated or ejected from his living, and remained in place until in 1646 he was appointed vicar of Bulmer, where in 1650 he was judged to be an able preaching minister: Newcourt, *Repertorium*, II, 405; ERO, D/P 358/1/1; Parliamentary Archives, HL/PO/JO/10/1/219 (16 Dec. 1646); Smith, *Ecclesiastical history of Essex*, p. 297.

[71] Although the minister of a donative living did not need institution or induction, he still needed a bishop's licence to preach. The last part of this article claims that Chamberlin read the 'second service',

Robert Harington, Edward Harington, Richard Purcas.
6. To his Sermon he prayed God, the Bloud of the Deputy of Ireland might not be required at our Hands.[72]
Martha Clark, Thomas Rainer.

fo. 27

7. He hath often left his Parish on Saboth Daies without any Supply.
Richard Purcas, Thomas Rayner.
8. In preaching he misinterpreted the Scriptures, saying some Part thereof was the very Spirit of Samuel which the Witch of Endor raised.[73]
Giles Crowne.
9. He said he would reade Masse if anyone would hire him.
Giles Crowne.
The Living is a Donative sine Cura, now in the Disposall of the Lady of Sir William Wiseman who gave 30[li] per Annum.
No Mention of this Man's Persecution in either Newcourt's Repertorium or Walker's Sufferings of the Clergy.

Ashen
[Depositions to which His Answer is retorned]
Depositions taken against William Jones Parson of Ashen Aprill the 10th 1644.[74]
1. He hath, or lately had, 3 Cures to serve at the same Time, viz: Ashen, Barfeld[75] and Brantham in Suffolk.
John Pledger, Richard Raymond, William Knight, George Warren, Stephen Bets.

that is the communion service, while standing at the altar rails and with his back to the congregation: see Introduction, p. xxviii and n. 104.

72 Thomas Wentworth, earl of Strafford, had been lord deputy of Ireland since 1633. One of Charles I's principal counsellors, he was accused of treason and impeached by parliament. He was executed in 1641: R. G. Asch, 'Thomas Wentworth, first earl of Strafford (1593–1641)', *ODNB*.

73 1 Samuel xxviii tells how the witch of Endor raised the spirit of Samuel, whose advice Saul sought about a forthcoming battle with the Philistines.

74 William Jones was the son of William Jones DD, a founder fellow of Emmanuel College, Cambridge, and from 1591, rector of Brantham, Suffolk, of which the church of East Bergholt was a dependent chapel. Jones senior was a godly minister but also a pluralist. While retaining his two churches in Suffolk, he was given dispensations to hold the Essex livings of Tendring (1613) and of Ashen (1617). William Jones junior graduated MA from Caius College, Cambridge in 1622. In 1624, he was appointed rector of Ashen, and in 1633 he also took over the living of Brantham and East Bergholt from his father, who died three years later. The articles against Jones did not lead to his sequestration. There is no record of it, and the parochial inquisition of 1650 stated that the cure was served by Joseph Skynner, clerk, 'by the choice of the parish and the consent of Mr Jones', and that Jones paid Skynner £60 a year. It appears that Jones was also allowed to keep his parish in Suffolk, providing a curate there. In 1654, Jones may have been formally deprived of Ashen, when on the death of Skynner the lords commissioners are recorded as appointing Samuel Symonds as rector. Whatever the position was in the late 1650s, in 1660 Jones was in possession at Ashen, but he died in 1661: Venn, *Alumni Cantabrigienses*, II, 488, 489; CCEd, Location IDs 11119, 11460, 20829; Smith, *Ecclesiastical history of Essex*, p. 302; Matthews, *Walker revised*, p. 156; BL, Add. MS 36792, fo. 84v; TNA, PROB 11/306/2.

75 'Barfeld' may be a reference to Great or Little Bardfield, but there is no other evidence that Jones ever served either parish: his livings are listed in the preceding footnote.

2. He hath bin non-resident from the said Parish of Ashen 6 or 7 yeares last past, not having preached there above 3 or 4 Lord's Daies in a yeare; and hath employed malignant Curats in his Place till of late.
Stephen Bets, John Pledger, Richard Raymond.
3. He published the Booke for Liberty on the Lord's Day in the Church.
Richard Raimont, John Pledger.

fo. 28

4. Being desired by the Church-warden to publish and give the Vow and Covenant, he answered he durst not doe it, for then he should run himselfe into a Praemunire, and so it was not taken in our Parish.[76]
John Pledger, Richard Raymond.
5. He chose for his Tenant in the Parsonage a notorious convicted Drunkard, as we conceive, to vex the Parish, because, said he, Now you shall know how kind I have bin to you.
Stephen Bets, John Pledger, Richard Raymond.
His Benefice is worth 80^{li} per Annum.
[They desire old Mr Blackaby may be their Minister.][77]
No mention of this William Jones, who was Doctor in Divinity, as to his Persecutions by these puritan Saints, either in Newcourt or Walker.

Additionalls to the Charge of George Crackingthorpe Viccar of Bradwell (in the 3rd Leafe) deposed unto besides and since his first Charge, taken the 21 Day of Aprill 1644. Phillip Prick the Wife of John Prick of Braintree deposeth that she hath seen him severall Times drunk comeing from Braintree by her House; And this knowes, because she saw him reele and stagger, and once or twice fall, and could not keepe right the way from falling into Ditches, so as once comeing into her yard he so misbehaved himselfe in his Speeches, as her Prentice Boy laughed, and showted at him.
Phillip Prick wife of John Prick of Braintree.

fo. 29

More Additionalls to the Charge of the said George Crackingthorpe taken May 1, 1644.[78] This Deponent saith that Thomas Lawson Schoolmaster to Sir William Maxie's Grandchildren did for about 2 Houres earnestly solicite him to testifie in Mr Crackingthorpe's Behalfe under his Hand, which this Deponent at first ~~refused~~[79] Mr Lawson told him he was afraid of Goodman Collins one of the Deponents telling

[76] See Introduction, pp. xxxi–xxxii, for the vow and covenant.
[77] The parishioners set their sights very high in aspiring to recruit the famed puritan preacher Richard Blackerby, for whom see Yiannikkou, 'Richard Blackerby', *ODNB*.
[78] See above p. 11 n. 33 for the Maxey family's support for Crackenthorpe. Lawson also was beholden to the family and tried to rally support for Crackenthorpe. Collins had given evidence against Crackenthorpe a month previously (p. 11 above). Evidently, Bridgeman was persuaded to give his support to Crackenthorpe, but to no avail. This 'additional' article has been omitted from the version at Leicester MS 31, fo. 22. It did not add any fresh accusation against the minister and did not reflect well on the process.
[79] Cole notes in margin: 'scratched out thus in the original ms'.

him further, he must either be for him or against him, throw whose Importunitie he did subscribe his Hand among others for the said Mr Crackingthorpe.
Edward Bridgeman Gent.
Can anything show more clearly the diabolical underhand Actings of these saint-like Devils? First to get all the idle Tales of every peevish old Woman against a Man, and then to make it a Crime and Article against him that a Friend solicited to give Evidence for him in his Favour?
See p. 12 for more against him.

V. p. 86.[80]
Depositions taken against John Crosse Viccar of Gosfeild May 1 1644.[81]
1. He hath beene negligent in preaching, many Saboth Daies not preaching at all, nor any for him, except of late when the Towne procured one, saying, preaching is but Man's Invention.
Widow Dale, Judith Bacon.
2. He read Propositions coming from the King, encouraging Men thereupon to give Mony to main-

fo. 30

taine War against the Parliament, saying, if it were never so little, the King would accept of it.
Richard Clarke, Richard Ruffle.
3. He reade the Booke of Sports on the Lord's Day, and exhorted the People to come to Church to heare it read, and to give Attention to it, and to observe it, saying it was fit to be read often, and the Booke being lost, he threatened the Church-wardens with the High Commission because they bought him not another to reade.
Richard Clarke, Richard Ruffle, then Church-wardens.
4. He usually sufferd profaneing Sportes by the youth on the Saboth Day; and used to sitt and looke on when they playd at Stoole-ball, Barley-break etc without reproving them.[82]
Thomas Nevill, William Syday.
5. He said on the Saboth to this Deponent, that the Saboth is noe longer to be observed than he is reading Divine Service, and that on any other Part of the Day, Men may take their Liberty and doe what they list, and that Holy-Daies ought to be kept as well as the Saboth.
Nicholas Clarke.

80 Cole here refers to what is now fo. 87 of BL, Add. MS 5829, where he quotes Zachary Grey's note, which in turn is a summary of the contents of the entry relating to Crosse in Leicester MS 31, fo. 24.

81 The early life of John Crosse is obscure: it seems most likely that he became vicar of Gosfield in 1622, having recently graduated from Trinity College, Cambridge (BA 1617–18, MA 1621). As is shown in Leicester MS 31, fos. 28v–29 and A31, Manchester decided on 18 September 1644 that Crosse should be sequestrated and ejected. He was replaced by John Norton and soon afterwards by William Smithies. Crosse's wife was awarded the customary fifth, which, as often, was not paid. Crosse died in 1655: Venn, *Alumni Cantabrigienses*, I, 426; Smith, 'Sequence of Essex clergy, 1640–1664', II, 45; Matthews, *Walker revised*, p. 149: Smith, *Ecclesiastical history of Essex*, p. 295.

82 Stool-ball and barley-break are both described in the *OED* as old country games, the former somewhat resembling cricket, the latter somewhat resembling prisoners' bars (a chasing game).

6. When the Communion Table was to be railed in and set Altar-wise, this Deponent asking him, why he was soe forward to charge the Towne in bringing in such an Innovation before it was in other Parishes, he then answerd, Wee shalbe the first that shall worship.
[Quaere][83]
7. He was very active and strict to observe the Innovations, using to reade Service at the Rayle, where few could heare him, bowing at the Name of Jesus, preaching with his Surplice, Hood and

fo. 31

Tippett, without any Prayer at the Ende of his Sermon.
Robert Digby, William White.
8. One Mr Wems preaching there, he would not suffer him to make any Prayer after his Sermon, but pulled the Pulpit Dore open twice whereon the cushion lay, so as the Minister was in Danger to fall downe and spoile himselfe.[84]
Robert Digby, William White, [John Dier].
9. When the godly Ministers preached there, he would usually looke upon them, and jeere and fleere at them whilest they were in their Sermon.
William Scott, William Webb, Elizabeth Webb.
The Benefice is worth betwixt 40 and 50^{li} per Annum. He hath a Wife and one Child. He hath at least 16^{li} per Annum of his owne, besides 150^{li} in Stock.
Ex
Mr Newcourt has not his Name among the Vicars of Gosfeild and Mr Walker mentions him not as a Sufferer.

Midleton: Depositions against William Frost Parson May 1 1644.[85]
1. He was very forward to procure the setting up the Railes, and then refused to give the Sacrament to such as would not come up to them.
Thomas Mills, Isaac Mullins.
2. [a] He read the Booke of Sports on the Lord's Day; And [b] thereupon the Youth said, They had Liberty to play, and would.
Margaret Wall[a], Katherine Prig, Anne Ellis.
3. He is a Tipler, and these Deponents have seene him so distempered with Drink that he could not speak plaine, nor goe right in the streets

83 In Leicester MS 31, fo. 28v, the deponent is named as Richard Ruffle.

84 Probably Patrick Weemes (Wemys), MA St Andrews, ordained at York and appointed vicar of Acomb, 1614. At an unknown date, he became curate of Pattiswicke, not far from Gosfield. It seems likely that Weemes was intending to follow his sermon by praying extempore: CCEd, Person ID 121519; Smith, *Ecclesiastical history of Essex*, pp. 207, 311, 409.

85 Frost was the son of John Frost, rector of Fornham St Genevieve, Suffolk. Like his father, he attended school in Bury and then Caius College, Cambridge (BA 1613–14, MA 1617). Frost became curate of Great Ashfield, Suffolk, in 1617 and rector of Middleton in 1624. The earl of Manchester decided to sequestrate Frost, as the entries in Leicester MS 31 confirm. He was briefly restored in 1660 but died the next year. Venn, *Alumni Cantabrigienses*, II, 182. The charges against Frost are lengthy, in this manuscript at fos. 31–3, 37 and 43–5, and consolidated in Leicester MS 31 at fos. 18–19v. Mostly concerning drink and sexual misconduct, they follow charges by parishioners in the 1630s on similar grounds which resulted in a judgment by the High Commission, on which see Introduction, pp. xxxiv–xxxv.

fo. 32

about 2 or 3 yeares sithence.
Mary Ollave, Katherine Prig.
And that in his Distemper with Drink, he came hallowing and whooping Home at unseasonable Times in the Night; and this was a little before Michaelmass last.
Anne Ellis.
That in one of his drinking Fitts at the Crowne in Sudbury he offerd to forgive a Woman divers Debts (which he pretended she ought him) if she would give him a Kisse.
Bartholomew Male Gent, Margaret uxor eius.[86]
4. He is a Man dangerously suspected of Incontinency, as may appeare by these Presumptions;
First, that he hath offerd to putt his Hand under a Woman's Cloths, in an obscene and uncivill Manner.
Margaret Wall.
2dly he hath lately kept Company with a Woman of a light Cariage, and kept a whore, vizt one Anne Hovell in his House for many Yeares together.[87]
John Kitson, John Waypoole.
3dly One Susan Ruggle[88] told this Deponent that her Mistris (Mr Frost's Wife) fell out with her threatning to turne her out of Dores; but she sayd, that if she did turne her out, she would make her Master for ever shewing himself in the Pulpitt any more.
So in the original. I suppose the word afraid may be wanting.
4thly Upon a Suite against him in the High-Commission upon the Crime of Bastardy, he was forced to find Compurgators to sweare for him, who were are (*sic in originall*) since most of them either sequestred or run away.[89]
Thomas Mills, Margaret Wall.
5thly Notwithstanding he was strictly enjoyned by the Ecclesiasticall Court, to put away the foresaid Anne Hovell and her Bastard out of his House, with

86 The deponents here are Bartholomew and Margaret *Wall*; the error is corrected in Leicester MS 31, fo. 18. Margaret Wall had been married previously to John Knopp, yeoman of Middleton. In September 1637, the widowed Margaret married Bartholomew Wall, a widower of Langford. Wall evidently moved to Middleton where in 1641 he was the resident most highly rated for the subsidy. He served as the parish's overseer in that year and in 1650 was appointed a juror for the hundred's parochial inquisition: he died in 1655. Margaret Wall's depositions (at fos. 31, 32–3 and 37) hark back to before her marriage to Wall: to the book of sports (1633), to the allegations made against Frost in the High Commission (1635) and to her claim that he had made sexual advances to her about eight years previously: TNA, PROB 11/173/77 (Knopp's will); ERO, D/P 212/1/1 (marriage of Bartholomew and Margaret, at Twinstead); TNA, E 179/112/646; Parliamentary Archives, HL/PO/JO/10/1/91/22; Smith, *Ecclesiastical history of Essex*, p. 292.

87 According to the evidence given to the High Commission in 1635, Anne Howell (or Hovell) was the sister of Frost's wife. She had an illegitimate child and lived with the Frosts, and common fame had it that Frost was the child's father: *CSPD 1635–6*, p. 114.

88 Susannah Wruggle was named in the High Commission case of 1635 as one of two maidservants with whom Frost had committed adultery: *ibid.*

89 Frost's compurgators are listed in *CSPD 1635–6*, p. 478, as follows: Henry [*recte* Edward] Glover, rector of Lamarsh (d. 1637); Charles Forbench, rector of Great Henny (sequestrated, 1643); John Lake, vicar of Great Saling (articled against 1644, d. 1646); Edward Jenkinson, rector of Panfield (sequestrated, 1643); Elisha Pratt, vicar of Lindsell (judged in 1650 to be 'a very honest and painful minister'); Richard Moore, vicar of Braughing (Herts), 1620–38; Richard Etkins, vicar of Kensington (Middlesex) 1608–41 (resigned); Job Eglington, vicar of Feltham (Middlesex), 1621–40 or later: Foster, *Alumni Oxonienses*, II, 572 and Newcourt, *Repertorium*, II, 361; Matthews, *Walker revised*, p. 152; p. 13 n. 40 above; Matthews, *Walker revised*, p. 156; Smith, *Ecclesiastical history of Essex*, p. 279; Newcourt, *Repertorium*, I, 809; *ibid.*, I, 681; CCEd, Person ID 62673.

fo. 33

whom hee was suspected, yet notwithstanding he hath since entertained them both againe.
Margaret Wall, Anne Ellis.
5. That amongst other Discourses about a yeare agoe, speakeing of the Wars he used these Words, we thinke it is an unnatural Thing to goe against our King, and to give away our Mony so basely and uglily as we doe to the Parliament.
Anne Ellis.
Ex
[See more against him fol 21 and 25].[90]
Neither Walker nor Newcourt mention this Persecution: only the last barely produces him as Rector of Middleton, but without any Date of Institution: see p. 36, 42, 43.

Oaten-Belchamp
Depositions taken against Joseph Bird Parson May 10th.[91]
1. Elizabeth Coote deposeth that having beene Mr Bird's Servant at 2 severall Times a yeare and 3 Quarters, she hath often seen him distempered with Beere in his own House, and sometimes sitting up drinking on the Saboth Day until 12 of the Clock at Night: And at one Time he was so unquiett for Beere that his Wife and this Deponent fetchd a Barrell of Beere and sett it in the Chimney Corner by him to drinke what he pleased.
Thomas Newton, William Martin, Elizabeth Smith, Robert Letch, and Sara Letch deposeth he is an excessive Drinker and often so distempered that he is unfitt for his Calling.

fo. 34

Upon Easter Monday being at Sudbury he was so distemperd with Drink that he behaved himselfe disorderly, disquieting the People at 10 a Clock at Night, and in these Distempers was taken by the Constable and the Watch and carried before the Maior, notwithstanding there was a Sacrament administered by him the Day before.
George Golding, Thomas Chaplin.
2. This Deponent while she lived with him hath heard him often swear by God, and other Oathes.
Elizabeth Coote.

[90] The further depositions against Frost (here referenced by the foliation of the original manuscript) are at fos. 37 and 43–5 below.

[91] The son of the rector of Boxford, Suffolk, Bird graduated from Pembroke College, Cambridge (BA 1621–2, MA 1625), and was appointed rector of Belchamp Otten in 1634. The committee considered the articles against Bird on three occasions, 10 May and 4 October 1644 (fos. 33–5) and 1 January 1645 (fo. 63). Bird must have submitted a defence, in which he had attacked the character of Elizabeth Coote, a deponent who had been a servant in his house. He asserted that she had been convicted of fornication and theft before Oliver Raymond JP, but Raymond testified that Bird's allegation was untrue. Isaac Wincoll added an account of an occasion when Bird had been drunk. Leicester MS 31 does not record the ejection and sequestration of Bird, but there is good evidence that this was the outcome. In January 1646, parliament's committee for plundered ministers awarded Bird's wife a fifth of the rectory's income, the record noting that the living had been sequestered by the earl of Manchester, and this was confirmed by the parochial inquisition in 1650. Probably, the record of the ejection was omitted from Leicester MS 31 in error. Bird was restored in 1660 and died in 1665: Venn, *Alumni Cantabrigienses*, I, 156; CCEd, Person ID 133777; BL, Add. MS 15669, fo. 239v; Smith, *Ecclesiastical history of Essex*, p. 302; ERO, D/P 214/1/1.

That he hath heard him swear as God should judge him.
William Martin.
3. That he hath often absented himself from his Cure 3 or 4 Saboth Daies together, either leaving no Supply at all, or else scandalous and ill-affected Men, many of them now justly sequestred for their professed Malignancy vizt: Mr Alsop, Mr Forbench and Mr Austin.[92]
Thomas Chaplin, Robert Letch, William Martin.
4. That they heard him say above a yeare since that the Parliament was guilty of all the innocent Bloud that hath been shed, and that it would be required at their Hands: and that they kept backe the King's Right. And, he said, if your Rights were kept back it would make you shedd Bloud.
Elizabeth Herd, Bridgett Betts.
His Benefice is worth 60 or 70^{li} per Annum.
He hath a Wife and 5 Children.
They know not of any temporal Estate he hath.
See more against him on the next Page, wrote in another Hand, and at p. 62.

fo. 35

[Additionall Depositions taken upon Oath against Mr Bird October 4th 1644 Parson of Otten-Belcham]
Sara Letch deposeth that the said Joseph Bird is an excessive Drinker and that she hath seen him above twenty Times drunke, and that about ii years since coming to hir House, he did drinke of her Beere against hir Will, that he was not able to open the Cover of the Tankard nor to put it to his Mouth without spilling most of the Beere in it, on his Clothes: and it is his usual Manner when he was drunke to fall on railing on his Neighbors and one Tyme on hir Daughter, calling hir Baggaige, and base Baggaige, because she would give him no more strong Beere, being about xii a Clock at Night.
Mary Wilson deposeth that somewhat above a yeare since, she saw Mr Bird in Ballingdon nie Sudbury, being about iii Miles from his Parish uppon a Satterday Night betwixt ix and x of the Clock at Night so drunke that he could not goe right in the Way, but was fayne to grope after the Wall and to leane on the House and there she left him standing.
There is no Notice taken of the Persecution of this Man either in Newcourt or Walker. These 2 last Depositions by the 2 Women, the first of whom was probably an Ale-Wife, as might be the 2nd, are wrote in a very different Hand from the rest of the Book, but at the same Time.

Paul's Belchamp
Depositions taken the same 10th of May against Robert Fisher Vicar.[93]
1. That he refused to administer the Sacrament to those that would not come up to the Rayles.

92 John Alsop (rector of Fordham), Charles Forbench (rector of Great Henny) and Edward Alston (rector of Pentlow) had all been ejected from their livings by parliament in 1643: Matthews, *Walker revised*, pp. 145, 152, 145.

93 Robert Fisher was appointed vicar of Belchamp St Paul at an unknown date in the 1620s: he signed the parish register as vicar every year from 1629 to 1653 and baptized three children of his own there in the 1630s. It is not clear if he was the man who graduated from Emmanuel College, Cambridge (BA 1622/3) or from Queens' College (MA 1624). As discussed in the Introduction (p. xlv above),

Captain Thomas Smith, Rose Hart, Alice Walford.
2. That he often sweareth by his Faith and Troth.
Captain Smith, Sara Browne, William Spark.

fo. 36

3. He hath sufferd * on the Saboth Day 4 or 5 yeares since without reproving.
**Sic MS*
William Sparke, William Jennings, William Owers.
4. That he published a Declaration that came from the King about a yeare since very audibly and distinctly; but at the same Time he read an Ordinance that came from the Parliament with a low Voyce, and [b] read but Part of it.
William Owers, Thomas Dier, [b] William Owers.
In this 20th page of the manuscript is a void Space left of about 2 Inches or 3 Inches, being a third Part of the Leaf, in Order, probably, to insert some fresh Accusation expected against him. I have wrote just about as much as the Vacancy.[94] *It then proceeds in this Manner*:
And at other Times the said Mr Fisher hath said that the King fights for the Protestant Religion: And what would you have more.
At another Time upon his Discourse with this Deponent about the Lawfulnes of the Parliament's taking up Armes, she siteing a Booke written to that Purpose, he blamed her for reading so much for the Parliament and so little for the King. And he commended a Booke which Prince Rupert had sett forth that he came hither to fight for the Protestant Religion.[95]
Mary Sparke.
That he said to this Deponent (being then Constable, who told him the Penalty of a Warrant that came from the Parliament coming for any) I marvell where is the Law for it, if they could tell me any Law for it.
William Sparke.

fo. 37

That he was very active to promote the late Petition for Peace, and was angry with those that opposed it.[96]
William Owers.
That he hath sufferd divers malignant Ministers to preach for him.
William Owers, William Sparke.
The People desire, that he may preach before my Lord's Chaplins, upon Triall.

Fisher was not deprived of his living, and consequently there is no mention of him in Leicester MS 31: ERO, D/P 408/1/1; Venn, *Alumni Cantabrigienses*, II, 143; CCEd, Person ID 163064.

94 The length of this note by Cole in MS 5829, and therefore of the gap in the original MS, is 3 inches (7.5 cm).

95 Prince Rupert, nephew of Charles I, was commander of the royalist cavalry during the first Civil War. The book which Fisher referred to was probably *Prince Rupert his declaration*, issued by him in 1642 to rebut accusations of harsh tactics and papist sympathy: Ian Roy, 'Rupert, prince and count palatine of the Rhine and duke of Cumberland (1619–82)', *ODNB*; BL, Thomason Tracts, E.242[32].

96 See Introduction, p. xxxi, for the petition.

That he usually keeps Company with profane Men.
Mary Sparke, Sara Browne.
No mention of this Man's Persecution by Newcourt, who has not his Name among the Vicars of Belchamp St Paul's, or by Walker.

Middleton
Additionalls to the Charge of Mr Frost fol:16. May 11.[97]
Margaret Wall deposeth that he did read so farr of the Booke for Sports as gives Liberty to the Boyes to play. And this was read in the Church, when she was there, it being about the usual Time when they went to Church. But what other Company was there shee doth not now remember.
To the 4th, she deposeth that about 8 yeares since she was the Person mentioned in the 4th Article of the Depositions taken against him the 1 of May under whose Coates he offered to put his Hand, meeting her alone in a strait Entry in her owne House.
See more taken June 17 fol: 25, 26, & 27. To his Charge May 1. fol: 16.
Vide p. 30 Ex

fo. 38

Farleborne *V. p. 85*[98]
Depositions taken the 15th day of June 1644 against Edward Strutt Parson thereof.[99]
1. Imprimis that the said Edward Strutt did upon Newyeares Day last was twelve-moneth in the hearing of divers Persons at Sir Edward Bullock's House, in his presence, say, that what the Parliament doe now they doe it without Law, for they have noe Law for what they doe.[100]
Thomas Herridge (mark), Bartholomew Hall.[101]

97 Here, the writer of the original manuscript refers to the earlier entry about Frost at fo. 16 of that volume, which was copied by Cole at fos. 31–3 of this manuscript. 11 May was a Sunday when the committee would not have met. '11 May' should perhaps read '1 May', the day of the first hearing: or these 'additionals' might perhaps have been deposed on 11 May by Mrs Wall, making a statement to the committee clerk, whose annotation 'Ex[aminatur]' confirms the accuracy of the text. This entry about Frost ends with a reference to further evidence, taken on 17 June 1644, printed at fos. 43–5 below.

98 A reference to fo. 86 of this manuscript, where Cole copied a note by Zachary Grey summarizing the charges against Strutt, as set out in Leicester MS 31, fos. 16v–17.

99 Edward Strutt was a graduate of Jesus College, Cambridge (BA 1602–3, MA 1606). He was presented to the rectory of Faulkbourne in 1617 and served there until, as confirmed by Leicester MS 31, fos. 16v–17 and A23, he was ejected by Manchester. Richard Chadsley was appointed to serve Faulkbourne in place of Strutt. In 1646, Strutt died and the patron of the living decided to displace Chadsley and appoint Richard Strutt, kinsman and probably the son of the late Edward, as the new rector. He remained rector of Faulkbourne until his death in 1675: Venn, *Alumni Cantabrigienses*, IV, 177; CCEd, Location ID 11253; ERO, D/P 375/1/1; *Lords Journal*, VIII, 644; Smith, *Ecclesiastical history of Essex*, p. 367.

100 Sir Edward Bullock owned the manor of Faulkbourne. Sir Edward was probably a royalist, as several members of his family were, but he did not take up arms, perhaps for reasons of age and infirmity; he died in September 1646, aged sixty-six: Morant, *History of Essex*, II, 117; Bullock, *Memoirs of the Bullock family*, pp. 31–2; TNA, PROB 11/197/603.

101 The second deponent was Bartholomew Wall. He was also a deponent against William Frost of Middleton (fos. 32 n. 86, 38, 39, 43, 44 above). That Wall was a guest in the Bullock house is no surprise: Wall had a farm at Faulkbourne, perhaps leased from the manor: Smith, *Ecclesiastical history of Essex*, p. 307.

2. Item upon young Mr Bullock's telling this Deponent upon the Saboth Day, at Sir Edward Bullock's House, about the Time when the Vow and Covenant was taken, as he remembers, upon that very Day, that the said Mr Bullock parted with his Money to the Parliament freely; to which Mr Strutt said so did not he, for, said he, if I did not, it would have beene better then it is.
John Tomson (mark).
3. Bartholomew Wall heard the said Edward Strutt say, that now there was noe Parliament, they are as a Body without a Head now the King is away: And the said Mr Strutt did further say that the Parliament is as deeply guilty of Treason as the Earle of Strafford: For, I pray, said he, what did he? He sought to bring the Land into an arbitrary Goverment and soe doth the Parliament. I pray else (said he) what meaneth this twentith Part? Soe they may come for a tenth Part, and at last for all.[102]
Bartholomew Wall.

fo. 39

4. Philip Harvy saith, That about a Weeke before the Vow and Covenant was to have beene taken in Falborne he heard Mr Strutt diswade Sir Edward Bullock from takeing it telling the said Sir Edward that Doctor Gawden and Mr Collins of Braintree and Mr Fuller of Stebbing and others did not take it, And that the said Vow and Covenant was called in againe.[103]
Phillip Harvy (mark).
Bartholomew Wall saith, that at the Time when the Vow and Covenant was to be taken, the said Mr Strutt did treat with this Deponent wishing him to take heed what he did, for, said he, it is a very dangerous Covenant: And I believe (said he) that not a quarter of the Kingdome will take it.
Bartholomew Wall.
John Tomson deposes that Mr Strutt did not for divers yeares together preach more than once on the Saboth Day untill about a quarter of a yeare since.
John Tomson (mark).
Bartholomew Wall, Thomas Herridge and John Thompson depose that the said Mr Strutt doth ordinarily sweare by his Faith, and sometimes in his Anger will sweare by God, and one time especially the Deponent Bartholomew Wall did heare him on the Saboth Day swear by God severall Times because his Dog was killed.
Bartholomew Wall, Thomas Herridge (mark), John Tomson (mark).
Jerome Skingly and John Tomson depose that when Mr Wright late Vicar of Wickham was called in Question before the Parliament about his profane and wicked Courses, they having Conference

[102] For Strafford, see fo. 26 above, n. 72. In May 1643, parliament established a tax on those people who had not already contributed voluntarily to the costs of the parliamentary forces. It could be levied at the rate of one fifth on annual income or one twentieth of the value of personal property: *Acts and ordinances*, pp. 145–55.

[103] See Introduction, pp. xxxi–xxxii above, for the vow and covenant. The argument that opponents of the oath included such well-respected clergy as John Gauden, Samuel Collins and John Fuller was persuasive. For Gauden, see Spinks, 'John Gauden', *ODNB*; for Collins, see n. 104 below; for Fuller, see Smith, *Ecclesiastical history of Essex*, p. 407.

fo. 40

with Mr Strutt about the same, He said to them, that the Parliament could not by Law take away his Living.
Jerome Skingly, John Tomson (marke).
The 3 Parishes of the Name of Wickham in Essex are all Rectories, where none of the Name of Wright occur as Rector: but one Francis Wright occurs Vicar of Witham, who, no Doubt, is the Person referred to, being ejected for his Loyalty, which joyned to other Frailties occasioned his being sequestred by the House about the Beginning of April 1643. See Newcourt's Repertorium vol: 2 p. 677 and Walker's Sufferings of the Clergy, p. 397, Part 2nd. The Mr Collins of Braintree mentioned in the 4th Article was the learned Dr Samuel Collins Provost of King's College in Cambridge.[104]
John Tomson deposeth that Mr Strutt hath for many Yeares usually frequented the House and Company of one Mr Leventhorpe, who is a knowne Papist.
John Tomson.
The value of Falborne Benefice is about 80li per Annum.
Mr Strutt's Estate is very small. He hath a Wife and ten Children, but they are all growne up to Men's and Women's Stature.
They desire   to be their minister.[105]
Mr Bartholomew Wall and Goodman Thomas Herridge are nominated Sequestrators.
Then follows in a large black Character, signed by the Informer Francis Scott himself, a fresh Accusation against Mr Strutt, which takes up the whole Leaf and is as follows.

fo. 41

Additional Deposition taken against Edward Strutt the 6th of September 1644.
Francis Scott deposeth, that within 3 or 4 years since he hath heard Mr Strutt Parson of Falborne in his ordinary Discourse at severall Times to sweare divers Oathes, as namely, by his Faith, by God shall save me, before God, and the like.
Francis Scott.
No Mention of Mr Strutt's Sufferings either by Walker or Newcourt. In an Extract which I had from Dr Z. Grey, it is said that the 19th June was the Day when the Depositions were taken: but my MS says the 15th, possibly Dr Grey might mistake in transcribing his Copy, or myself from the Doctor's.[106]

---

104 Cole was right on the first point: see also fo. 47, n. 119 below for Francis Wright of Witham. Cole was, however, mistaken about Collins. Dr Samuel Collins, provost of King's College, Cambridge and the possessor of two livings in Cambridgeshire from which he was ejected by parliament (d. 1651), was never vicar of Braintree. A namesake held that position from 1611 until his death in 1657. Presented to the living by the first earl of Warwick, this Collins was a diligent minister of Braintree and on good terms both with Laud and with leading puritans: Nicholas W. S. Cranfield, 'Samuel Collins (1576–1651)', *ODNB*; CCEd, Location ID 11159; Smith, *Ecclesiastical history of Essex*, pp. 33–4, 148, 169, 361.

105 At the time when the Cole's committee book was written, the parishioners had apparently not chosen their new minister. By the time when the committee's conclusions were sent to the earl of Manchester, the parishioners had decided that they wished to recruit Robert Chadsley, late curate to Mr Herring, the rector of Doddinghurst: Leicester MS 31, fo. 17.

106 See Leicester MS 31, fo. 16v, where the date of the hearing is given as 19 June, which Grey had correctly copied.

Oulting
Depositions taken against William Hull Viccar of Oulting.[107]
John Covell saith that upon Michaelmas Day last Mr Hull came to the House where this Deponent now dwells, so distempered with Beere that he staggered and reeled so that he was likely to fall into the Fire, and after he had taken a Pipe of Tobacco, he went to the Table and fell asleepe all the while this Deponent was at Supper, and so he left him there when he went to Bedd, and found him in the House the next Morning.
John Covell.
Amos ....* saith that upon Michaelmas Day last he saw Mr Hull at .....* going toward the foresaid John Covell's House, reeling and staggering in the Street, so as he could hardly stand upright.
The marke of Amos.*
*** *Sic in originali Ms^to^.*

fo. 42

Richard Lunt deposeth that about a yeare and a halfe since, Mr Hull came to this Deponent's House much distempered with Drinke, and tumbled downe as he came into his House, and that he doth too often frequent Alehouses.
The Marke of Richard Lunt.
Richard Lunt doth also further depose that the said Mr Hull told him when the Parliament Officers came to Sir Henry Mildemay ......* Monsons House for his Armes, that they were none but a Company of Rogues and Rascalls.[108]
* *Sic in orig.*
Thomas Lake and Abraham Lake depose that Mr Hull doth ordinarily frequent Alehouses and that they have seene him divers times distempered with Beere, and that he doth constantly goe from Maulden either very late on Saturday Night or on the Saboth Day Morning to his own Parish of Oulting.
Thomas Lake and Abraham Lake.
Abraham Lake deposeth that Mr Hull doth ordinarily sweare by his Faith and Troth and is reputed a common Liar.
Abraham Lake.
Mr Hull did openly before the whole Committee confesse, he had not taken the Vow and Covenant.
His Benefice is worth betwixt 30 and 40^{li} per Annum.
He is a Widower and hath 4 Children, but they are all grown up.
His personall Estate is little or nothing, for he spends it at the Ale-house so soone as he gets it.

107 William Hull was a local man, born at Witham, and educated at Pembroke College, Cambridge (BA 1617–18). He was ordained in 1621, then aged twenty-six, and was appointed curate at Aldham. In 1626, Hull was appointed vicar of Ulting. In 1644, the articles printed here were submitted to the north Essex committee but there is no evidence that Hull was ejected: there is no entry in Leicester MS 31, and in 1650 the parochial inquistion reported that he was the incumbent and that 'he doth not neglect the cure, but is not a godly preaching minister'. He retained the living until his death in 1669: Venn, *Alumni Cantabrigienses*, II, 429; ERO, D/P 208/1/1; Smith, 'Sequence of Essex clergy, 1640–1664'; Smith, *Ecclesiastical history of Essex*, p. 306; CCEd, Location ID 11489.

108 The reference here is probably to Sir Henry Mildmay, member of parliament for Maldon. He was active for parliament in the Civil War. The nature of the incident involving Monson's house and the latter's identity are obscure.

They desire that ....* may be their minister.
* *Sic in Ms*[to].
Sequestrators Abraham Lake, Henry Adams.
No Notice of this Persecution in Newcourt or Walker.

---

fo. 43

Additions against Mr Frost of Midleton June 17, 1644.
M[ris] Anne Hubbert deposeth, that she hath heard it reported, that Mr Frost had used some light and uncivill Cariage towards some Women; and that once comeing to her House in the Morning to speake with her Husband before she this Deponent went out of hir Bedd, he came up into her Chamber and kissed her being in Bedd, having no Occasion that he acquainted her with that he came to her about; but onely on her Maide's telling him that she was not well.
Anne Hubbert.
Vincent Cocke and Thomas Mills say and depose that Mr Frost preaching about the Nature of Vowes and Covenants on that Saboth when the Vow and Covenant was to be taken, he did, after many Cautions given us about the Danger of Breach of our Vowes, soe presse upon us what protestations the King had taken for defending the protestant Religion, that we were thereby much disheartened from takeing the said Vow and Covenant, untill Mr Wall one of the Parish did perswade us thereunto.
Vincent Cocke, the Marke of Thomas Mills.
Sibill Kidson deposeth that upon the Day for the publicke Thanksgiving[109] Mr Frost did come to this Deponents House then at Twinsted upon noe Occasion which she knew of; and followed her out of one Roome into another, and kissed her by Force, insomuch as she called in her Husband, and told him of Mr Frost's Cariage to her. And at another Time, (being as she remembers about 6 Weekes after), the said Mr Frost came againe to her House un ....[110] to aske her the Way to Robert Frier's House, who dwelt hard by (which he as well knew as she) and she letting

fo. 44

him goe the nighest Way through her Barne, he kissed her at the same Time, goeing a little further with him he kissed her againe by Force, pulling her by the Apron; And she breaking from him, he told her she was very quick, but she said not quick enough for you.
The marke of Sibill Kidson.
Bartholomew Wall and Margaret Wall depose that Mr Frost did (as they now remember) about the Time that the King's Army went first against the Scotts, read a Paper publikly in the Church, which was to this Effect, that though that the Scotts pretended their Coming was for Maintenance of the Gospell and Liberty of the Subject, yet the End

109 This may have been the day of thanksgiving ordered by parliament to mark the thwarting of a royalist plot led by Edmund Waller against the city of London, 15 June 1643 in London but 13 July elsewhere: *National prayers*, I, 395–7.

110 The incomplete word (wholly omitted in Leicester MS 31, fo. 19) might have been 'unbidden' or 'unnecessarily'.

of their Coming was to take away our Estates and abuse our Wives, and other Words to that Purpose.[111]
Bartholomew Wall, The marke of Margaret Wall.
Mr Frost's Benefice is worth 80^{li} per Annum. He hath a Wife, but noe Children. His reall Estate is worth, as we conceive, about 12^{li} per annum. And he hath about C^{li} in personall Estate.[112]
For sequestrators Bartholomew Wall Gent, Edmond M.[113]
See more next Page.
More additional Depositions against Mr Frost
Vincent Kidson deposeth that William Frost preaching on a Saboth Day about the Vow and Covenant, he wished them to be very carefull what they did, And told them, that they who had taken the first Protestation, if they should take this, must needs be forsworne; and used this Reason, because in the first Protestation the King joined with the Parliament. But in this last, the Parliament tooke up Armes against the King without his Consent.

fo. 45

Vincent Kidson also further deposeth that William Frost Minister of Middleton [about Christmass was 12 Months, was so distempered with drinking as he could not goe over a Bridge above 3 yards wide, so as this Deponent and his Wife being of his Parish and going homewards did lead him a good Part of the way, this was] at Sudbury about a 12 Month since: And since that Time also he hath likewise seene Mr Frost so distempered that he could not goe without leading: And about September last, he heard Mr Frost aske M^{ris} Frost his Wife why she went not to Church, and she said to him, that she had better stay at Home then come Home with broken Legs as he did.
Mr Wincoll hath these last two Depositions under Kidson's Hand.

What follows is wrote in a very different hand from the rest of the MS, viz from p. 28 to p. 39.
Depositions against Daniel Faulconer Parson of Aldham in Essex this xxiiith Day of July 1644 at Halsted before Thomas Cooke, Isaac Wincall, John Elistone, Robert Crane and Richard Harlakenden Gent taken uppon Oath.[114]

111 In 1639, Charles I raised an army with the aim of forcing the Scots to adopt certain changes in the Scottish church. A royal proclamation of 27 February 1639, to be read in churches throughout England, informed 'our loving subjects … of the seditious practices of some in Scotland, seeking to overthrow our regall power under false pretence of religion'. Frost may have dwelt on a passage in the proclamation which claimed that the king was forced to take up arms 'which is for no other end, save onely for the safety and security of this our kingdom … and the suppressing of such as have misled and abused our subjects there [sc. in Scotland] and would (if not prevented) do the like here': *Stuart royal proclamations*, II, 662–7; Bowen, 'Royalism, print and the clergy', pp. 300–10.

112 In Leicester MS 31, fo. 19, the benefice is valued at £70 per annum and Frost's personal estate at £200.

113 At Leicester MS 31, fo. A24 (p. 97 below), the sequestrators are named as Bartholomew Wall, Edmond Marsh and Vincent Cocke.

114 Daniel Falconer graduated BA 1618, MA 1621 from Gloucester Hall, Oxford and was collated by the bishop of London to the rectory of Aldham in 1624. Aldham parish register records that Falconer and his wife Elizabeth had five children there between 1625 and 1633. The living was a good one, valued in 1650 at £114 a year. There is no doubt that Falconer was sequestrated and ejected, despite the absence of a record in Leicester MS 31. On 13 September 1645, the committee for plundered ministers noted that Falconer 'late minister of Aldham … hath complained that hee was sequestered

1. Imprimis he did publish the Booke of Sports for prophaneing the Lord's Day on a Saboath in his owne Church without any Disswation of his People from that Sinne.
John Jacksonn, John Sommersom, David Coxes, Robert Golding.[115]
2. He is a frequent Swearer by his Faith and Troth, and Robert Strutt hath heard him some yeares since sweare by God and other deepe Oathes.
John Sommerson, John Norton, John Besouth, Robert Strutt.

fo. 46

3. He was very active to promote the late Innovations, as comeing to the Rayles, standing upp at Gloria Patri.
John Sommerson, William Bolton, John Besouth.
4. Item he denyed the Sacrament to Elizabeth Cockrell, Elizabeth South and Sara Little except they would come upp and kneele at the Rayles.
Elizabeth Cockrell, Elizabeth South, Sara Little.
5. Item he preached in a Sermon that the King's Cause was innocent and that God would bless his innocent Cause.
Jane Dier.
6. Item on a Fast Day morning he desired some of his parish to pray for the King and the Company with him, for they were his good Councellours: But the Parliament were drawen away by the People.
Stephen Peachie.
7. Item he told Stephen Peachie in private, that he did believe if the King gett the Day the Soldiers would be better paid then they are by the Parliament.
Stephen Peachie.
8. He said if ever the Tymes come to be as they have beene (as I hope they will) I will try a Suite with every one of those who are the Ceassers[116] and Collectors, by which Meanes some Persons have beene much discouraged in the Service to the Parliament.
John Norton, John Sommerson.
9. Item he declared at a Christening, that he hoped to see the Booke of Common Prayer and the Ceremonies used againe in the Church, one replyed, he hoped it would never be as long as he lived, Yes said Mr Faulconer, I will warrant you.[117]
Mr William Dyer, Elizabeth South.

... without being heard on his parte or admitted to be heard'. When the committee finally heard Falconer's appeal, on 23 May 1646, they concluded that he had been sequestered by Manchester and 'it was affirmed by divers members of this committee' that the decision was taken 'upon full hearing of him'. They dismissed his appeal and on 20 June 1646 they reiterated this and confirmed that Gamaliel Carr, 'a godly and orthodox divine', should continue to serve the cure. Falconer died in 1653: Foster, *Alumni Oxonienses*, II, 487 (as Venn points out at *Alumni Cantabrigienses*, II, 126, Foster was probably in error in attributing three additional parishes to 'Fawkener'); ERO, D/P 208/1/1; *VCH Essex*, X, 20; BL, Add. MS 15669, fo. 166; BL, Add. MS 15670, fos. 93, 113; TNA, PROB 11/225/598.

115 This parish's seventeen deponents were mostly complaining about events in the 1630s. John Sommerson and David Coxes were churchwardens in 1637, when the episcopal visitation found that the communion table had already been railed, surely a matter of lasting regret to these and other parishioners: London Metropolitan Archives, DL/B/A/002/MS 09537/015, fo. 20.

116 That is, cessors (assessors, *OED*), those appointed by parliament to assess the liability of individuals to taxes based on wealth or income.

117 The Book of Common Prayer, though long subject to objections by puritans, was still lawfully in use at this time: it was finally banned by parliament in January 1645. William Dyer had his son Benjamin christened in 1641; if this was the occasion for the exchange recorded here, perhaps Dyer had asked

fo. 47

10. Item he bestowes much of his Tyme about worldly Imployments as dressing Corne, pitching Cart, and that sometymes on Satterday Nine a Clock at Night, when it were better he were in his Studdy.
William Dier, John Sommerson, John Norton.
11. Item he hath taken upp young Apple-trees in other Mens Grounds and sett them in his Orchard, and fished other Mens Ponds with Netts, and sett Grams[118] to catch Hares etc, and such like is his frequent Imployment.
John Sommerson, John Norton.
12. Item he is an ungifted and unfitt Man for the Ministry and imployeth scandalous Ministers to preach for him, as Mr Elmer now sequestred, and one Richardsonn a drunken Minister, and Mr Write a sequestered Man, whom he kept in his House to secure him from the Parliament Officers.[119]
John Sommerson, William Bolton, John Jackson.
13. That in visiting the Sicke, he onely useth the Booke of Common Prayer, and being sent for to one John Tawler a very godly Christian in his Sicknes, he told him it was just with God to lay that Affliction uppon him for going from his Ministery.
David Coxes, William Bolton.
14. Item that at Mr Whitgift's Child's baptizeing he had drunke so much as he ran his Head against the Wall and there shamefully vomitted.
Elizabeth South.
15. Item that at Colchester he dranke more then was fitt for him to drinke and Mistress Whitgift charged hir Man he should not speake of it, he being in his Company a drinking.
William Chapman.

fo. 48

16. Item, that at an Alehouse in his owne Parish he continued halfe a Day in disorderly Drinkeing with John Baxter and John Gibson, that Baxter's Wife desired the Constable to lay hir Husband by the Heeles, which he was loath to doe because the Minister was there, whereuppon she went hirself and brake the Potts.
John Sommerson, Richard Webb.
17. Item, that he refused to baptize Children of his Parish, when they were presented to him in the Church on the Lord's Day in the Fore-noon.[120]
David Cocks, John Cleare.

Falconer (or his curate) to omit the sign of the cross, and Falconer had agreed, under protest: *Acts and ordinances*, pp. 582–607; ERO, D/P 208/1/1.

118 Cole transcribed this word as grams, but marked the reading as doubtful. 'Grains', perhaps in the sense of 'refuse malt left after brewing' (*OED*, *sub* grain, 4.b.), might be the meaning.

119 A. G. Matthews suggests that Mr Elmer was Edward Aylmer, rector of West Hanningfield, who was ejected by parliament in 1643: *Walker revised*, pp. 151, 145. Richardson has not been identified. 'Mr Write' was probably Francis Wright, vicar of Witham, also ejected by parliament in 1643. Wright had been rejected by the godly Lady Katherine Barnardiston, who lived at Witham but gadded to Terling to hear the preaching of Thomas Weld: *ibid.*, p. 170; Gyford, 'Lady Katherine Barnardiston (née Banks)', *ODNB*.

120 Falconer was presented for this offence in the court of the bishop's commissary in 1635: ERO, D/ABA 7, fo. 123v.

18. He prosecuted one Aron Little a godly young Man of his Parish to his Death, for going to heare the Word of God at other Places; and when he was dead refused to bury him and sent his Sonn to forewarne the Sexton not to make his Grave, and yet exacted ii^{s} for his Buriall.[121]
His Living is worth 100^{li} per Annum and he hath a Wife and 4 Children, the youngest 12 yeares old: his temporall Estate is worth 30^{li} per Annum or thereabouts.
They desire   for their Minister.
No mention of him in Walker's Sufferings of the Clergy and Mr Newcourt has not his name among the Rectors of Aldham.

fo. 49

Depositions taken at Halsted the 16th of August 1644 against Stephen Nettles Minister of Lexden.[122]
He saith, that the said Stephen Nettles is a Frequenter of Tavernes and Ale-houses and one private House vizt of Roger Warran, whose Wife, by common Fame, is reputed a light Woman.
James Gibson to the vith.[123]
That he is a Man that often gives ill-Language, and hath sworne by his Faith.
James Gibson to the viiith.
That he is an unprofitable Preacher.
Edward Griffin, John May, James Gibson to the first.
That he did not stir up his Parishioners to take the Vow and Covenant neither did he take it himselfe with them, but gave it to Boyes that came out of the Streets from Play.
John May to the 4th.

121 The parish register records Aaron Litle's burial on 26 April 1641: ERO, D/P 208/1/1. No witnesses are named for this article, but Sarah Little, who swore to article 4 above, may well have been a relation of Aaron, and the deponent.

122 Nettles graduated from Queens' College, Cambridge (BA 1599, MA 1602), and was a fellow there for some years. He proceeded BD in 1611. In 1610, he was appointed rector of Lexden and in 1617 vicar of Great Tey, a living which he exchanged in 1623 for that of Steeple. The articles against Nettles led to his sequestration, although there is no entry to that effect in Leicester MS 31. On 28 June 1645, the committee for plundered ministers ordered Nettles 'from whom the rectory of Lexden is sequestered' to explain why he kept possession of the parsonage house and glebe from Gabriel Wyersdale, 'to whom the rectory is sequestered'. Nettles and Wyersdale were also in dispute over tithes, and the committee requested parliament's committee at Colchester to get Wyersdale speedy possession and the dispute settled. Whether they did so in 1645 is unclear but in 1647 Nettles was occupying the parsonage and glebe and attempting to assert a right to tithes, and the committee for plundered ministers ordered the sheriff and JPs to help Wyersdale to get possession. Nettles was finally ejected from Lexden. He was also ejected from Steeple. See also p. lii above, n. 7, for more on the sequestrations. He died in 1657, and John Nettles, probably his son, was appointed rector of Lexden: John Walter, 'Stephen Nettles (fl. 1599–1647)', *ODNB*; BL, Add. MS 15669, fos. 98v, 134v; BL, Stowe MS 842, fo. 4v; BL, Add. MS 15671, fos. 162, 171v; BL, Stowe MS 842, fo. 28; Newcourt, *Repertorium*, II, 389.

123 This and subsequent references to ordinal numbers must refer to the written articles submitted to the committee, which are not included in our manuscript: their content can, however, be inferred from the evidence given in support of them. James Gibson, the deponent, had been in dispute with Nettles for two years. James and John Gibson owned two mills which brought in £40 a year in rent, on which tithes had customarily been paid, but for the last two years the sums of £4 per annum had been withheld. Nettles blamed this shortfall in his income for his failure to pay recent taxes levied by parliament. Parliament's committee for Colchester, sitting on 7 Aug. 1644, ordered the Gibsons to pay £6 to the tax collectors: BL, Stowe MS 842, fo. 31v–31. Elizabeth and Grace Gibson were also deponents: their relationship to James is not known.

Saith, that he never gives Notice of keeping the Fast, and when that Day comes, teacheth them but little to any purpose for Edification.
Andrew Hall to the second.
He used to begin the Fast Day not till Eleaven of the Clocke, and then spend little above an Hower, and after Sermon he goes home to Dinner and invites others to dine with him, and after Dinner he spends Parte of the Day in the Taverne, and sometymes drinking in private Houses.
Andrew Hall to the third.
That he hath neglected to take the Vow and Covenant, wholly slighting it, saying we might take it if we would, or we might let it alone.
Andrew Hall to the iiii^th^.

fo. 50

That he hath suffred Bowling and Football on his owne yard on the fasting Day.
Ambrose Foulsham to the second.
That he hath often seene him at Tavernes drinking, and at a private House of Roberte Warrein, whose Wife is counted light, into whose Plackett this Deponent hath seene Mr Nettles at his House put his Hand upp to the Elbow, hir Husband sitting next to hir on the other side: and that he hath seene eight or tenn Payer of Cards[124] in his House, and Company playing with them.
Ambrose Foulsham to the vi^th^.
That he hath seene Bowling and Football on Mr Nettles his owne yard on the Fast-Day, and seene himselfe crosse the yard at the same Tyme. And that he preaches and prayd not above an Hower on that Day.
John Adkinson to the second.
That uppon July 28th last, being Lord's Day, at night, he went to the Taverne and there tarried till above eleaven of the Clocke, and when he came forth he went into the House of Roger Warrein aforenamed.
John Adkinson to the vi^th^.
Saith, that he said the Booke of Common Prayer is an absolute Rule to walke by.
George Ashley to the 5th.
That uppon July 28th last, being the Lord's Day at night, he went to the Taverne and there tarried till about xi of the Clocke and when he came forth he went into the House of Roger Warrein aforenamed.
George Ashley to the 6th.

fo. 51

Sayeth as Adkinson, verbatim.
James Deeplocke to the vi^th^.
That in his kissing of Women he putteth his Tongue into their Mouthes, as he hath offerd to doe to this Deponent more than once.
Sara Foulsham to the vii^th^.
That she saw him kissing Warrein's Wife wantonly at Warrein's House under the Stayres covring her with his Gowne.
Sara Foulsham to the vth.

[124] A pair of cards means a pack of cards: *OED*.

Sayth, that about 4 yeares since, he, comeing to the House of Deponent in hir Husband's Abscence, as she sate in hir Chayre, held hir downe and offred to pull upp hir Clothes, and said unto hir, I wonder such a lusty young Woman as thou art hast no Children, saying, didst ever use the Meanes by trying any other Man besides thy Husband, she answered, she durst not committ such a Sinne, for she thought God would not pardon it, he replyed, God forbidd but that we should thinke God able to pardon such a Sinn, and his haveing hir in his Armes, desired to have his Will of hir, askeing hir, whether she would doe it for Love, or if not for Money: But she withstood him, and at last one comeing by, he left hir.
Margery Stow to the viith.
That in kissing of hir this Deponent, he offerd to put his Tongue into hir Mouth.
Sara Foulsham to the viith.
That last Sommer she saw him at Warrein's House with Warrein's Wife on his Knee, and

fo. 52

his Hand under hir Clothes.
Sara Foulsham to the 4th.
That kissing hir, he offerd to put his Tongue into hir Mouth.
Elizabeth Gibson to the viith.
To the viith, say that Joseph Mason said he saw Mr Nettles go into an Arbour in his owne Ground, and a Woman presently following him went into the Arbour and there were presently at it, and were so earnest, that he could have taken him by the Gowne before he could have knowen it.
Richard Stacy and Richard Walteere.
That denying to read a Briefe, being spoke to by this Deponent he some few Dayes after tooke Occasion to rayle uppon him and call him Jacke Rascall and Shacke and such other Termes.[125]
John Makin.
That he often sweares by his Faith.
Grace Gibson.
One John Nettles is mentioned by Mr Newcourt vol: 2, p. 389 as Rector of Lexden in 1657, who dyed in 1669. He also mentions one Stephen Nettles S.T.B. who was Vicar of Tay-magna in Essex to 1637: it would be hazarding too much to suppose that John is a mistake for Stephen, especially as one John Nettles occurs Vicar of St Peter's Colchester in 1663. Yet if that was allowed, I would also suppose the year 1657 to mean 1637, when Stephen Nettles resigned Tay-magna. However that be, certain it is that Stephen Nettles was Rector of Lexden in 1644 and probably then ejected, though the former Account of his Persecution mentions nothing of it and though his Name occurs not as such in Newcourt's List of those Rectors. He was born in Shropshire and admitted a Pensioner in Queens College in Cambridge June 25 1595, and made Fellow of the same Oct:11.1599. He tooke his Degree in Arts and afterwards

[125] A brief was a royal letter patent licensing a collection in churches throughout England for a specified charitable purpose. During the Civil War and Commonwealth parliament issued briefs on its own authority. Nettles may have objected to a brief which he thought was designed to raise funds for a parliamentary cause: W. A. Bewes, *Church briefs* (1896), p. 19. 'Jack' could mean a 'person of low social status, … a rogue': *OED*, under 'jack' n. 2, I.2.a. 'Shack' meant 'an idle, disreputable fellow; a vagabond': *OED*, under 'shack', n. 2.

fo. 53

proceeded Bachelor in Divinity. He was the learned Author of the Answer to the Jewish Part of Mr Selden's History of Tithes, printed in 1625 in 4to at Oxon. Mr Walker says that he was dispossessed of his Living at Lexden by Force of Armes, but was unacquainted with the Particulars of his ill Usage: Sufferings of the Clergy, Part 2, p. 318.

It is probable that all this Trumpery against him proceeded from his Contempt of the Covenant: yet it is a Pity that a Man of his Learning should be branded down to Posterity in this Manner by his fanatical neibours, only for some Levities, magnified, no doubt, according to the ill Will they bore him, not only for his Conformity, but for having signaliz'd himself in writing in Favour of an Argument which Committee Men disrelished and particularly for having dared to attack so famous a Champion of the puritan Cause as the very learned Mr Selden.

Mr Morant in his History of Colchester, Book 2, p. 25, says that Stephen Nettles Rector of Lexden near Colchester was removed from thence in 1644 and Gabriel Wyersdale put in his Room.[126]

Vide p. 14 Additionalls taken against Mr Lake uppon oath at Halsted October 4. 1644.

Richard Emberson saith, that about iii yeares since he saw Mr Lake so drunke at Braintrie Fayer as he could not go upright in the Streets, and one Goodwife Bigbone now deceased, that knew him formerly, haveing beene his Mayd Servant, led him then away.

Thomas Powlter saith, that another Tyme about iii yeares and Quarter since, he was so drunke at Braintrie on the Markett Day, where he stayd drinking till 9 or 10 a Clocke in the Evening, that he was unable to goe Home alone, but this Deponent was fayne to lead him, and yet he

fo. 54

could not keepe him upp, But he had a great many Falls by the Way, and comeing out at the Towne's End, Mr Lake called at the George for more Beere; but he had drunk so much before, that he was able to drinke but little of that; And as he was going homewards, he reeling, fell downe amongst Bushes and rent his Coate, and when this Deponent did helpe him upp agayne, he swore by God he had rent his Cassocke.

Richard Rumzie and Thomas Powlter depose, That he hath formerly and within this halfe yeare caused or suffred Drunkennes in his House, so as John Thurgood and divers others have gone from his House in Drinke and so disguised as they could not speake or goe right, and hath kept Company with other drunken Company since, as with one Martyne Steele.

Richard Emberson saith, he hath heard him sweare before God within this Quarter of a yeare at Braintrie Markett.

Josias Smith saith, he hath heard him sweare by his Faith, on the Sabbath day, after his Sermon, in the Church yard, about a yeare agoe.

[126] See n. 122 above for a summary of Nettles's career. In his commentary, Cole also notes that Nettles was the author of *An answer to the Jewish part of Mr Selden's history of tithes* (Oxford, 1625), in which Nettles argued that the scriptures gave authority for the imposition of tithes. In this, as in other respects, he would have incurred the disapproval of some of his parishioners.

Thomas Powter heard Mr Lake say, his Dogg being shucked[127] by Richard Wenden's Dogg, he comeing downe from his Studdy, A Poxe take you and your Dogg, you have done me one shrewd Turne already by God, and now you have done me

fo. 55

another, by God, I shall never beware of you, and rann about as if he had been madd; and this was about ii yeares agoe.
All these Deponents say they have never seene any such Evydence of Reformation or Repentence in him, as he pretends: And also that they conceive him to be a Man not qualified with fitt Gifts and Abilityes for the Ministery, either for preaching or praying.
Henry Smith, Josias Smith, Richard Rumzie, Richard Wenden, Thomas Powter, Richard Emberson.
After this Evidence of their Conceits of his Abilities, whereof, no Doubt, they were very proper Judges, follows a blank Space, probably for another Information to be inserted: though it being the bottom of the Page, it is more probable, the Writer would not begin a new Deposition in that Place.

Depositions taken uppon Oath against John Mow Curate of Bardfeild magna the 8th of November at Thaxted Fryday.[128]
Theise Deponents say that about a yeare and a half since, Mr Mow being requested by Isaac Rich, then Church-Warden, to read a Booke of the Remonstrance of Parliament, which he refused, and the said Isaac Rich reading the same himselfe, Mr Mow drew forth a Letter of the Lord Pagett's and said, heere is my Lord Paget's

fo. 56

Letter who is as worthy a Parliament Man as any of them all, untill he saw the Parliament's Treachery against the King, and then he turned from them to the King. And so he drew away as many of the People as he could into the Chancell to hear him read Lord Pagett's Letter, and William Edwards saith he read it with a loud Voyce.[129]
Isaac Rich, William Mathew, William Edwards.

[127] The *OED* records 'shuck' as a dialect word for a 'spectre hound'. The sense might be that Wenden's dog had made a frenzied attack on Lake's dog. A similar meaning would follow from emending the text to 'shocked': *OED*, under 'shock' v.2, 2, 'to assail with a sudden and violent attack'.

[128] By his own account reported at fo. 56 below, John Mow was a Scot who had come south in disgust at the Scottish National Covenant of 1638, which he considered required him to take up arms against the king. He may have been the man of that name who graduated MA in 1609 from King's College Aberdeen. See Introduction, p. xlvi, for Mow's appointment at and his retention of Great Bardfield: *Roll of alumni in arts of the university and King's College of Aberdeen, 1596–1860*, ed. P. J. Anderson (Aberdeen, 1900), p. 3.

[129] It seems unlikely that the document read by Rich in mid-1643 was the Grand Remonstrance of 1641. It could have been *A remonstrance of the Commons in parliament* (of June 1643), which was a spurious piece of propaganda in support of parliament: BL, Thomason Tracts, E.105[23]. Mow evidently responded with *The copie of a letter sent from the right honourable the Lord Paget, unto the honourable house of parliament, declaring the reasons of his departure from the parliament, unto the kings most excellent majesty at Yorke* (1642): BL, Thomason Tracts 669.f.6[35]. This latter text may also be spurious, but it conveys correctly the fact that Paget, who had been serving parliament, had a crisis of conscience in mid-1642 and defected to the king at York. By November 1644, when the charges against Mow were being heard, Paget had returned to the parliamentary fold: Gordon Goodwin (rev. John Sutton), 'William, 6th Baron Paget (1609–78)', *ODNB*.

Theise Deponents say, that about Easter, next after the Parliament began, as they remember, at the Baptizeing of two Children in Finchingfeild, Mr Mow in the presence of Mr Paynell of Stamborne and Mr Fitch of Bumsted,[130] said that he came not out of Scotland for any Fault of Life or Doctrine, but by reason of one Clause in the Covenant which he said was that they could defend themselves and their Religion against all Manner of persons, and said in doing so I must take upp Armes against my Prince which I ought not to doe, for if he were not a religious King we ought not to take upp Armes, For the Weapons of the Church were Prayers and Teares.
Amos Rushmer, Thomas Titterell.
Thomas Paynell was instituted Rector of Stamborne in 1578: probably it was a Descendant of his, who is mentioned in this Article: as to Mr Fitch, there occurs none of that Name in either of the 2 Bumsteds as Parsons there: in that of Bumsted Helion none of any other Name but mine, and my Relations were possessed of that Rectory from 1580 to 1700, except one of the Name of Smith, my Ancestors being Patrons of that Living for

fo. 57

many Generations: in the North-West Window of the North Isle of which Church is as old and curious a Coat of Arms of my Family, as any I ever met, being at least 400 years old: viz: Argent a Chevron Gules inter 3 Scorpions Sable. Which see in my 5th vol: depicted. But this by the by; to gratify a little Family Vanity, it being no unusual or illaudable Thing, for those of a decayed or modern Family to claim Kindred to those of an antient one: my father was of a good Gentleman's Family, but decayed, he being the youngest of 16 Children, who were all born at Ashen, the very next Parish to Bumsted-Helion, and the most contiguous to Cambridgeshire.
Theise Deponents say that about a year agoe, when the Vow and Covenant was to be taken in the Church, Mr Mow refused the takeing of it and thereupon fledd towards Ingerstone, where he being apprehended, he tooke it, as this Deponent saith he heard Sir Martyne Lumely report.[131]
Bartholomew Note, William Mathew.
These Deponents say, that they heard Mr Mow say, those that had taken the Protestation to mayntayne the Parliament were forsworne for voteing out the Popish Lords, aludeing to that of Joshua concerning the Gibeonits, that although they were of the Canaanites, yet for his Oathes sake he spared them, because of the Oath; and that was presently after the taking of the second Protestation.[132]
Mr Joseph Hull, Isac Rich.

130 At the time in question, Easter 1641, John Paynell was rector of Stambourne: CCEd, Location ID 11440. Zachary Fitch had only recently graduated from Emmanuel College, Cambridge and may have been employed locally, perhaps at Steeple Bumpstead, as curate. His later career is recorded in Venn, *Alumni Cantabrigienses*, II, 145.

131 For Lumley, see Introduction, p. xlvi.

132 In early 1642, parliament was considering a bill, enacted on 14 February, which deprived bishops of their membership of the House of Lords. In the same month, many parishes were taking or had recently taken the protestation oath which bound its subscribers to defend both the king's person and estate and the power and privilege of parliaments. Mow was therefore accusing parliamentarians who supported the ejection of the bishops from the House of Lords of breaking the oath which they had sworn in the protestation, and comparing their conduct unfavourably with that of Joshua and the Israelites, who had honoured a treaty made with the Gibeonites, although the latter had practised a

fo. 58

Mr Hull further saith, that Mr Mow said, the Parliament sett base Fellowes, such as a Weaver and a Miller, to take such as he was.
James Rich saith also, that he heard Mr Mow say, they were all forsworne which subscribed the Petition for voteing of Popish Lords out of the House, the same Lords being all as good Subjects as they, till they were convicted: for which he brought the Example of the Gibeonites, that after the Covenant with Joshua let them remember of the Oath and this was above a year since.
Arthur Borley deposeth, Mr Mow went about to gett Hands to the Petition for Peace.
Robert Dawkin deposeth, that Mr Mow comeing in at the Chancell Dore did use to bow towards the Rayles, and that he, with one Mr Barnard, came to the Deponent's House and would not leave him untill he had gotten his Hand to the Petition for Peace, about Christtide 1642: which he was loath to have done, because he saw it was carried about by Malignants and Ministers that way disposed.[133]
Daniel Rich deposeth that he saw Mr Mow carry the Petition for Peace from House to House to gett Hands: and on New Years Day after, he did reprove those that would not sett thir Hands to it in his Sermon, quoting for that purpose John 14, My Peace I leave, etc.
John Bond deposeth that Mr Mow came to him to gett his Hand to the Petition for Peace, which he denying, Mr Mow

fo. 59

was very angry with him.
Daniel Rich deposeth, that Mr Mow useing in his Discourse his Faith and Troth, being, as this Deponent heard, reprooved for it, did after in his Sermon, say that there were many that would not sweare, but would lye like the Devill, and so left it.
Austen Boswell deposeth, that he heard Mr Mow in his Sermon say, that many would not sweare but would lye like Devills. And farther this Deponent saith, Mr Mow said at this Deponent's M[r's] House, all the best of the Towne were on his Side, and there were none against him but a few of the Devill's Children.
Theise Deponents say that about some Difference concerning Tith of Pigg and Apples betweene the said Mow and the Deponent Mary Scott, he wished she might live in Want until his Pigg were restored again. And because the said Mary Scott did not give him so much for hir Tithe Apples as he required, he wished shee might perish; and this he wished severall Tymes.
Mary Scott, Judeth Lorkin.
And Judeth Lorkin deposeth further, that because she told him that she would pay him Tith when the King and Parliament were agreed, he said (as she conceiveth out of his distast to the Parliament, because he hath done nothing for the Parliament) Are yow one of those? and thereuppon and often since called her separate.
Isaac Rich saith that he heard Mr Mow swear by God.

deception in negotiating it. For the protestation, see Introduction, pp. xxx–xxxi above; Shaw, *History of the church 1640–1660*, I, 118–19; Joshua ix, 1–27.

133 For the petition for peace, see Introduction, p. xxxi. Richard Barnard was a gentleman who was rated third highest in the parish for ship money: ERO, T/A 42/1, p. 4.

fo. 60

Richard Wood deposeth, that he saw Mr Mow and Mr Pakenham bow towards the Rayle as they went upp to receive the Sacrament.
William Mathew deposeth, that Mr Mow being to receive the Sacrament, Mr Pakenham comeing up with him to the Rayle to receive, they both made three Congees to the Rayles.
And further, this Deponent saith, another Tyme he would not preach in the Afternoon because, he said, he was afraid the Rayles should be pulled upp which, he said, were a fine Ornament for the Church.
I meet with John Packenham who was instituted Rector of Bardfeild-magna in 1615, who probably was the Rector to whom Mr Mow was Curate. Newcourt vol. 2, p. 30.
Bartholomew Nodes deposeth that about three yeares since, on the Lord's Day, Mr Mow refused to go to Church, for Feare the Rayles should be pulled upp, as he himselfe told them, and so there was neither Sermon nor Service that Afternoone.[134]
And farther, this Deponent saith that he delivered in a Sermon about a yeare agoe, that many would runn three miles to a Sermon, when they might have as good at Home, and, if they were examined, they had no more Religion in them than a Dogg: saying that a Man ought not to go a Mile on the Sabbath Day: for the Jewes, he said, would not goe seaven Furlongs.

fo. 61

John Addams saith that about 3 Quarters of a yeare agoe, Mr Mow haveing appointed a Satterday to examine People for the receiveing of the Sacrament the next Day, they comeing to Church found him not there, and repayreing to his House, they heard he was at the Taverne, where they saw him after come out, and wholly neglecting that Worke of preparation he pretended.
William Surrey, John Bond and William Edwards Depose that Mr Mow, haveing passed by one John Haukes in giveing the Bread in the Sacrament, being told thereof by the Church-Warden, he bad the Church-Warden carry it him, which he did in the Cover of the Cupp, and Haukes tooke a Peice of it, and this was above a yeare agoe.
John Haukes deposeth, that Mr Mow did not give him the Bread in one Sacrament but it was brought him by the Church-warden: as he conceiveth, it was sent by Mr Mow.
Robert Daukin deposeth, that Mr Mow would not pay him his Collection for the Poore, untill he had made him promise not to give any to the Widdow Carder, because she did not keepe her owne Church, but goe to heare at other Churches where there were good Ministers.
Sara Carder deposeth, that Mr Mow told hir she would have no Collection because she went to other Churches to heare good Ministers, she being an old poore Woman and, as she saith, could not understand him.

[134] See Introduction, p. xxxvi, for the attempt by the House of Commons in September 1641 to enforce the removal of altar rails. No doubt at that time there was talk in Great Bardfield of implementing this policy. It is not known when the rails in that church were in fact removed, but they surely had been by the time of the deposition.

fo. 62

Mary Wallis deposeth, that she, not being able to edifie by Mr Mow and going to other parishes, he did and doth with hold from hir Gifts given to the Poore, because she went to other Churches to heare.
Robert Godfrey deposeth, that as Mr Mow came from Mr Bendlowes,[135] in some Discourse Mr Mow said that the Parliament were not ordeyned by the Word of God as Kings were, but were meerely by the Favour of the King to his Subjects.
Isaac Rich deposeth, that about two yeares since he publiquely taught, that none were to meddle with the temporall Sword but the King and whom he should appoint: but now the Commons did easily prevyle with the People to take up Armes against the King, and brought in Absolon for an Example.[136]
Joseph Hull deposeth, that he heard Mr Mow say the Oath taken in Scotland was against the King; the latter parte of it especially and he said he came away
This Article seems imperfect and unfinished and Room is left to fill up the Page with other Informations: but probably here was enough to out poor Mr Mow from his Curacy. On the other Side of the Page is an Attestation or two of these godly Hypocrites: the 2^{d} is enough to make one sick of the Hypocrisy of those sanctified Tymes, and (though we now live in an Age quite the reverse of them, being ashamed to own even any Pretence of Religion) to bless ones self that we have not to do with such sanctified Villains. This is wrote in quite a different hand from all the rest of the MS.

fo. 63

For that parte of Mr Bird's Defence which chargeth Elizabeth Coate for being convicted for Fornication and Theft before Mr Raymond, I doe utterly deny that any such Conviction was ever before me, Witness my Hand the 1 Day of January 1644.
Oliver Raymond.
As touching Mr Bird, this of my own Knowledge I can witnes, that the said Mr Bird was once or twice much disguised with Beere or Wine at Castle-Hedingham, so that he was scarce able to speak common Sence, uttering such Words to me who was a meere Stranger to him, 'O thou man of God, take up the Busines betweene me and my Neighbour touching the Tyth Calfe, for I know thou hast the Spirit of God in thee: I will stand to thy Judgment whatever it be.
Isaac Wincall.
What is certified by the Witnesses produced to theise and the former Articles, we do believe to be Truth, and some of us haveing long knowen him, and all of us beleeveing were right he departed thense [illeg] certified concerning the matter of Drunkenness.

This Page is wrote in so wretched an Hand, that it was with Difficulty I could read it: yet I am sure it is all right, but 2 words in the last Line, which I would not give myselfe any more Time to study about, having considered it longer then it deserved: however I found out one by giving it another Look, which is Drunkeness. It refers to Joseph Bird Parson of Oaten-Belchamp, for whose Depositions against him see p. 32. What follows is wrote at the other End of the MS and is sewed up the wrong End upwards and is imperfect, beginning on the second Page, so that the Title is lost.

135 See Introduction, p. xlvi, for Edward Bendlowes.
136 Absalom rebelled against his father King David, and was killed as a result: 2 Samuel, xv–xviii.

fo. 64[137]

5. He is a common Ale-house Hanter, and hath bin severall Times distempered with drinking Night and Day.
John Bets, James Thorpe.
6. He is very obscene in his Speeches in Women's Company.
John Bets.
7. He is a usuall Swearer by his Faith.
John Spurgion, James Thorpe.
His Benefice is worth 40^{li} and his temporal Estate 20^{li} per Annum. He hath a Wife and Child.
[Sequestrators nominated: John Rye, Simon Wrench, Edmond Withers.][138]
See more fo. 8.
But as there never was more than 6 Leaves to the Book, and they single paged, so if each Side of the Leaf was paged, folio 8 would be what is now folio 4 and relates to Dr John Jarvis, who, I have reason to believe, is the Person the 3 above said Articles refer to. It does not mean Dr Jarvis.[139] *What I have put in Crochets above and throughout this whole Transcript is wrote in a different Hand from the rest of the MS.*

fo. 65

[Depositions. his Answer is retorned]
Gregory Holland Parson of West Bergholt-Sackvill.[140]
1. He preached, it was not fit for Farmers or Tradesmen to know the Mistery of their Salvation, but only for himself, and such as he was.
Thomas Read, John Smith.
2. He published and allowed of the Booke for Liberty of prophaning the Lord's Day.
Peter Sadler, Thomas Read, Thomas Martyn.
3. Usually coming into the Church he went up to the Raile to his Devotions.
Christofer Stamford, Thomas Reade.

137 As recorded by Cole immediately above, the following section of the original manuscript was contained in a separate booklet sewn into the main volume: see also Introduction, p. xi. The first and last leaves were missing so that the articles numbered 5–7 below are the later part of the articles against Joseph Long of Fingringhoe. Fortunately, the complete articles are found in Leicester MS 31, fo. 23: notes about Long are given there.

138 This list of sequestrators has been entered in the manuscript by a later hand and in error, being a duplication of the entry for Greenstead by Colchester (fo. 68 below). Leicester MS 31 contains a different and more credible list of sequestrators: Leicester MS 31, fo. A27.

139 'It does not mean Dr Jarvis' is clearly an afterthought by Cole, to indicate that on reflexion the three articles numbered 5–7 do not refer to Jarvis. As noted above, they do in fact refer to Joseph Long of Fingringhoe.

140 Holland was a graduate of Christ's College, Cambridge (BA 1604–5, MA 1609). In 1613, he was appointed rector of West Bergholt. Despite the charges set out in these articles, Holland was not sequestrated: there are no records of this in Leicester MS 31 or elsewhere. He was still in possession in 1650, but it was reported that he was aged and consented to the appointing of a curate by the parish 'for the better supply of the cure'. (In 1638, Holland had been suspended by the archdeacon's court for failing to wear the surplice and to pray for the king, possibly signs of premature ageing rather than ideological conviction.) The parish register records Holland's burial on 17 September 1658, specifically identifying him as 'rector': Venn, *Alumni Cantabrigienses*, II, 393; Newcourt, *Repertorium*, II, 56; Smith, *Ecclesiastical history of Essex*, p. 309; ERO, D/ACA 53, fo. 185v; ERO, D/P 59/1/1.

4. He deferd the Sacrament till the Raile were finished, and then in giving it, he protested before God and the Congregation, he would not come out of the Raile though he lost his Living for it, and yet at that Time came out to some that would not come up.
David Cosens, John King, Thomas Read, Peter Sadler.
5. Having subscribed 10^{li} to the Parliament he said before he would pay it, he would goe to Prison, and that he would doe no more for the Parliament than he was forced to.
Thomas Martyn, Thomas Read.
6. He published the Scots to be Rebells, and prayd for their Confusion.
Thomas Read, Christopher Stamford.
7. He said the King and Cavaleers stood to maintaine the true Protestant Religion.
Thomas Read, Thomas Martin.

fo. 66

8. He is a prophane Swearer not forbearing in the Church.
Thomas Martin, David Cozens.
9. He is a Haunter of Innes and Taverns and divers Times drunk.
Thomas Read, Christopher Stamford, David Cozens.
His benefice .... 100^{li}.
His temporal Estate per Annum .... 37^{li}.
By his Wife per Annum .... 20^{li}.
His Wife living and 5 Children.
This Man's Persecution by these reforming Hypocrites is neither taken Notice of by Newcourt or Walker. It is probable he was ejected to make Room for some Relation of that great Saint Dr Lazarus Seaman, as I find one Nat. Seaman his Successor in the Rectory of Bergholt, who, if my Conjecture is right, possibly might conform at the Restoration, before which time it is probable that Mr Gregory Holland died, for the Successor died possessed of it in 1679.[141]

Colchester Mary Magdalen's Parish. Gabriel Honifold vicar.[142]
1. Having Charge of the Parish 28 yeares, he preached seldome and that * and unprofitably.
**sic in MS.*
Cornelius Tunbridge, Thomas Heckford, John Inman for 7 yeares.

[141] As noted above, Holland was not ejected and died in post in 1658. At that point, Nathaniel Seaman was appointed as rector, a position which he retained until his death in 1679. Seaman was the son of a Chelmsford draper and is not known to have been a kinsman of Lazarus Seaman: Venn, *Alumni Cantabrigienses*, IV, 37; Tai Liu, 'Lazarus Seaman (d. 1675)', *ODNB*.

[142] Gabriel Honifold graduated from Corpus Christi College, Oxford (BA 1597, MA 1602). Elected a fellow, he proceeded BD in 1610. In 1614, he was appointed vicar of Ardleigh, four miles east of Colchester. Shortly afterwards, Honifold was appointed master of St Mary Magdalen hospital in Colchester, a position in the gift of the lord chancellor which brought with it the rectory of the parish of St Mary Magdalen. As a loyal conformist who sometimes sat as surrogate in the archdeacon's court, Honifold became a target of puritan critics in Colchester. In 1642, his house was ransacked by an angry crowd, and he was unable to obtain help from the town's authorities. He left Colchester, resigning his living at Ardleigh and arranging for another local minister, Samuel Cock, to preach at St Mary's and to look after the hospital. See Appendix 2, p. liii n. 8, for discussion of whether Honifold was sequestrated; there is no evidence that Manchester took such action. Responsibility for the parish and the hospital was not settled until 1646 when the committee for plundered ministers ordered that Alexander Piggott should serve the cure and govern the hospital. Shortly afterwards, Honifold died: Foster, *Alumni Oxonienses*, II, 739; CCEd, Location ID 11115; Walter, *Understanding popular*

2. He hath bin non-resident this yeare and half last past, and hath not preached there since.
Thomas Hill, John Inman, William Love.
3. He hath placed in his Roome a Plu-

fo. 67

rallist who preaches there but once a Fortnight.
William Love, Richard Barker.
4. He does commonly sweare by his Faith.
Thomas Hill, Thomas Finch.
5. He ordinarily plaies at Cards and Tables on the Lord's Day. And Hill saith that he enticed him often to play betwixt Forenoone and Afternoone Service: And Linton, that when he came out of Towne on Saturday Night after his Returne to his owne House.
Thomas Hill, Alice Linton.
This last Article, being towards the Bottom of the Page, does not seem to be finished, Space being left to add 2 or 3 Lines more. Such were the Articles these Wretches brought against this old Gentleman, which outed him of 2 Livings, viz the Vicarage of Ardley near Colchester and that of St Mary Magdalen's in Colchester: though according to Mr Newcourt there is no such Parish: at least there is none mentioned by him. He puts him down S.T.P. in the List of the Vicars of Ardley, yet the Mercurius rusticus p. 12 says that he was only S.T.B. and 70 yeares of Age, where an exact Account of their barbarous Usage of him may be seen: particularly by a Namesake of mine, an Alderman of Colchester.[143] *It is said in Newcourt that he resigned Ardley in 1642, so that, probably, he was only outed from his Vicarage in the Town of Colchester.*

fo. 68

April 2d 1644

[To which his Answer is retorned.] Depositions against John Jarvis Dr of the Civill Law Parson of Greensted.[144]

1. He hath often said this Parliament are a Company of factious Fellows and aime at nothing but their owne Ends.
William Rie, Edmond Withers.

violence, pp. 169, 173, 187–8; BL, Add. MS 15670, fos. 108, 228v; also Bodleian Library, MS 324, fo. 81; ERO, D/ACW 14/168.

143 Honifold, having been robbed, sought help from the mayor, whereupon Alderman Cole told him that 'he wond[e]red he would offer to come abroad, being a man so much hated': Walter, *Understanding popular violence*, p. 41.

144 John Jarvis matriculated at Brasenose College, Oxford in January 1622, aged eighteen, and obtained the degree of BA in that year, proceeding MA at All Souls in 1625, BCL 1627 and DCL 1632. In 1631, he was presented to the rectory of North Fambridge. Later, probably in 1638, he was additionally presented to the rectory of Greenstead by Colchester, some thirty miles distant from North Fambridge. It seems that he lived at North Fambridge and served Greenstead by hiring curates. Jarvis was a civil lawyer and it is clear that he succeeded for a while in contesting the sequestration: there is no record of his ejection in Leicester MS 31, which was probably written in spring 1645. Jarvis signed the parish register of North Fambridge in early 1646, but he was finally sequestered by the committee for plundered ministers from both livings on 28 April 1646. Jarvis died in 1648: Foster, *Alumni Oxonienses*, II, 803; Newcourt, *Repertorium* II, 253, 287; London Metropolitan Archives, DL/B/A/002/MS 09537/015, fo. 23; ERO, D/P 206/1/3; BL, Add. MS 15670, fos. 75v, 85, 141; Matthews, *Walker revised*, p. 156; *Lords Journal*, X, 237.

2. He said the Parliament sought nothing but Bloud, instancing the Earle of Strafford and the ArchBishop.
Edmund Withers.
3. He hath 2 Benefices, this of Grinsted and another at North-Fambridge.
Thomas Martin, Henry Bones, Robert Bretton.
4. Oftentimes his Cure is wholly neglected on the Lord's Day.
Henry Bones, Richard Gregory, Edmund Withers.
5. He is a common Swearer by his Faith and Troth.
Henry Bones, Edmund Withers.
6. He is a Man of very idle Conversation, being a great Frequenter of Ale-houses, and associates himself with Drunkards and prophane persons.
[Sequestrators John Rye, Simon Wrench, Edmond Withers.]
His Benefice at Grinsted is worth [80li] per Annum.

fo. 69

He hath a Wife and 5 Children.
His Benefice at North-Fambridge is worth 60li per Annum.
[They desyer Nehemia Longe to be theyr Minister, who is known to Mr Harlakenden].
Dr Jarvis's Persecution is omitted by Walker and Newcourt. One Nehemiah Long was Rector of Denge in Essex 1661 and continued so to his Death in 1678. This Mr Harlakenden was Commissary General to the Earl of Manchester and Major of Horse for the County of Essex, and was of a puritanical Family of good Antiquity at Earl's Colne in Essex. See my 10th vol: p. 25.[145]
See more p. 72.[146]

Depden [Noe Answer]
Thomas Wilson Doctor of Divinity Parson of Depdin.[147]
1. He is a Pluralist, having 3 Benefices, vizt. Depdin, Wimbish and Fulborne where his Family live.
Thomas Hamond, Daniell Hockley.

[145] In 1644, Nehemiah Long had recently graduated from Emmanuel College, Cambridge (BA 1640, MA 1643) and was shortly to be intruded into Runwell following the sequestration of Symon Lynch (Leicester MS 31, fos. 3–4 and A14). Long moved on to other parishes later; in 1650, at Matching he was reported as having been presented there by the earl of Warwick and being a 'godly able payneful preacher'. At Dengie in 1662, he conformed. It seems more likely that the Mr Harlakenden mentioned by the parish as knowing Mr Long was not William Harlakenden but his cousin Richard, who had probably sat as a committee member to hear the evidence against Jarvis. Cole's 10th volume, p. 25, is now BL, Add. MS 5811, fo. 29: Venn, *Alumni Cantabrigienses*, III, 102; Matthews, *Walker revised*, p. 158; Smith, *Ecclesiastical history of Essex*, pp. 274, 382; CCEd, Location ID 11229; for the Harlakendens, see Introduction, p. lx.

[146] A reference to fo. 73 below where further charges are made against Jarvis.

[147] Thomas Wilson (BA, Trinity College, Cambridge, 1604/5) was elected a fellow of St Catherine's College in 1606. He proceeded MA 1608, BD 1615 and DD 1623. In 1626, he was appointed rector of Fulbourn St Vigor (Cambridgeshire), and married the widow of Dr John Hills (late rector of the parish and master of St Catherine's). He became a prebendary of Westminster in 1626 and of Lincoln in 1631. In 1629, he was also appointed rector of Debden, where he employed John Debnam as curate, being himself largely absent. During the 1630s, he also held the *sine cura* rectory of Wimbish, neighbouring Debden. In 1643, Wilson was arrested by order of the Commons for delinquency (probably a refusal to pay parliamentary taxes or fines) and suffered sequestration. The charges set out below led Manchester to sequestrate all three parish livings. Wilson continued to contest these decisions,

2. He hath bin non-resident from *, ever since he had * Living, being about 12 or 13 yeares,* never coming there for the most part but to receive money or compound for his Tithes.
John Mead,[148] William Eldred.
** Sic in ms. This must mean Debden Living, the Time answering pretty well to this Deposition, he being instituted to it 22 December 1629: for supposing this Deposition to have been made in 1644, it would have been 14 or 15 years since he had been in Possession of it.*

fo. 70

3. He hath employed a Curate there who hath for the most Part not preached above once on the Lord's Day, and on the Fast Day.
Daniell Hockley, William Eldred.
4. He hath bin so notorious an Innovator, as that he sett up the Railes at his owne Chardge, and that a yeare or 2 before any Injunction.
Thomas Hamond, Daniell Hockley, John Meade.
5. He used to bow to the East End when he came into the Church, and at the naming of Jesus.
William Eldred, John Mead.
6. He is a knowne Delinquent, and his Estate sequestred and himselfe apprehended: but where he is, we know not.
Thomas Hamond, John Mead.
The Benefice of Depdin is worth 200li per Annum. His Benefice at Wimbish worth 100li per Annum.
He hath a Wife and no Child.
They desire Mr Glover of Finchingfeild may be their Minister.
Dr Wilson was Prebendary of St Paul's, Archdeacon of Westminster, Rector of Debden and Wimbish in Essex and Fulborne St Vigor's in Cambridgeshire, where he resided during the Usurpation. He was carried away a Prisoner by Captain Turner to London, as I learn from a MS Note in my own Hand writing in my Copy of Walker, and taken from Dr: Z. Grey. Walker is mistaken, as I guess, in Respect to the Name of one of his Preferments in Sussex, where probably another Dr Thomas Wilson might have been settled.[149]

---

without success, and died in 1652 or 1653: Venn, *Alumni Cantabrigienses*, IV, 432; J. Le Neve, *Fasti Ecclesiae Anglicanae 1541–1847*, ed. J. Horn *et al.* (13 vols., 1969–2013), VII, 73, and IX, 89; Newcourt, *Repertorium*, II, 209, 674; Matthews, *Walker revised*, pp. 169–70; Leicester MS 31, fos. 26v–27v and A30; TNA, PROB 11/232/21.

148 The identity of John Mead(e), swearing here to four articles, cannot be conclusively established. It is possible that he was the gentleman of Finchingfield – a nearby parish – who was a member of the north Essex committee. If so, he may have wanted to promote the prospects of Hugh Glover, curate at Finchingfield, as Wilson's successor in this lucrative living. The parish did ask for Glover, and he was appointed to serve at Debden: see Introduction, p. lxi, for John Meade; Matthews, *Calamy revised*, p. 225, and Smith, *Ecclesiastical history of Essex*, p. 283 (Hugh Glover).

149 Here, Cole refers to Zachary Grey's notes drawn from his study of Leicester MS 31, fo. 27. Walker's attibution of the parish of Pulborough (Sussex) to Wilson was surely based on a misreading of 'Fulbourn'.

fo. 71

Trinity Parish in Colchester. Thomas Newcomen Parson there.[150]
[Noe Answer]
1. He hath bin non-resident 19 months last past. And when he was in Towne he preached very seldome for some Moneths before: And since his Cure we have bin wholly unprovided for.
Nathaniel Cross, William Bowler.
2. [a] That in his preaching he said that the Scots were damnable Rebells for invading the Kingdome, gathering where they scattered not and reaping where they sowed not, [b] at other Times he affirmed to be Rebells and Traytors *(sic in MS)*.
[a] William Bowler, Edward Firmyn, [b] James Bisco, Edward Furmyn.
3. An Infant being brought to be baptised, not being suffred to cross it, used these Words, We doe not receive this Child into the Congregation of Christ's Flock, neither doe wth (*sic in orig*) signe it with the Signe of the Crosse, in token that hereafter it shalbe ashamed to confesse the Faith of Christ crucified, and not manfully to fight against the World, the Flesh and the Divill, and not continue his faithfull Soldier, perverting the Forme of that part of the Liturgy.
Robert Sida Father of the Child, Nathaniel Crosse.
4. He denied to administer the Sacrament to all that would not come up to receive it at the Rayle, for which divers were prosecuted in Ecclesiasticall Courts to their great Expence and Trouble.
Robert Sida, William Bowler, Edward Firmyn.

fo. 72

5. He was carried to Prison as an Actor at Sir John Lucas his House, as an Assistant to him in promoting his Designe, as is supposed, when provided and attempted to carry Horses and Ammunition to the Cavaleers at Notingham.
Nathaniel Crosse, William Bowler.
The Value of his Living is 24^{li} per Annum.
See an account of his sufferings in Mercurius rusticus, transcribed into Newcourt vol 2 p. 182 and Walker Part 2nd. p. 318.[151]

St Giles Colchester. April 3rd 1644 Samuel Cock Minister.[152]
[His Answer is retorned]

150 The son of Stephen Newcomen, vicar of St Peter's Colchester, Thomas Newcomen attended the grammar school there and graduated from St John's College, Cambridge (BA 1625, MA 1628). He was appointed rector of Holy Trinity, Colchester in 1628; he was also appointed curate of St Runwald, Colchester. In the 1630s, Thomas became notorious in Colchester for his loyalty to the Laudian programme and for assisting in the prosecution of John Bastwick. His work there ended in 1642 when he played a part in Sir John Lucas's plan to join the king: Newcomen was severely beaten by protestors and later imprisoned by parliament. After his release, he did not resume his parish duties. He was articled against in 1644, but there is no evidence that he was sequestrated. In 1645, he obtained a new living in Hampshire, moving to Clothall (Hertfordshire) in 1653, a living he retained until his death in 1665. He never returned to his Colchester parishes. For more on Newcomen, see Introduction, pp. xxiv–xxv (and n. 87), xxvi and liii–liv n. 8; Webster, 'Matthew Newcomen', *ODNB* (this article also covers Thomas Newcomen, 1603–65).

151 The account of Newcomen's sufferings is given in *Mercurius rusticus*, pp. 2–3 and 6–7.

152 Samuel Cock graduated from Pembroke College, Cambridge (BA 1611–12). In 1619, he was appointed rector of St Giles, Colchester, receiving a dispensation to succeed his father, William

1. We conceive he is an unable Man for the Ministry, and we desire he may be tried by some judicious Divines, [vizt. to Mr Owen of Fordeham nigh Colchester, and to Mr Ellis of St Peter's in Colchester: if my Lord pleases].[153]
John Tillet, Robert Drake, John Erbery.
2. He hath of late taken another Cure and resides there.[154]
John Tillet, Robert Drake, Robert Knop.
3. At the last Sacrament after he had delivered the Bread and before he delivered the Wine, he read on in the Liturgy the Conclusion [of the Sacrament] till the Clark put him in mind, he had forgot to deliver the Wine.
John Tillet, Robert Drake, William King.

fo. 73

4. He hath promoted the late Innovations, refusing to administer the Sacrament to such as durst not receive at the Raile, prosecuting some of them to Excommunication.[155]
Thomas Elger, John Erbury.
5. He did not prepare his People to take the Covenant according to the Ordinance of Parliament: But refused some that desired information, saying he had no such Command.
John Tillet, Robert Drake.
His Benefice is worth above 30^{li} per Annum. He hath a Wife and 3 Children.
[Sequestrators Robert Drake.]
[Its desyerd that a Letter may be writ to the Earle to acquainte him with that Ministers Insuffitiensy].
No notice of this Person's Persecution in Newcourt or Walker.

Cock, who died about that time. There is no documentary evidence that Manchester sequestrated the living of St Giles or arranged the appointment of a successor, and in 1650 the living was reported to be vacant and the church ruinated. In 1646, Cock was ordered to vacate the parish and hospital of St Mary Magdalen, which Gabriel Honifold had passed to him on leaving Colchester (see p. 48 and n. 142 above), and thereafter Cock is absent from the record. He did not seek to recover St Giles in 1660 and may well have been dead by then: Venn, *Alumni Cantabrigienses*, I, 362; CCEd, Location ID 11207; Smith, *Ecclesiastical history of Essex*, p. 318; BL, Add. MS 15670, fos. 108 and 228v; Bodleian Library, MS 324, fo. 81.

153 Both men were recent recruits to the area. John Owen had been intruded into the rectory of Fordham in 1643; soon he was minister of Coggeshall, and then, after serving with Cromwell in Ireland, dean of Christ Church Oxford. He was perhaps the leading figure among Congregationalists in the 1650s: Richard L. Greaves, 'John Owen (1616–83)', *ODNB*. John Ellis, a former fellow of St Catherine's College, Cambridge, had earned a reputation for godly preaching in Cambridge and was appointed a lecturer at St Peter's Colchester: E. C. Vernon, 'John Ellis (d. 1681)', *ODNB*; Andrew Barclay, *Electing Cromwell: the making of a politician* (2011), pp. 50–60.

154 Presumably this refers to Cock's agreement with Gabriel Honifold to preach at St Mary Magdalen and act as master of the hospital.

155 At Easter 1637, fifteen parishioners who refused to receive the sacrament in the Laudian mode were presented in the archdeacon's court and some were excommunicated. They were following the lead of Thomas Lamb, who a year previously had protested that 'he would be brained before he would receive the holy sacrament after this manner'. In the 1640s, Lamb became the baptist minister of 'the most notorious sectarian church in London during the English civil war': ERO, D/ACA 52, fo. 67v; D/ACA 51, fo. 122; M. Tolmie, 'Thomas Lambe, soapboiler, and Thomas Lambe, merchant, general baptists', *Baptist Quarterly*, 27 (1977), pp. 4–17, quotation at p. 7. The church was located in Bell Alley, Coleman Street. Lamb also preached in Essex and other counties, earning Tolmie's judgment that he was 'the greatest of the itinerant evangelists of the 1640s': *ibid.*, p. 8.

Greensted Additions to Dr Jarvis his charge taken the 21. of June.
Edmond Withers, Simeon Wrench, John Rie, Henry Bones and William Rie depose that Dr Jarvis, being a Doctor of the Civill Law, is as they, who are his Parishioners, doe verily beleeve, a very insufficient Man for the Ministry

fo. 74

he not being able to deliver any Thing in his Sermons more than what he reads out of his Booke, pointing with his Finger, for the most Part, to every Line he reads: and the Matter of his Sermons is also very weake and unprofitable: and for further Discovery of his Insufficiencie we desire that he may be tried by the Earle of Manchester's Chaplins, or some other able Ministers in these Parts.
Subscribed by Edmond Withers and Simeon Wrench. Signed with the Mark of John Rie, the Marke of Henry Bones, And the Marke of William Rie.
Also Edmond Withers and John Rie depose, that Dr Jarvis is an excessive Drinker and that they have seen him often drunk.
Edmond Withers. The mark of John Rie.
William Rie deposeth that he saw Dr Jarvis once so.

Thus imperfectly ends my MS of the Committee's Tyranny in Essex: it is probable there was a great Deal more of it, now lost: but by this, it easily appears, from the Number of the Sufferers in one small Part of the County of Essex unnoticed as such by Walker, what an Addition might be made to his Collections, had he been furnished with proper materials.
As I have made some Additions to my Copy of Walker, cheifly from MS Notes added on the Margin of Dr: Zach: Grey's Copy of the same Book, which he kindly lent me; and as the said Copy may be dispersed one Day or other, with my Library, I shall inscribe them here, as they belong to the same Argument.[156]

[156] In the next section of his collection (BL, Add. MS 5829, fos. 75–90), Cole has transcribed additional information about the purges of scandalous ministers, including much relating to counties other than Essex. The additional material about Essex ministers derives from notes which Zachary Grey had made during his examination of Leicester MS 31, lent to him by Philip Williams. As the full text of Leicester MS 31 itself is printed below at pp. 55–100, it is unnecessary to reproduce Cole's transcriptions of the notes made by Grey.

University of Leicester Library, Special Collections, MS 31 (Leicester MS 31)

fo. 1

Essex

Depositions of witnesses against John Fenwicke[1] Minister of Chignall St James in the said County taken upon oath before the Committee for Scandalous Ministers 28th March 1644.

1. Imprimis John Boosey and Edward Boosey of Chignall aforesaid yeomen, sworne and examined, depose that the said Mr Fenwicke was very devout at all times to kneele at the Rales, and power out his devotion towards the East window of the church where was a picture of the Virgin Mary, and when he had soe done, he called up the Alehouse keeper to helpe him on with the surplice Tippett and Hood, then in the deske he reades in the service booke the Letany, and at the end of every Psalme he saith Glory be to the Father &c earnestly urging his people, both men, woemen and children, to stand up, and answer him with a loud voyce (amen) saying he would have them answer him like a Thunder clapp, and used to bow at the name of Jesus.
2. John Empson and Sarah his wife depose that the said Mr Fenwicke did force his parishioners to come up to the raile to receive the sacrament saying he did not desire to leave a Puritan in his parish.
3. John Boosey and William Crow depose that when some of the neighbour parishioners came to heare another Minister preach at Mr Fenwickes church he chidd them, telling them that they troubled his people, soe that they could not kneele downe nor rise up when he would have them, according to the manner he had taught them and that they came to heare 2 sermons a day, but they should have but one, and thereupon commanded his curate to preach but once a day.[2]
4. John Empson and Sara Empson likewise depose that the said Mr Fenwicke did say in a sermon about 2 or 3 yeares agoe yow are to offer upp the Calves of your lipps; but

1 Fenwick was a graduate and fellow of Christ's College, Cambridge (MA 1626, BD 1639). He became rector of Chignal St James in 1639, having been presented by the University of Cambridge; the patron, Lady Gerrard, was a catholic recusant and therefore disqualified from acting. The inclusion in the book of these articles against Fenwick and of the (undated) warrants for his sequestration and ejection at p. 94 below strongly suggest that he was indeed ejected by Manchester in 1644. It is, however, recorded that he was the rector in 1650 (when he was described as 'an able preaching minister'), and that he resigned the living in January 1652. It seems probable that he was ejected in 1644 and subsequently restored: Newcourt, *Repertorium*, II, 138; Venn, *Alumni Cantabrigienses*, II, 132; Smith, *Ecclesiastical history of Essex*, pp. 116, 254; Cambridge University Library, MS Mm. 1.42, 266.

2 A visiting preacher, probably invited to preach by godly parishioners, had attracted an audience from outside the parish who had discouraged the local congregation from observing the procedures specified in the Book of Common Prayer. Differences of opinion about the frequency and content of sermons were a common cause of conflict between clergy and godly parishioners. Charles I's attempts to control puritan preaching included an instruction of 1629 that afternoon sermons should be replaced by catechizing by question and answer: see Introduction, p. xxviii and n. 107.

in Malachy the Lord complaines yow have robbed me of my tythes and I am sure if yow were noe forwarder in paying your tythes then in offering up the Calves of your lipps yow would pay them but slowly and soe fell a laughing in his pullpitt.[3]
5. John Boosey and Edward Boosey likewise depose, That the said Mr Fenwicke did say in a sermon, since this parliament began, there is a Parliament but what doe

fo. 1v

they doe, nothing but sitt and Fumble, they can enact nothing without the king. And in his prayer he alwaies prayed that the Lord would turne the heartes of the Parliament to the heart of the king.
6. John Empson and Sara Empson, Further depose that the said Mr Fenwicke did say that whatsoever the king setts up in matters of religion, we ought to obey, affirming that the difference betweene the king and the Parliament was not about matter of religion but the Parliament laied heavy taxes upon the people which the King would take of.[4]
7. John Empson and Sara Empson likewise depose that an honest woeman of the said parish told Mr Fenwicke that the descent of the Bishops was from the Pope at which he flung about and was angry telling her she knew not what a Pope was and that Christ was a Pope.[5]
8. John Empson further deposeth that the said Mr Fenwicke would not suffer him, being one of his parishioners, to take the Protestation of the 5th May but said he was a foole and would foresweare himselfe, affirming that the protestation was to uphold and maintaine Ceremonies and so snatched it out of his hand in somuch that the said Empson was forced to complaine to a Justice of Peace.[6]
9. John Sager and John Hall of Chignall aforesaid Husbandmen, sworne and examined, depose that the said Mr Fenwicke did desire the said John Hall to fetch in hay for him on a Fast day about a yeare since which he refused to doe but Mr Fenwicke hired 2 of the said Hall's servants and they unloaded one load, and fetcht in another that day.[7]

[3] Hosea xiv. 2: 'Take with you words, and turn to the Lord: say unto him, Take away all iniquity, and receive us graciously: so will we render the calves of our lips': that is, offerings in the form of praise. Fenwick referred also to Malachi, iii, 7–10, where the Lord accused the Israelites of robbing him of tithes and offerings. Fenwick jokingly accused his parishioners of being slow in their responses both in church and in paying their tithes.

[4] 'take of[f]', that is remove, abolish.

[5] Some puritan critics of the Church of England sought to abolish episcopacy, arguing that it was a relic of the Roman church. In responding, Fenwick may have argued that the office of bishop in the English church descended from Jesus Christ through the apostles and succeeding generations of bishops, a succession which was not broken by the Refomation: hence the Church of England was both catholic and reformed.

[6] See Introduction, pp. xxx–xxxi, for the protestation, ordered to be printed by parliament on 5 May 1641. It committed the swearer to 'defend the true reformed religion expressed in the doctrine of the Church of England, against all popery and popish innovation within this realm'. Fenwick's argument was that the doctrine of the church included various ceremonies prescribed in the church's canons and the Book of Common Prayer, such as bowing at the name of Jesus, which many puritans refused to do. In order to deal with that point, parliament soon added an 'Explanation' to the protestation, which said that the doctrine of the church was not to be interpreted as covering 'any form of worship, discipline, or government; nor any rites and ceremonies of the said Church of England'. The meaning of the protestation was contested from the outset: Walter, *Covenanting citizens*, pp. 62–3, 95–108.

[7] For public fasts under parliament, see Introduction, p. xxx n. 120.

10. John Hall and Thomas Wooleward depose that the said Mr Fenwicke is a frequent swearer and sayd in his pullpit the last sabbath day that by Faith and by Troth is not swearing, and that he useth to curse, saying a pox on it, in his wrath.
11. Edward Boosey and John Boosey further depose that the said Mr Fenwicke is a common frequenter of Alehouses and the deponent Edward Boosey complaining to him, the said Mr Fenwicke, of the Alehouse in the Towne, he said it was convenient it should be there, and hee hath beene there oftentimes 3 dayes in a weeke drinkeing. And he hath confessed to him the said Deponent that he

fo. 2

was there in companie, when the Hostesse was Christened and named Northumberland by one, whoe made himselfe the Godfather, whose name was Northumberland.
The Benefice of Chignall St James is worth 100^{li} per annum. Mr Fenwicke hath neither wife nor children.
Wee gave him time to putt in his answer which he hath done in a large manner which is herewith Transmitted, and there is a petition for Mr Sanders to have the living, who is an honest, Godly man, and well thought of in this County.[8]
Henry Holcroft, Richard Everarde, William Martin, Robert Maidstone, Carew H Mildmay, William Astwood.

fo. 2v blank

fo. 3

Essex
At Chelmesford
Depositions of witnesses against Symon Lynce,[9] Minister of Runwell, taken upon oath before the Committee for Scandalous Ministers etc March the 28th 1644.
1. Imprimis John Crane of Runwell aforesaid yeoman, and Edward Turner of the same husbandman, sworne and examined, depose, That the said Mr Lynce is a common haunter of Alehouses and a company keeper with common swearers and he doth often keep companie with Mr Thorpe a Minister[10] whom they have seene drunke and they have many times seene Mr Lynce very full of drinke.

8 Neither document is copied into this manuscript. Mr Sanders may well have been Philip Sanders, a graduate of Sidney Sussex College, Cambridge. Sanders had been suspended from his position as curate at Hutton in 1634. He remained active in the area, however, said to be doing 'much hurt among people inclined to faction'. He was not appointed to Chignal, but was soon intruded into the living of Magdalen Laver: Smith, *Ecclesiastical history of Essex*, pp. 47, 50, 57, 270.

9 Simon Lynch, a graduate of Queens' College, Cambridge (MA 1625), was appointed rector of Runwell in 1630. He was presented by his father, also Simon, vicar of North Weald, who had acquired the right of presentation *pro hac vice*. Having been ejected from Runwell, by 1647 Lynch had obtained appointment as curate of Blackmore, a position he held until 1660, when he died. This was despite the comment by the parochial inquisition of 1650 that the patron of Blackmore had appointed Lynch without the consent of the well-affected parishioners: Newcourt, *Repertorium*, II, 511; Venn, *Alumni Cantabrigienses*, III, 121; Matthews, *Walker revised*, p. 158; Smith, *Ecclesiastical history of Essex*, pp. 148–9, 253.

10 Presumably this was Edward Thorpe, rector of the nearby parish of Nevendon, who held that living from 1638. He was still at Nevendon in 1650, and said to be an able preaching minister, apparently

2. John Crane John Turner senior and Richard Abbot depose, that the said Mr Lynce did not reade an order from the house of Commons for the lending of money to releive the Lord Fairfax, the said Order being brought to the Towne.[11]
3. Henry Carter of Runwell aforesaid husbandman deposeth that the said Mr Lynce did suffer his men to saw and cropp wood on a Fast day, about a quarter of a yeare since till eleven of the clocke in the forenoone, and upon the 28th of February last, being a Fast day, his servant did chop wood in his yard in Service time and the noyse of the chopping was heard lowder in the church then the Ministers voyce.[12]
4. Edward Turner Junior further deposeth that the night before the Thanksgiving for the deliverance from the plott against London, the said Mr Lynce was drinkeing in an Alehouse at Runwell with Mr Byatt Mr Benison and others from sun setting, till eleven or 12 of the clocke in the night, which Byatt and Benison did misuse this deponenent and another, being then upon the watch.[13]
5. Edward Turner Junior further deposeth that about the time when the Parliament did put out Mr Stevens, Minister of South Hanningfield, the said Mr Lynce did say in a sermon, now I have shewed yow what evill Ministers of Satan are risen up, and have cast out their poore brethren, and trodden the horsemen and charriots of Israell under their feete, and is this to doe as yow would be done by. John Crane and Edward Turner senior doe likewise depose that they heard Mr Lynce speake the same words, or to that effect.[14]

fo. 3v

6. Edward Turner Junior deposeth that the said Mr Lynce reading a warrant to the Constables for the keepeing straight watch and ward did direct them to looke well to the Alehouses, and the watch searching the Alehouses that weeke according to his direction, found him the said Mr Lynce and Captaine Chester there about 8 or 9 of the clocke drinkeing.
7. The said deponent further saith that comeing from Billarecay, he saw Mr Lynce Captaine Chester and Mr Thorpe a Minister sitting, drinking, and taking Tobacco, in a Ditch on the backe side of an Alehouse in Runwell, because as it is reported Captaine Chester had sworne not to come into that Alehouse for a yeare.[15]

not challenged on account of drinking or any other misconduct: Newcourt, *Repertorium*, II, 436; Smith, *Ecclesiastical history of Essex*, p. 238.

11 Lord Fairfax was the general commanding parliament's forces in the north. On 17 August 1643, the House of Commons ordered that 'the aid and assistance of the Lord Fairfax shall be especially and respectively recommended to the counties of Norfolke, Suffolke, Essex and Lincolne', such aid to be in the form of men, money, plate, horse or ammunition. Lynch was accused of refusing to have the order read in church; see fo. 5 below for a complaint that Francis Gouldman refused to contribute to the appeal: *Commons Journal*, III, 209; Andrew J. Hopper, 'Ferdinando Fairfax, second Lord Fairfax of Cameron (1584–1648)', *ODNB*.

12 See Introduction, p. xxx, for fast days. 28 Feb. 1644 was the regular fast day for that month.

13 For this thanksgiving, see above, Cole MS, fo. 43 n. 109. The drinking session evidently took place on 12 July 1643.

14 South Hanningfield was a neighbouring parish to Runwell. Evidently, Thomas Stevens, the rector, had been ejected by parliament in the preceding months; the date is unknown. On 30 April 1644, the committee on plundered ministers ordered Seth North, the intruded minister, to pay Stevens's wife one fifth of the income of the living: Matthews, *Walker revised*, p. 163.

15 For Mr Thorpe, see n. 10 above. Captain Chester may have been Robert Chester Esq. of Wickford, a neighbouring parish: ERO, Q/SR 315/30, T/A 42/1, p. 84.

8. Henry Caster[16] likewise deposeth, That the said Mr Lynce dehorted the people in the church, from takeing the League and Covenant telling them that after they have taken it they must sell all they have to maintaine warres, or words to that purpose. John Crane and Edward Turner depose that they heard Thomas Parker confesse that Mr Lynce told him the same, or to that effect.[17]

9. Edward Turner senior Edward Turner Junior Richard Carter further depose That the said Mr Lynce did not joyne with his neighbours in the association and gave onely an old bowle of 24[shill] price to the propositions, his spirituall Living being worth an 100[li] per annum, and his Temporall neere four score, and that he did not send his armes when they were required for the defence of the Countrey.[18]

10. Edward Turner senior and Richard Abbot depose that the said Mr Lynce doth still use the service booke and did usually pray for Bishopps and curates etc till within these 6 weekes.[19]

11. Henry Carter and Edward Turner further depose that the said Mr Lynce on Fast days doth commonly use a printed service booke formerly appoynted by the Bishopp to be used on Fast dayes.[20]

Wee that were the Committee then present doe certify of our owne knowledge that when the said Mr Lynce came before us he was very farre in drinke and smelt soe that he was very offensive to some of us and being charged with it he confessed he had beene drinking and takeing Tobaccoe.

16 'Henry Caster' is probably a misreading of 'Henry Carter', listed twice in these articles as a deponent.

17 See Introduction, pp. xxxii and xxxvii–xxxviii, for the solemn league and covenant, an oath of great importance for the clergy.

18 Lynch is accused of failing to contribute adequately, or at all, to parliament's war effort in response to three separate demands. The article refers to them in reverse chronological order. First, in June 1642, the county of Essex executed parliament's militia ordinance: Lynch, along with his colleagues in the clergy and the better-off laity, will have been required to contribute arms to the county militia. Also in June 1642, parliament adopted 'propositions for money and plate', inviting voluntary contributions to the cause. By July, subscriptions were being sought in Essex, and the deponents claim that Lynch's contribution was worth only 24s. In early 1643, parliament set up the Eastern Association, bringing together five (later seven) eastern counties, including Essex, in a military alliance against the king. Parliament also encouraged its county committees to convene meetings at which the people would enter into an association with one another for mutual defence, and contribute arms and money for the war: Holmes, *Eastern Association*, pp. 34–5; Fletcher, *Outbreak*, pp. 336–8; Holmes, *Eastern Association*, pp. 62–5.

19 Some puritans objected to the Book of Common Prayer, for example because of its set forms of prayer, or because some of its rubrics imposed ceremony which they believed to be idolatrous, and in the early 1640s verbal and physical attacks on the prayer book became common: Walter, 'Confessional politics in pre-Civil War Essex'; idem, 'Popular iconoclasm and the politics of the parish in eastern England 1640–46', 274–7. At the time when this article was deposed, the Westminster Assembly of Divines was still deliberating over a new service book, and it was not until 1645 that parliament endorsed *A directory for the public worship of God*, and banned the use of the prayer book: Shaw, *History of the church 1640–1660*, I, 338–56. Lynch's continuing use of the prayer book in 1644 was therefore lawful, although many ministers in Essex had probably ceased to use it by this date, and Lynch himself had apparently recently stopped using parts of it which he must have decided were best avoided.

20 The service book which Lynch used on fast days may have been *A forme of common prayer to be used on the eigth of July: on which day a fast is appointed by His Majesties proclamation, for the averting of the plague, and other judgements of God from this kingdom, set forth by His Majesties authority* (1640). This day of fasting and prayer, called during the interval between the first and second 'bishops' wars' between England and Scotland, was intended to avert sickness and war. The book contained forms of morning and evening prayer. It had been composed under the direction of the English bishops, who were ordered to circulate it throughout the kingdom: *Stuart royal proclamations*, II, 714–15.

The living worth 100li per annum. Mr Lynce hath a wife and many children. His Temporall estate is worth neere 80li per annum.

fo. 4

He hath put in his answer which is herewith sent.[21]
Henry Holcroft
William Martin
Richard Everarde Car H Mildmay
William Astwood
Robert Maidstone.

fo. 4v blank

fo. 5

Essex
Depositions of witnesses against Francis Gouldman[22] Rector of South Okenden taken upon oath before the Committee for Scandalous Ministers for the said County, at Ongar 9th April 1644.[23]
1. Imprimis, William Reinolds of South Okenden aforesaid, yeoman, sworne and examined doth say that the said Mr Gouldman about the time of the propositions did say in his pullpitt that those that raise armes against their Anoynted are Anoynted knaves, and that the Parliament raise armes against the king.
Bartholomew White and John Patch depose the same.[24]
2. Robert Beomont, John Patch, and Bartholomew White of South Okenden aforesaid, yeomen, depose that the said Mr Goldman did say in his pulpitt about last winter was twelve month, that an asses head was once sold for eighty peices of Silver, but he hoped they would be at a cheaper rate, for there were many gathered together.[25]
3. William Reinolds further deposeth That the said Mr Goldman refused to reade divers Ordinances of Parliament appointed to be read in the Church, saying they were not fitt to be read in the Church, and he looked to heare from the Bishopp first.

21 This and other answers submitted by ministers in their defence were not included in the manuscript.

22 A graduate of Christ's College, Cambridge (MA 1630), Francis Gouldman became rector of South Ockendon in 1634, on the death of the previous incumbent, George Gouldman, archdeacon of Essex. Both men hailed from Norfolk and were probably kinsmen, but the exact relationship is unknown. After ejection from the living in 1644, Francis seems to have moved to London, where he published books on theological subjects, including *Fur praedestinatus* and *Articuli Lambethani*, both in 1651: he was not the author, but he may have sympathized with their Arminian standpoint. In 1652, he and the printer Thomas Dugard were in difficulties with parliament over the publication of the *Racovian catechism*. Gouldman also wrote a Latin dictionary, published in 1664. He regained possession of his rectory in 1660 and lived until 1688: Venn, *Alumni Cantabrigienses*, II, 229; Matthews, *Walker revised*, p. 153; Janet Bately, 'Francis Gouldman (c. 1607–1688/9)', *ODNB*; *Commons Journal*, VII, 113–14; Harold Smith, 'South Ockendon clergy 1640–60', *The Essex Review*, 32 (1923), 8–13.

23 These articles against Gouldman were copied from this manuscript by Thomas Baker: Cambridge University Library, Mm. 1.38, 464, whence Smith, *Ecclesiastical History of Essex*, pp. 135–6.

24 See fo. 3v and n. 18 above for the propositions for money and plate.

25 2 Kings vi. 25: 'And there was a great famine in Samaria: and behold, they besieged it, until an ass's head was sold for fourscore pieces of silver.' Presumably Gouldman was thought to be referring to parliament or its supporters as the asses gathered together.

4. All the said deponents further say, that the said Mr Gouldman never prayed for the Parliament.
5. John Patch deposeth That the said Mr Gouldman refused to joyne in the association, and said there would come an Army out of the North which would prevent all these Taxes. This was spoken about the time when the Lord Gray went out.[26]
6. John Patch and William Reinolds further depose that the said Mr Gouldman refused to lend anything to the Lord Fairfax, saying Shall I take my childrens bread and give it to my Lord Fairfax.[27]
7. All the forenamed Deponents doe further say that the said Mr Gouldman preached but once on the Sabbath or on Fast days, and never catechised his parishioners for the space of nine yeares together or thereabouts.[28]
8. John Patch and William Reinolds likewise depose that the said Mr Gouldman is an enemy to frequent preaching and Lectures, and hath lately sayd in his pulpitt, the people cannot be contented now to have the word preached on the sabbath, but they must have Lectures forsooth.

fo. 5v

9. William Reinolds and Robert Beamont likewise depose that the said Mr Goldman had a cart brought Broome to his house all day long on a Fast day, and that day he said, what, must we fast still? William Reinolds further deposeth that the said Mr Goldman did say, it went against his conscience to pay the Rates to the Parliament.
10. All the forementioned Deponents further depose that Mr Blunt, Curate to the said Mr Gouldman, said in the pulpit in the heareing of Mr Gouldman, that our saviour Christ had nothing to leave us but his crosse, and his crowne of Thorns and his Nailes and the Appertinances thereof, the beautifying of the Church and the engraveing and the needleworke: and the Separatists, Brownists, Anabaptists and Schismatiques take away these our Legacies which our Saviour left us.[29]
11. And that the said Curate the last Sabbath day, did say in the heareing likewise of the said Mr Gouldman, we must now have a new upstart reformation forsooth and

[26] As noted above (n. 18), in early 1643 parliament had encouraged its county committees to convene meetings at which the people would enter into an association and contribute arms and money for the war. Supporters of the king, hoping for relief from parliamentary control and taxation, looked north, where the earl of Newcastle commanded a royalist army. Gouldman's remarks were apparently made around July 1643, when Lord Grey of Warke, the commander of the Eastern Association forces, was dismissed: Holmes, *Eastern Association*, pp. 62–5, 87, 91–2.

[27] See fo. 3 and n. 11 above for Simon Lynch's alleged reaction to Fairfax's appeal.

[28] For the frequency of preaching, see n. 2 above. The Book of Common Prayer set out a catechism which every child should learn before confirmation. The prayer book also required the parish minister to instruct and examine such children on Sundays and holy days for half an hour before evening prayer. Parish clergy did not always comply, nor could they always rely on parishioners to send their children to be catechized: *The Book of Common Prayer: the texts of 1549, 1559, and 1662*, ed. Brian Cummings (Oxford, 2011), pp. 150–6; Ian Green, *The Christian's ABC: catechisms and catechizing in England c. 1530–1740* (Oxford, 1996), pp. 129–39.

[29] Gouldman's curate was probably William Blunt, an Essex man who, like Gouldman, was a graduate of Christ's College. In January 1645, he was appointed rector of Corringham, a few miles to the east of South Ockendon, but by September of that year he had been sequestrated for opposition to parliament: Venn, *Alumni Cantabrigienses*, I, 170; Matthews, *Walker revised*, p. 146.

none are so well liked of now, as those who delight to preach and pray by the Spiritt (as they call it) and they are never out, because they are never in.[30]

The Parsonage of South Okenden is worth 120li per annum. Mr Gouldman hath a wife and five children: his personall estate is near 50li per annum.
We returne his answer: he appeareth to be ill affected and an Idle minister.

Richard Everarde	Henry Holcroft
William Masham	William Martin
Edward Bickhead	Carew H Mildmay
	William Astwood

fo. 6 blank

fo. 6v

Essex
Depositions of Witnesses against John Russell[31] Parson of Chinkford taken upon oath before the Committee for Scandalous Ministers at Ongar 9th Martii 1644.[32]
1. Imprimis John Crouch and Ralph Dell of Chinkford aforesaid yeomen and Elizabeth Heyward sworne and examined depose that the said Mr Russell is a common Gamester, and a common swearer and curser. John Crouch saith that the said Mr Russell hath very often played at Tables with one Mr Dobson and others: Elizabeth Heyward deposeth that the said Mr Russell doth use to play at Tables constantly and to sweare and curse very much saying, the divell take them, a pox on them, to the dice, and such like cursing and that he hath sate up at Tables sometimes all night, until a little before day, and began the morning before. Ralph Dell likewise deposeth that the said Mr Russell is a common Gamester, and he hath told this deponent that he would play at Tables with any man in England and the said Mr Dobson hath likewise told this deponent that he hath wonne of Mr Russell a Marke at a time at Tables.
2. John Burton of Chinkford aforesaid husbandman sworne and examined deposeth that Mr Russell did say a pox, and a plague upon the witnesses that were deposed in a tryall of law against Mr Boothby some 5 yeares agoe. Capt: Dawges that he was seldom in Mr Russells companie without heareing some oathes from him.

30 Harold Smith suggests that Blunt may have meant that ‘they never lose the thread of their discourse, because there is none to lose’: ‘South Ockendon clergy 1640–60’, p. 9.

31 John Russell was a graduate of Magdalene College, Cambridge (MA 1632), and was appointed rector of Chingford in December 1634. He had disputes with parishioners in the 1630s over tithes and over the railing of the communion table and re-flooring the chancel. But the case against him in 1644 was mainly concerned with his alleged gambling and swearing, and his attitude to parliament. He was ejected in 1644, and restored in 1660, the parish having been served by a series of five intruded ministers in the interval. Russell continued as rector until his death in 1688: Venn, *Alumni Cantabrigienses*, III, 500; Newcourt, *Repertorium*, II, 148; *VCH Essex*, V, 102, 109; Smith, *Ecclesiastical history of Essex*, pp. 61–2; Matthews, *Walker revised*, p. 162; TNA, PROB 11/389/300.

32 If this case really was heard on ‘9th Martii 1644’ (that is 9 March 1645 in modern practice) it is seriously out of order in the book, being the last hearing by a considerable margin. Moreover, 9 March 1645 was a Sunday. If ‘1644’ is a mistake for ‘1643’ (that is 1644 in modern practice) it would be the first hearing in time in the book, and theoretically possible as Manchester appointed the Essex committees on 24 February 1644. It seems most likely, however, that ‘March’ is a mistake for April: on 9 April 1644, also at Ongar, the same committee plus one member (Birkhead) heard the evidence against Gouldman, the preceding case in this manuscript.

3. Jeremy Wells of Chinkford aforesaid sworne and examined saith that he heard Mr Russell say (upon the apprehending him, upon a warrant from the Deputy Leiuetenants for this County), a plague of God confound him, this Deponent, body and soule for a Damned Rogue.
4. Rebeccah Sanders deposeth that she heard Mr Russell say (being demanded whether he would reade some Ordinances of Parliament) noe not he, he would curse them with bell, booke and candle.
5. George Burton and John Burton further depose that they have often delivered Ordinances and Orders of Parliament to the said Mr Russell to reade in church, and he carried them home and never read them.
6. Jeremy Wells George Burton and John Burton likewise depose that the said Mr Russell hath severall times threatened the Collectors saying that he would make two men pay all that he lost, and that there were heavy things comeing against them, and that there would be a difference made betweene

fo. 7

them that gave their money freely and him from whome they forced it, when the kings army came amongst.
7. All the forementioned deponents further say that the said Mr Russell hath beene a constant bower at the name of Jesus and unto the Altar, as well since as before the order of Parliament and hath beene and is a constant frequenter of a Papists house in the Towne although he was warned to the Contrary by John Burton.[33]
8. Jeremy Wells and John Burton further depose that the said Mr Russells constant practise is to slight the Parliament and to speake unworthyly of them and their actions and he told the Under Collectors of his parish that if they obey such Ordinances of Parliament they were undone, askeing them if they did not see the kings proclamation to the contrary.
9. Anne Moore sworne and examined deposeth that upon the execution of the Earle of Strafford, the said Mr Russell did say there were a company of Round headed Divells belonging to the Parliament.[34]
10. John Smyth of Chinkford aforesaid husbandman deposeth that he hath seene Mr Russell soe drunke that he could not goe but as he was helped by Captain Blincoe and being sett upon his horse by the said Captaine, he fell over his horse.
11. It was reported before us by a coppy of a verdict out of the Kings Bench dated 15º Caroli Regis that Mr Russell was there found guilty of the subordination of one Francis Taverner, to have borne false witness in a suite then depending: and this was also proved by a writing under the hand of the said Francis Taverner.
12. John Briskett Jeremy Wells and George Burton likewise depose that the said Mr Russell did say at Ongar when the witnesses were examining against him, that the Earle of Manchester had nothing to doe to question the matter against him.

[33] For the requirement that the minister and congregation should bow at the name of Jesus, see Introduction, p. xxviii and n. 106; for the practice of bowing to the altar, see Introduction, p. xxvii and n. 103. The 'order of parliament' mentioned by the deponents probably refers to the order approved by the House of Commons on 1 September 1641, instructing churchwardens to abandon the Laudian policies concerning the communion table, bowing in church and observance of the Lord's day: see Introduction, p. xxxvi and n. 158.

[34] See Cole MS, fo. 26 n. 72 for Thomas Wentworth, earl of Strafford.

13. Mr Herring a Minister deposeth that the same day that the said Mr Russell tooke the League and Covenant with the rest of the Ministers, he said openly at Dinner that he had taken this Oath against the Tyrannie of the Hierarchy and not against the Hierarchy, and that Christ did not appoint a parity amongst Ministers for there must be an order, not confusion, and that by the rule of Nature, those that are superiour in gifts ought to have the rest as slaves to them, and he said at the same time that the times may change.

fo. 7v

14. Mr Willis a Minister likewise deposeth that pressing the Parenthesis of the second article in the Covenant concerning Prelacy, the said Mr Russell said it was not in the Latin Covenant according to which he tooke it, and that some of the synod were of his mind.[35]

The Parsonage of Chinkford is worth nere 120^{li} per annum. Mr Russell hath noe wife nor children.

The answer is returned, and as for the order with which he imagines to rise of the Articles[36]

wee send it likewise but there was never any proceedings upon it, he hath beene and is a malicious Malignant and his father hath reported he will spend 500^{li} to keepe him in, in dispite of them that oppose him.

Richard Everarde Henry Holcroft
Car H Mildmay William Martin
William Astwood William Masham.

fo. 8 blank

fo. 8v

Essex

Depositions of Witnesses against Raboshire Dove[37] Minister of Fowlness taken upon Oath before the Committee for Scandalous Ministers at Mauldon on 17° April 1644.

35 See Introduction, pp. xxxii and xxxvii–xxxviii for the solemn league and covenant. Russell attended a meeting at which he took the oath, then sought, in discussion with fellow ministers, to justify his compliance. Mr Herring, probably Theodore Herring, rector of Doddinghurst, deposed that Russell had defended the continued existence of the church hierarchy. Then Mr Willis, probably John Willis, rector of Ingatestone, pointed out that Russell in taking the oath had sworn to endeavour to extirpate prelacy, which a parenthetical clause clearly defined as government of the church 'by Archbishops, Bishops, their Chancellors and Commissaries, Deans and Chapters, Archdeacons and all other ecclesiastical officers depending on that hierarchy'. The Latin version to which Russell referred cannot have been an official text approved by parliament, if indeed it existed at all. In 1660, Russell published *The solemn league and covenant discharg'd* (BL, Thomason Tracts, E.1048[1]), arguing that parliament, which had imposed the covenant, could release those who had taken it from their obligations under it.

36 The script is hard to read here, but the sense seems clear, that Russell had quoted an order which he thought would enable him to refute the articles. We do not have the text of Russell's answer, and the content of the order which he cited is unknown.

37 This man's forename is found in several different forms. Named Rabosh by Walker, in Venn (*Alumni Cantabrigienses*, II, 58), he was Robosher Dove, ordained in 1619 without a degree after attending Emmanuel College, Cambridge. He was instituted rector of Foulness in 1626 and ejected in 1644, after which little more is known of his career. His wife was granted fifths in 1645. The earl of

1. Imprimis Jeremy Justice, Nicholas Justice, John Justice and Eustace Kennet sworne and examined doe say that the said Mr Dove is a man very scandalous in his life, a Common Alehouse-haunter and a Drunkard, and that he hath sometimes satt in the Alehouse a whole night together drinkeing, after he had preached on a sabbath day, and that upon Fast dayes he hath beene drunke in the afternoone. And that he was drunke the next day after he should have appeared at Chelmsford to have taken the League and Covenant.
Jeremy Justice likewise deposeth that the said Mr Dove hath urged him to drinke whole potts at a time, or else he would not pledge him, and that he would not drinke unlesse he dranke an whole pot at a draught.
John Justice further deposeth That the said Mr Dove urged another man in the sight of this deponent about a yeare agoe to drinke whole potts at a draught, and continues still urging men to drinke.
Eustace Kennett, Nicholas Justice and Susan Justice depose that since Cristmas last they saw the said Mr Dove goe reeling from an Ale-house.
2. Jeremy Justice and Eustace Kennett further depose that the said Mr Dove doth bow towards the Communion Table, and at the name of Jesus. Susan Justice deposeth the same, and that within these two months did bow at the name of Jesus and useth it still.[38]
3. Nicholas Justice, Jeremy Justice and Susan Justice further depose that the said Mr Dove did reade the booke of sportes to be used on the Sabbath and did exhort the people to observe the same.[39]
4. Nicholas Justice and Jeremy Justice further depose that when the shipp money was to be payed the said Mr Dove did say that those that refused to pay it were noe better then Rebells and what becomes of Rebells they must be hanged and quartered.[40]

fo. 9

5. Eustace Kennet, Jeremy Justice, and John Justice further depose that the said Mr Dove on the same day, when the vow and Covenant should have beene taken in July last 1643, did say in the pullpit the people might take it if they would, it was all one with the protestation, onely here was the difference, that was for the king and Parliament, this was for the Parliament against the king, and soe it was not taken at all.[41]
6. Edward Hawknett of Foulness aforesaid Husbandman, sworne and examined, deposeth that the said Mr Dove did say in his owne house about a yeare agoe in favour of Drunkeness, that he had more hope of them that followed the blacke pott then of them that follow sermons.[42]

The Living of Foulness is worth 40^{li} per annum.
Mr Dove hath a wife and 3 children.

Warwick was patron of the living. Assuming there was some substance in the accusations against Dove, it is surprising that Warwick did not pay more attention to the conduct of his appointee: Matthews, *Walker revised*, p. 150; CCEd, Location ID 11260; Donagan, 'The clerical patronage of Robert Rich', 398.

38 See fo. 7 n. 33 above for bowing.

39 See Introduction, pp. xxviii–xxix and n. 111 for the book of sports.

40 Ship money was an ancient tax, revived and levied controversially by Charles I during the 1630s. Dove's alleged attack on refusers would not have been welcome to the earl of Warwick, landlord of Foulness, patron of the living, and leader of the county's opposition to the tax: Kelsey, 'Robert Rich, second earl of Warwick', *ODNB*.

41 See Introduction, pp. xxxi–xxxii for the vow and covenant.

42 A black pot, otherwise black jack, a 'large tar coated leather jug for beer', *OED*.

Wee have sent his answer.

Richard Everarde	Henry Holcroft
William Masham	William Martin
	Carew H Mildmay
	Robert Maidstone.

fo. 9v blank

fo. 10

Essex
Depositions of Witnesses against Elizeus Burges[43] Minister of Canoudon taken upon Oath before the Committee for Scandalous Ministers at Maldon 16° Aprill 1644.
1. Imprimis Timothy Ottley, Thomas Row, Isaac Rich, and Israell Sweeting, sworne and examined, depose that the said Mr Burges is Non Resident at Canoudon, and Plurallist, haveing another Living in Kent called Southfleete, he is also Archdeacon of Rochester, and Prebend of Ely, and he hath preached at Canoudon but very seldome these ten yeares.
2. The said Timothy Ottly further saith that the said Mr Burges doth slight the pious observation of the Monthly fast, and that in November last the said Timothy Ottly being at Mr Burges his house in Kent, on the fast day, he saw his servants about their ordinary imployments.[44]
3. Timothy Otly likewise affirmeth that the said Mr Burges refuseth to pay the Assessments imposed by the Parliament, insoemuch that the Inhabitants have beene enforced to satisfy the same out of the Tythes remaining in their hands.

The Living of Canoudon is worth 140^{li} per annum.[45]

Hee hath made noe answer beinge Non-resident.

Richard Everarde	Henry Holcroft
William Masham	William Martin
	Carew H Mildmay
	Robert Maidstone.

fo. 10v blank

43 Elizeus Burges was a graduate and fellow of St John's College, Oxford (MA 1619, BD 1625). During Burges's early years at the college, William Laud was president, having replaced John Buckeridge in that *rôle* in 1611. Burges left the college in 1625 for a series of appointments in Kent, including as archdeacon of Rochester, where Buckeridge was bishop. In addition, Laud, as bishop of London, collated Burges to the vicarage of Canewdon in 1630. Burges was only occasionally seen there, serving through curates. He was ejected from Southfleet (Kent) by parliament and from Canewdon by Manchester. He died in 1652: Matthews, *Walker revised*, pp. 212–13; *A biographical register of St John's College, Oxford, 1555–1660*, ed. Andrew Hegarty (Woodbridge, 2011), p. 27.

44 Presumably Ottly was visiting Burges in connexion with parish business. A Timothy Ottly, yeoman of Canewdon, left his son Timothy lands said to be worth £600 in his will of 1646: ERO, D/AEW 21/245. For the fasts, see Introduction, p. xxx and n. 120 above.

45 This would have been an unusually large income for a vicarage. In 1650, the value was said to be £100 a year: Smith, *Ecclesiastical history of Essex*, p. 259.

fo. 11

Essex
Depositions of Witnesses against Mr Vicars[46] Minister of South Fambridge, taken upon oath before the Committee for Scandalous Ministers for Essex at Maldon 16° Aprill 1644.
1. Imprimis Edward Emerson gent, Thomas Malt and Edward Englesby, sworne and examined, depose that the said Mr Vicars is Non-resident at South Fambridge, and that he never served his cure himselfe, for a quarter of a yeare together, and all the time of his absence, he had noe Curate but Mr Joseph Roades, a knowne Drunkard, and that the said Mr Vicars is suspected to be a Romish Preist in regard he hath beene at Rome.
2. Thomas Mulliens gent deposeth that the said Mr Vicars was amongst those that presented the mutinous petition at Guildhall,[47] and that he this deponent had in his hand at the signe of the Grayhound in Smythfeild, in Mr Vicars his chamber, halfe a dozen sheets of paper which Mr Vicars told him would turne a sword that should be thrust against him, at which time he uttered these words, wee cannot be heard now but wee will be heard hereafter.
3. Mr Church[48] deposeth that the said Mr Vicars caused a sermon to be printed out of the 19th of Luke, 12, 13, 14, 15 verses, which was full of Malicious invectives against the Parliaments proceedings. The said Mr Emersome further deposeth that the said Mr Vicars is in prison for preaching the said sermon as he hath heard.[49]
4. Thomas Malt further deposeth that he saw a booke which the Constable told him was sent downe to the parishioners by Mr Vicars, which booke contained invectives against the Parliament, wherein those times were commended, in which men might appeale to Caesar, as Paul did, but now they could not, but must be judged by Inferiour ones, or words to that effect; and this Deponent further saith that the said Mr Vicars

[46] John Viccars (*c.* 1604–53?) is not to be confused with John Vicars (1580–1652), the presbyterian poet and chronicler. Viccars was a graduate of Christ's College, Cambridge (BA 1622, MA 1625), and at first a rebel within the church. In 1624, he was presented for preaching at a conventicle at Waterbeach, near Cambridge; by 1627, he was rector of St Mary, Stamford (Lincolnshire), but was soon ejected for keeping conventicles and heresy. In 1635, after a period of imprisonment, he recanted and made his peace with the church. He travelled abroad, visiting Rome, and in 1639 published a learned commentary on the psalms, showing mastery of oriental languages. He was appointed rector of South Fambridge in 1640, but according to the articles, was non-resident. Manchester sequestrated him in 1644. He may have become rector of Battlesden (Bedfordshire) in 1645. He seems to have died in the 1650s: Cambridge University Library, EDR B2/40, fos. 198v–199; Toomer, revised Auger, 'John Viccars', *ODNB*.

[47] On 12 December 1642, the mayor and aldermen of London, meeting at the Guildhall, were pressed by a crowd to support their petition for peace. The petitioners were angry about parliamentary taxation and the impact of the Civil War on trade. In the ensuing disorder, some soldiers were injured: Gardiner, *History of the Great Civil War*, I, 74–5. It seems likely that Viccars was imprisoned as a result of these events, as discussed below.

[48] Mr Church was probably Josiah Church, rector of the neighbouring parish of Ashingdon. Church took over the parish of Southchurch in 1645, moved to Hawkwell in 1656 and was ejected from there in 1662: Matthews, *Calamy revised*, p. 116.

[49] See Introduction, p. xxv and n. 89 above, for Viccars's imprisonment and absence from his parish. Peter Auger has shown convincingly that Viccars was the author of three sermons published in 1643, including *A discovery of the rebels*, on Luke xix, 12–28, published on 6 March: Peter Auger, 'Attribution of three works to John Viccars (*c.* 1604–53?)', *Notes and Queries*, 61 (2014), 362–6; BL, Thomason Tracts, E.88[16] and E.92[1]. All three sermons name the author as 'J. V. prisoner'. The events described in the preceding article and note suggest that the description 'prisoner' on the title-pages referred to Viccars's current situation, not to his imprisonment in the 1630s mentioned in n. 46 above.

preacht a sermon about two yeares agoe, wherein he said these words, John[50] pretended Zeale but did all in Hypocrisy, and soe some now in these dayes pretend greate Zeale, and reformation, but those that will forsake their king, will forsake their God.

fo. 11v

5. Joseph Bennett deposeth that the said Mr Vicars refuseth to pay all taxes to the Parliament and also forbids his Tennants to pay.
6. All the said Deponents doe say that the said Mr Vicars was formerly committed to prison for malignancy against the Parliament, and there remaineth still for ought they know.

The said Mr Vicars is Non resident therefore he makes noe answer.
The Living is worth 100li per annum.

William Martin
Henry Holcroft
Carew H Mildmay
Richard Everarde Robert Maidston
William Masham

fo. 12 blank

fo. 12v

Essex
Depositions of Witnesses against Mr Holmes,[51] Minister of Southchurch, taken upon oath before the Committee for Scandalous Ministers at Maldon the 16th of Aprill 1644.
Article 1. Imprimis, Barrowes of Southchurch aforesaid gent, sworne and examined, deposeth that the said Mr Holmes is a Plurallist and non resident at Southchurch, and he never preached for these ten yeares last past. John Newton of Southchurch yeoman deposeth the same.

[50] The reference to John who pretended zeal but did all in hypocrisy is puzzling. I suggest that 'John' is a mistranscription, from an earlier version of the articles against Viccars, or from an auditor's sermon notes, of 'Jehu'. In his sermon *The Great Antichrist*, published in 1643, Viccars made an extended attack on the king's hypocritical enemies. He likened them to Jehu who, according to 2 Kings, chapter 10, claimed to be zealous against idolatry, but did not eliminate it from Israel: BL, Thomason Tracts, E.92[1], 39–40.

[51] A graduate of Trinity College, Cambridge (MA 1622), by 1626 Walter Holmes had been appointed chaplain to John Buckeridge, bishop of Rochester, vicar of Frindsbury (Kent) and rector of Southchurch. The latter parish was part of the archbishop of Canterbury's peculiar of the deanery of Bocking. The deponents said that Holmes was not resident at Southchurch and unfit for duty by reason of mental illness, a view which the south Essex committee endorsed, adding a recommendation that he should receive 'favourable consideration'. The living was sequestrated by Manchester but the decision was disputed. The committee for plundered ministers finally settled the matter in 1645, confirming sequestration but awarding Holmes and his family half of the income of the living. This seems to have been accepted by all, including the intruded minister, Josiah Church, for whom see n. 48 above: Venn, *Alumni Cantabrigienses*, II, 399; CCEd, Location ID 11437; Matthews, *Walker revised*, p. 155; BL, Add. MS 15669, fos. 207v, 221; BL, Add. MS 15670, fo. 25; Smith, *Ecclesiastical history of Essex*, pp. 261, 368.

2. They likewise depose that the said Mr Holmes is altogether unfitt to officiate the office of a Minister, hath beene a greate favourer of Innovations and a promoter of the Bishopps orders.
3. Mr Barrowes and John Newton further depose that the said Mr Holmes is altogether unfitt to officiate the office of a Minister, by reason that he is often destracted.
4. Theophilus Braithwaite gent deposeth that the said Mr Holmes is sometimes not well, but melancholly, and that he is troubled with Lunacy, usually about Midsummer. Wee who were then the Committee and tooke the depositions against Mr Holmes doe certify that when he came before us he appeared to be a weake man, and noe waies fitt to be continued in the Cure, but we referre him to your favourable consideration. Hee made noe answer. The Living is worth 140^{li} per annum but Mr Holmes hath lett it out by Lease for 80^{li} per annum
he hath a wife and three children.

Richard Everarde	Henry Holcroft
William Masham	William Martin
	Carew H Mildmay
	Robert Maidstone.

fo. 13 blank

fo. 13v

Essex
Depositions of Witnesses against Francis Kindleton Minister of Magdalen Laver taken upon oath before the Committee etc at Ongar the 10th of Aprill 1644.[52]
Article 1. Imprimis Phillemon Parmitter sworne and examined deposeth that the said Mr Kindleton did compell women to weare a vaile when they came to church to give thankes for their safe deliverance in Childbirth till within these twelvemonths last past or thereabouts. Francis Hadsley deposeth the same.[53]
2. Phillemon Parmitter likewise deposeth that the said Mr Kindleton did reade the booke of sports and commended it to be a thing very usefull and convenient.
3. Phillemon Parmiter further deposeth that Mr Kindleton used to bow at the name of Jesus and taught the people soe to doe.
4. The said Mr Parmiter further deposeth that the said Mr Kindleton used to bow at the Rales three or 4 times in a day.
5. Phillemon Parmiter and Amos Wignold depose that the said Mr Kindleton taught in the pullpitt that those ministers that were conformable had a greate share in the

[52] George Kindleton was a graduate of Jesus College, Cambridge (BA 1623/4, MA 1627, BD 1635). His name is sometimes spelled Kendleton and in Leicester MS 31 his forename is given as Francis. George Kindleton is, however, the correct name, as attested by several sources including the parish register of Magdalen Laver. The articles accuse him of numerous religious failings and of refusing the solemn league and covenant (probably the leading cause of his sequestration). He is not recorded as holding any other appointment until 1662, when he was restored to his parish. He died in 1667: Venn, *Alumni Cantabrigienses*, III, 17; CCEd, Location ID 11328; ERO, D/P 62/1/1.

[53] The wearing of a veil by women during churching was customary but not required by the prayer book, and was resisted by puritans who thought it popish. Under Laud, some bishops sought nevertheless to enforce it by their visitation articles. For churching and the veil, see Introduction, p. xxviii and n. 105; David Cressy, 'Purification, thanksgiving and the churching of women in post-Reformation England', *Past & Present*, 141 (1993), 106–46, especially 132–9.

forgiving of sins, else what should become of those that were sicke of infectious deseases, when their neighbours dare not come at them, in such cases the Common Absolution, read every Sunday, will serve to bring them to heaven, and that the prayers of the church are most effectuall, therefore the people must confesse their sins to their minister or else he cannot pray for them.[54]
6. The said Parmiter further deposeth that the said Mr Kindleton taught that the people had nothing to doe to read the scriptures, more then the Creede, the Lords prayer and the ten commandments.
7. The said Parmiter further deposeth that the said Mr Kindleton taught in the pulpitt that the common people had nothing to doe to question the Ministers Doctrine, but everyone must meddle with his Calling and be ruled by the church.[55]
8. Phillemon Parmitter and Francis Hadsley likewise depose that the said Mr Kindleton often used to preach in the surplice, and said that it shewed forth his integrity of life.

fo. 14

9. The said deponents further depose that the said Mr Kindleton compelled the people to kneele at the railes when they received the sacrament of the Lords Supper.
10. Phillemon Parmiter likewise deposeth that the said Mr Kindleton told him that the sabbath was arbitrary, and men might chuse whether they would keepe it or noe.
11. The said Parmiter likewise deposeth that the said Mr Kindleton did say, the other Parliament was broken up, because the House of Commons tooke upon them to meddle with church goverment which they had nothing to doe withall, for it belonged to the Convocation.
12. The said Parmiter further saith That the said Mr Kindleton did say the Parliament did unjustly in putting the Earle of Strafford to death.[56]
13. Phillemon Parmiter and Amos Wignold further depose that the said Mr Kindleton taught in the church that originall sin is washed away in Baptisme. And in his prayer before sermon, when he comes to confession of sins he saith Lord we doe not meane Original sinne for that is washed away in Baptisme.
14. William Sumner deposeth that the said Mr Kindleton counselled his trained souldier to run away to the king, if ever he came upon service.
15. Francis Hadsley, John Greene, William Crabb and William Reade depose that the said Mr Kindleton refused to take the League and Covenant himselfe, and also disheartened his people preaching out of the fifth of James, and the 12th, on these words (sweare not at all), and he hath ever since absented himselfe from his parish soe that none of the parishioners have taken it though they much desire it.[57]

[54] This charge stems from the puritan view that ministers did not have authority to give absolution and that auricular confession was a popish practice. The Church of England permitted auricular confession, notably in the visitation of the sick, and in the 1630s it was encouraged by some bishops: Nicholas Tyacke, *Anti-Calvinists: the rise of English Arminianism c. 1590–1640* (Oxford, 1987), pp. 221–2: *Visitation articles*, 136.

[55] Parmiter claims that Kindleton preached that everyone should remain within his own proper sphere ('meddle with his Calling') and laymen should leave matters of doctrine to the clergy.

[56] For Strafford, see Cole MS, fo. 23 and n. 72.

[57] James v. 12: 'But above all things, my brethren, swear not, neither by heaven, neither by the earth, neither by any other oath: but let your yea be yea; and your nay, nay; lest ye fall into condemnation.' After refusing the solemn league and covenant, preaching against it and then leaving the parish, Kindleton cannot have been surprised by the ensuing sequestration.

16. Thomas Aylett gent sworne and examined saith that the said Mr Kindleton did not take this last Covenant himselfe, neither gave it to his parishioners, and did preach as in the precedent article and hath absented himselfe ever since.[58]

His answer is herewith sent. The Living of Magdalen Laver is worth 80^{li} per annum.
Mr Kindleton hath neither wife nor childe.

Richard Everarde William Masham Henry Holcroft
Carew H Mildmay William Astwood William Martin.

fo. 14v

fo. 15 blank

fo. 15v

Essex
Depositions taken upon oath at Halstead April 9th 1644 against William Evett pretended parson of Yeldham parva.[59]
In primis, notwithstanding a pretended presentation to the Rectory of the said parish yet he hath never either by himselfe or any other for him officiated there soe as for about[60] the space of 12 months last past the parish hath beene wholy destitute of any meanes for the good of their soules, except what they procured by their private purses.
William Harlakenden gent, Thomas Rande, John Brimacam.[61]
2. That it appeares by a Letter under his hand, received July 29th 1643, that he contemned the power of Parliament threatening the parishioners, in their obedience thereof, because of the kings proclamation.
The letter itselfe produced.
The value of the Living is about 60^{li} per annum and the parishioners doe desire Mr Benton may be their minister whome some of us alsoe doe know and approve of.[62]
A Barnardiston[63]
Thomas Honywood
Richard Harlakenden
Isaac Wincoll
John Ellistone.

58 Thomas Aylett's testimony adds weight to the depositions. He was a wealthy resident, and his brother John was lord of the manor and had presented Kindleton as rector in 1631. It should not be assumed that Thomas was a godly man or hostile to Kindleton. In later life, the two men seem to have been on good terms; in his will of 1664, Thomas Aylett left Kindleton £100 and made him joint executor: Newcourt, *Repertorium*, II, 371; ERO, D/AEW 23/221.

59 These articles are carried forward from Cole MS, fo. 23, but include several amendments made by the north Essex committee. See the Cole MS version for additional notes on the case.

60 Cole MS, fo. 23, has 'above' twelve months.

61 Cole MS, fo. 23, omits the names of the deponents. For William Harlakenden, the cousin of Richard Harlakenden who sat as a committee member on this case, see Introduction, p. lx.

62 Probably Jeremy Benton, a recent graduate from Emmanuel College, Cambridge. It seems that he was appointed to serve at Little Yeldham, but he moved on by 1646/7, when Robert Chadsley took up the cure: Venn, *Alumni Cantabrigienses*, I, 137; Bodleian Library, MS 324, fo. 140 (where the intruder is named 'one Mr Bentham'); Matthews, *Calamy revised*, pp. 50, 107.

63 The scribe has attempted to reproduce the signature which he found in the original document. The initial letter could easily be read as 'J' (as it was by Zachariah Grey, see Cole's note at Cole

fo. 16 blank

fo. 16v

Fawlkebourne Witham halfe hundred.
Depositions of Witnesses taken the 19th day of June 1644 against Edward Strutt parson of Fawlkbourne at Witham before Arthur Barnardiston Esq, Sir Thomas Honnywood Knt, Richard Harlakenden, Henry Barrington, Isaac Wincall, Robert Crane Esqs.[64]
Imprimis that the said Edward Strutt did upon Newyeares day last was twelvemonth, in the heareing of divers persons, at Sir Edward Bullockes house and in his prescence, say that what the Parliament doe now they doe without law, for they have noe law for that they doe.
Bartholomew Wall, Thomas Herridge.
Item upon yong Mr Bullockes telling this Deponent upon the Sabbath day, at Sir Edward Bullockes house, about the time when the vow and Covenant was taken (as he remembereth upon that very day that the said Mr Bullocke parted with his money to Parliament, freely,) the said Mr Strutt said that soe did not I for (said he) for if I had not, it had beene better then it is.
John Tompson.
Item this Deponent did heare the said Edward Strutt say that now there was noe Parliament, they are as a body without a head, now the king is away, and the said Mr Strutt did further say that the Parliament is as deepely guilty of treason as the Earle of Strafford, for (I pray saith he) what did he? he sought to bring the land into an arbitrary Goverment and soe doth the Parliament. I pray else (said he) what meaneth this twentieth part, soe they may come for a tenth part, and at last for all.
Bartholomew Wall.
This Deponent saith that about a weeke before the vow and Covenant was to have beene taken in Fawlkbourne he did heare Mr Strutt diswade Sir Edward Bullocke from takeing of it saying to the said Edward that Doctor Gawdin and Mr Collins of Braintrie and Mr Fuller of Stebbin and others did not take it and that the said vow and Covenant was called in againe.
Phillip Harvey.
This Deponent saith that at that time when he was to take the vow and Covenant the said Mr Strutt did wish this Deponent to take heede what he did for (said he) it is a very dangerous Covenant and I beleive (said he) that not a quarter of the kingdome will take it.
Bartholomew Wall.
They depose that the said Mr Strutt doth ordinarily sweare by his faith and sometimes in his anger will sweare by God, and one time especially, the Deponent Bartolomew Wall did heare him on the sabbath day sweare severall times by God, because his dogg was killed.
Bartholomew Wall, Thomas Herridge, John Thompson.

MS, fo. 23, above), but in fact is 'A' for Arthur. This is confirmed by comparison with Barnardiston's actual signature in the parish register of Terling, in which in 1653 he entered a memorandum recording that William Ward had been sworn in as the new register 'by me Arthur Barnardiston Esq one of the Justices of the Peace': ERO, D/P 299/1/3.

64 See Cole MS, fos. 38–41, for the earlier version of these articles against Edward Strutt. The footnotes on the Cole MS, numbered 99–106, are applicable to the articles printed here.

fo. 17

Francis Scott saith that within 3 or 4 yeares space, he hath heard Mr Strutt in his ordinary discourse at severall times sweare by divers oathes, as by his faith, by God shall save me, before God and the like.
Francis Scott.
That Mr Strutt did not for divers yeares together preach more then once on the sabbath day, untill about a quarter of a yeare since.
John Tompson.
They depose that when Mr Wright, late vicar of Witham, was called in question before the Parliament about his prophane and wicked courses, they haveing conference with Mr Strutt about the same, he said to them that the Parliament could not by law take away his Living.
Jerome Skingly, John Tompson.
That Mr Strutt hath for many yeares usually frequented the house and company of one Mr Leventhorpe, who is a knowne papist.
John Tompson.
The valew of Fawlkbourne Benefice is about 80^{li} per annum.
Mr Strutts owne estate is very small, he hath a wife and ten children, but all growne to men, and woemens estate.
They desire Robert Chadsey, Clarke, late Curate to Mr Herring, parson of Dodinghurst, may be the minister.[65]
Bartholomew Wall and Thomas Herridge are nominated sequestrators.
A Barnardiston
T Coke
Henry Barrington
Robert Crane
John Ellistone.

fo. 17v blank

fo. 18

Essex
Depositions taken at Halstead May 1° 1644 against William Frost parson of Middleton before Arthur Barnardiston Esq, Sir Thomas Honnywood kn^{t} and Richard Harlakenden, Isaac Wincall, John Elliston Esquires.[66]
He was very forward to procure the setting up of the Rales and then refused to give the sacrament to those that would not come up to them.
Thomas Mills, Isaac Mulling.
2. He read the booke of sportes on the Lords day, and thereupon the youth said they had liberty to play, and now they would play.
Margaret Wall, Katherine Pregg, Anne Ellis.

[65] Robert Chadsley was indeed appointed to replace Strutt, but was soon displaced, as noted above, Cole MS, fo. 38 n. 99. He quickly moved to serve at Little Yeldham, 1646–62, noted above, n. 62.
[66] In the Cole MS, the articles against Frost are set out in three separate sections, at fos. 31–3, 37 and 43–5 of that manuscript. Here they are brought together, with some reordering of the articles, but with essentially the same content. See the Cole MS entries for notes on Frost and other matters.

3. He is a Tipler, and they have seene him soe distempered with drinke as he could not speake plaine, nor goe right in the streets, and this was 2 or 3 yeares since.
Katherine Pregg, Mary Oliver.
In his distempers of drinke, he came hollowing and whooping at an unseasonable time in the night, and this was about Michaellmas last.
Anne Ellis.
And in one of his drinking fitts at the Crowne at Sudbury, he offered to forgive a woeman divers debts that he pretended she ought him, if she would give him a kisse.
Bartholomew Wall gent, Margaret his wife.
4. He is a man dangerously suspected of Incontinency, as may appeare by these presumptions.

> 1. That he hath offered to putt his hand under woemens cloathes in an obscene and uncivill manner.
> Margaret Wall.
> 2. That he hath lately kept companie with a woman of a light carriage and kept a whore in his house for many yeares.
> John Waypoole, John Kettson.
> 3. That Susan Ruggle told this Deponent that her Mistress Mr Frosts wife fell out with her threatening to turne her out of doores but she said that if she did turne her out she would make her Master for ever shewing himself in the pulpitt anymore.[67]
> 4. That upon the generall crime of Bastardy he was forced to finde Compargators to sweare for him, who are now most of them either sequestred or ran away.
> Mrs Wall, Thomas Mills.
> 5. That notwithstanding he was strictly enjoyned by the Ecclesiasticall Court, to put away Anne Hovell and her Bastard out of his house, by whome he was suspected, yet notwithstanding since he hath entertained them both.
> Mrs Wall, Anne Ellis.

fo. 18v

5. That amongst other discourses about a yeare agoe, speakeing of the warres he used these words, Methinkes (said he) it is an unnaturall thing to goe against our king, and to give away our money so basely, and ugly, as we doe to the Parliament.
Anne Ellis.

A Barnardiston
Thomas Cooke
Henry Barrington
Robert Crane
John Ellistone.

Essex
Additional Articles against Mr Frost deposed the xviith of June 1644 at Hallstedd.
Vincent Kidson deposeth that William Frost preaching upon a Sabbath day about the vow and Covenant, he wished them to be very carefull what they did and told them that they who had taken the first protestation if they should take this must needes be forsworne and used this reason because in the first protestation the king joined with

[67] No deponent is named for this article. See Cole MS, fo. 32, for Cole's conjecture that it should read 'she would make her Master *afraid* for ever shewing himself' (my emphasis).

the Parliament but in this last the Parliament tooke up armes against the king without his consent.

And further he deposeth that William Frost, Minister of Middleton, about Cristmas last was twelvemonth, was soe distempered with drinkeing, as he could not goe over a bridge above 3 yards wide, soe as this deponent and his wife being of his parish and goeing homewards did leade him a greate part of the way, and since that time hath seene him soe distempered that he could not goe without leading, and about September last he heard Mr Frost aske Mrs Frost why she went not to church, she said to him that she had better stay at home then come home with broken leggs, as yow doe.

Sibill Kidson deposeth That upon the day of publique thanksgiving Mr Frost did come to this Deponents house then in Twinsted upon noe occasion that she knew of, and being in her house followed hir out of one roome into another, and Kissed her by force, insomuch as she called in her husband and told him of Mr Frosts

fo. 19

carriage to her, who then went away, and at another time, being about six weekes after as she remembereth, he came againe to hir house, pretending to aske hir the way to Robert Fryotts who dwelt hard by (which he as well knew as she) and she letting him goe through her barne the nighest way, he kissed her, and at the same time goeing a little further with him, he kissed her againe by force, pulling her by the Apron, and she breakeing from him, he told her she was very quicke, but she said not quicke enough for him.

Mrs Anne Hubbert deposeth that she hath heard it reported that Mr Frost had used some light and uncivill carriages towards some woemen and that once comeing to hir house in the morning to speake with hir husband before this deponent was out of hir bedd he came up into her chamber and kissed her being in bedd haveing no occasion that he acquainted hir with to come to hir about, but onely on her mayds telling him that she was not well.

Vincent Cocke and Thomas Mills. These deponents say that Mr Frost, preaching about the nature of vowes on that sabbath when the vow and Covenant was to be taken, he did after many cautions given us about the danger of breach of our vowes, soe presse upon us what protestation the king had taken for defending the protestant religion, that we were thereby much deterred from takeing the said vow and Covenant, untill Mr Wall one of our parish did perswade us thereunto.

Bartholomew Wall and Margaret his wife. To the 9th Article these deponents say that Mr Frost did as they now remember about the time that the kings army went first against the Scotts, reade a paper publiqly in the church which was to this effect, that though that the Scotts pretended that their comeing was for maintenance of the Gospell and liberty of the subject, yet the end of their comeing was to take away our estates and abase[68] our wives, and other things to that purpose.

Mr Frost his Benefice is worth about 70^{li} per annum. He hath a wife but noe children His reall estate is worth as we conceive about 12^{li} per annum. And he hath about 200^{li} and upwards in personall estate.[69]

68 Cole MS, fo. 44, has 'abuse our wives'.

69 Cole MS, fo. 44, states that Frost's benefice was worth £80 per annum and that his personal estate was about £100.

fo. 19v

For sequestrators Bartholomew Wall gent and Edmond Marsh.
Margaret Wall. This deponent sayth she was the woman mentioned in the first branch of the 4th Article under whose coates he offered to put his hand, meeting her alone in a straight entry in hir owne house.
A Barnardiston
Isaac Wincall
Thomas Cooke
Robert Crane
John Ellistone.

fo. 20 blank

fo. 20v

Essex
Depositions taken upon Oath against Christopher Newstedd Parson of Stistead xxth of March 1643 at Halstead.[70]
1. That he hath beene a greate promoter of the late Innovations, as bowing to the Alter, towards the East, reading the second service and churching woemen there, prosecuteing tender consciences that durst not observe those Innovations, affirming it to be Treason not to obey the same.
John Dawes, Richard Norton.
2. That he preached that the sin of Ignorance is but a small sin, and easily pardoned,[71] and that a papist might be saved as well as a Puritan, but that (said he) a papist must goe a little further about, and that that sin which makes some men Infamous, made Mary Magdalen Famous.
William Drake, John Browne, John Dawes, Richard Norton, these 2 last witnesses by Information from Abbington.
3. That he hath buried many dead Corps with Crosses on their breasts, and there being in his church at Abbington the pictures of God the father, and of purgatory, he caused to be razed out some scriptures, which were upon the walls, shewing the unlawfulnes of them, and others to be putt up, falsely quoted and applyed to justify and maintaine them, as 1 Peter 3. 19th and affirmed that Lent was observed for more then politiq ends, and being told there was an act of Parliament shewing that it was but for politiq ends (he said) what care I for an act of Parliament.
John Dawes, Richard Norton, by Information from Abbington.
4. That he is noe waies gifted nor fitly qualifyed for the Ministry, and negligent to prepare his people for the sacrament by preaching concerning that Ordinance.[72]
John Dawes, Richard Norton, John Browne.

[70] See Cole MS, fos. 18–20, for the earlier version of these articles and notes on the case. In a number of places, the earlier version has been edited in the present text, as noted below.
[71] The words 'and easily pardoned' have been added to the original text in the Cole MS.
[72] Cole MS, fo. 19, has 'negligent to prepare his People for the Sacrament by *not* preaching concerning that Ordinance' (my emphasis). In either case, the sense must be that in the view of the deponents it was Newstead's duty to preach in support of the ordinance which rescinded the Laudian policy for the communion service, and thus prepare the congregation for the change, and he failed to do so.

5. That his Curate in Catechizing, shewing that Christs death was sufficient for all, but not effectuall to all, he interrupted him, commanding him to goe noe further, and next Lords day preached that Christ died for all, proveing it by the Catechize in the Common prayer booke, Christ died for mee and all mankinde etc.
John Dawes, Richard Norton, by Information from Abbington.
6. That he hath declared his Malignancy against the Parliament, in particular against my Lord Say, saying he was noe good subject.
John Dawes, Richard Norton, by Information from Abbington.
7. That his Conversation hath beene most familiar with Malignants and ill affected persons, chusing those of the most base, and lewd life for his Churchwardens.
John Dawes, Richard Norton, by Information from Abbington.
8. That when Mr Roode Minister of Abbington before him was imprisoned by the High Commission, unjustly, he the said Newsted, in the absence of Mrs Roode, threw their goods out of the house, and also their children, exposing them to the extremity of the Cold, barefoot.
John Dawes, Richard Norton, by Information from Abbington.

fo. 21

9. At his takeing possession of Stisted Living last summer was Twelvemonth,[73] he said he must goe to his Master the king.
William Drake.
10. That he behaved himselfe soe evill at Abbington, that his parishioners were about to exhibite a bill against him, which he haveing notice of, resigned his Living to prevent them, and did binde some of his parishioners not to sue him.
John Dawes, Richard Norton, by Information from Abbington.
11. That he had preached that God had sparing mercies for the damned in Hell.
Arthur Owers, Marrion George.
12. That he would not take the Vow and Covenant, being asked if he would give that to others, which he would not take himselfe, he said ye must not doe as I doe, but as I say soe it was never taken in his parish.
Robert Dyer, Robert Wood, Barnaby Warren.

A Barnardiston
Thomas Cooke
Robert Crane
Henry Barrington
John Ellistone.

fo. 21v blank

[73] Cole MS, fo. 20, has 'At his taking Possession of Stiested Living last Summer, he said'. Here, the text has been corrected to indicate that Newstead took possession and spoke the words in summer 1642, not 1643. This is a tacit acceptance that Newstead's institution in June 1642 was lawful (although ineffective because of obstruction by parishioners).

fo. 22

Depositions taken upon oath against George Crakenthorpe Parson of Bradwell March the 22th 1643, at Halstead.[74]

1. He usually sweares by his faith and Troth.
Thomas Collins, John Raven.
2. That he is a Common Tipler, and often drunke, as at Baintrie[75] a quarter of a yeare since, whence he could not come without reeling into the hedges, and this is usuall with him, and about a yeare since he was soe distempered with drinking there that he fell to hollowing and hooping till he lay downe to sleepe.
Roger Emory, John Bernard.
3. That he refused to take the vow and Covenant in the expressions thereof, but altered it and soe reade it, but in the afternoone refused to take it, but bade them often take heede what they did and said he would not take it otherwise then he had framed it though he lost his Living.
Joshua Raven, Robert Francke, Anthony Blackbone.
4. That he hath preached about a yeare since that almes purge away sin, and good workes deliver from death.
Thomas Collins.

Phillip Pricke the wife of John Pricke deposeth that she hath seene Mr George Crakenthorp severall times drunke, comeing from Baintrie, by hir house, and this she knowes because she saw him reele and stagger, and once or twice fall, and could not keepe in the right way from falling into the ditches, soe as once comeing into hir yard, he soe misbehaved himselfe in his speeches, as her prentice laughed, and howted at him.

Arthur Barnardiston
Thomas Honywood
Robert Crane.

fo. 22v blank

fo. 23

Essex
Depositions taken upon Oath against Joseph Long parson of Fingringho April the 1° 1644 at Colchester.[76]

74 For the earlier version of these articles and notes thereon, see Cole MS, fos. 13–14, 28–9. This later version omits two sections of the Cole MS: the information about Crackenthorpe's income and family at Cole MS, fo. 14, and the deposition by Edward Bridgeman at Cole MS, fo. 29.

75 Braintree is the town referred to here and below.

76 Articles against Joseph Long of Fingringhoe are recorded in both the Cole MS and here, in Leicester MS 31, but Cole's version has the first part missing: see Cole MS, fo. 64 and n. 137. Long graduated from Christ's College, Cambridge (BA 1625–6, MA 1629), and was appointed vicar of Great Clacton in 1629. In 1638, he was given a dispensation to hold also the vicarage of Fingringhoe. According to his parishioners, he was non-resident at Fingringhoe, appointing poorly paid and idle curates to serve. As these articles and the draft warrant (below, fo. A27) show, Long was sequestrated from Fingringhoe by Manchester, but he was not challenged at Great Clacton, which he retained until his death in 1662: Venn, *Alumni Cantabrigienses*, III, 102; Newcourt, *Repertorium*, II, 154, 267; CCEd, Location ID 11257; *VCH Essex*, XII, part 1, 278 (Great Clacton).

1. That he hath two Livings and hath beene Non-resident there, ever since he had it, and since Michaelmas last there hath beene seldome any preaching and but one Fast day kept, and yet was very Cruell in exacting Tythes.
John Nun, Joseph Clarke, Robert Beckwith, Samuel Whittering.
2. That he hath beene an Innovator, and refused to give the sacrament to those that would not come to the Raile.
Samuel Witring, John Nunn, Robert Beckwith.
3. That Notwithstanding his Non-residency he would allow not above 10 or 12 pounds per annum for a Curate, and hath procured noe other for them, but Idle and Lazy ones.[77]
John Nunn, Richard Stone, Jonash Tye.
4. Being desired to come and live at Fingeriho, he said there were such a companie of Puritans, he would not live amongst them, and being told the Parliament had ordered that noe Minister should have two Livings, he said the Parliament had nothing to doe to order it, without the kings hand and consent.
John Nunne.
5. That he is a common Alehouse haunter, and hath beene severall times distempered with drinking, night and day.
John Betts, James Thorpe.
6. And that he was very obscene in his speeches, being in company with a woeman.
John Betts.
7. He is a usuall swearer by his faith.
John Spurgion, James Thorpe.
his benefice worth about 40^{li} per annum, his temporall estate 20^{li} per annum he hath a wife and a childe.

Arthur Barnardiston
Thomas Honywood
Henry Barrington
Robert Crane
John Ellistone.

fo. 23v blank

fo. 24

Depositions taken upon Oath against Timothy Clay, Parson of Wickham St Paul, March 22th 1643, at Halsted.[78]
1. That he used to preach but once a day, nor any for him, and then railing against Godly and painfull Ministers saying it was not lawfull to call the people from their worke on the weekeday to heare a sermon, abusing the fourth Commandment to proove it.
Richard White, Elizabeth Grange.
2. That he deferred a sacrament by him appoynted and provision made, till the Rale was sett, and when it was up, reade the second service at it threatening those with the High Commission that would not receive there.
John Perry, Richard Golding.

77 George Smith is reported to have been the curate at Fingringhoe in 1640, but nothing else is known of him: CCEd, Location ID 11257. Certainly £12 a year would not have been an attractive stipend.
78 See Cole MS, fos. 16–18, for the earlier version of these articles and for notes on Clay and other matters.

3. That he hath lyen out Drinkeing, seaven or eight dayes till he was distempered unto distraction, that Mr Ady his Physitian sent him word that if he would not leave his drinking of Sacke he would be starke madd, and in his drinking fitts, he with another parson (now gone to Oxford) kept a noted whore with them (sometimes in private) the most part of two dayes and nights to the expence of above 5 poundes, for their partes, from Monday to Fryday, in these disorders.
Robert White, John Perry, Richard Golding, John Strutt, Thomas Hedgman.
4. he is a prophane swearer.
Robert Digby, William Ellistone, William Saward.
5. That he said he was sure that God made a king, but not a Parliament.
Samuel King.
6. That he Dranke a Health to Prince Rupert saying the Queene and Prince Rupert were right for us, but the king would come to the Parliament if he could, and said he, but we have gott him and will keepe him, and that there were never merry dayes since the Bishopps went downe, and that he would venture his life for the king, and goe to him if he could, and would dye in the Rome[79] rather then yeild to the Parliament.
The value of his Living 60^{li} per annum.
Mr Clay had notice to take a Copy of these Depositions, to make his defence thereunto but he refused to doe the same, onely returned a Letter the Copy whereof followeth, filed to these depositions.

Thomas Honywood
Thomas Cooke
Richard Harlakenden
A Barnardiston
Isaac Wincoll
Robert Crane.

fo. 24v blank

fo. 25

Depositions taken upon oath against Rowland Steward Parson of Alphamstone, March the 22th 1643 at Halstead.[80]
1. That he is a common swearer by deepe Oathes as by God etc.
Isaac Wincall Esq, Salomon Clarke, William More.
2. That he is a discourager of the service of the Parliament, as appeares by his preaching (at the time of the propositions comeing forth) about Almes, he said there is a giving, now I doe not like that, for that makes the breach bigger, and also by his neglect to pray for the army, and blaming one of his neighbours for letting of his sonne goe Volunteir, and when some of them were killed said to one of his neighbours I told yow what would come of it, affirming the contrary forces to be the stronger.
Robert Harrison, Robert Moyce, John Clarke, William More.

[79] This word is spelled ‘roome’ in the Cole MS, fo. 18. See there, n. 49, for the meaning.
[80] See Cole MS, fos. 11–12, for the earlier version of these articles and for notes on Steward and other matters.

3. That he hath neglected and slighted the keepeing of the Fast.
William More, Robert Moyce.
4. That he hath beene a Common frequenter of the Companie of Papists and other Lewd persons, at Inns, their houses and also his owne.
William More, Robert Moyce, John Clarke, Solomon Clarke.
5. He hath beene a Notorious Common Gamester, at Dice and Cards.
Solomon Clarke, Robert Harrison, William More, John Clarke.
6. That he hath beene an excessive drinker, urging others there unto by Drinking healthes, and that on his knees, boasting that he had beene Drunke twenty times at one house.
William More, John Clarke, Henry Leffingwell.
7. That he hath played at Catt and Trapp with the boyes of his parish on the Lords day, and constantly was a Looker on, and teaching his children therein, on that day.
William More, John Clarke.
8. That he hath bragg'd that he hath had the use of divers woemen, besides his wife, and this he hath spoken in her presence.
William More, John Clarke.

fo. 25v

That he hath beene alwaies negligent in his function.
Robert Harrison, William More, John Clarke.

Examinatur per Johannem Smyth cl Com Scand Min[81]
A Barnardiston
Isaac Wincoll.

his Living 70^{li} per annum
he hath 10 children
his personall estate thought to be 400^{li}.

fo. 26 blank

fo. 26v

Essex
Depositions taken upon Oath against Dr Wilson Doctor in Divinity parson of Depden, April 2 1644 at Colchester.[82]
1. That he is a Plurallist haveing 3 Livings at least, vizt Depden Wimbish and Fullbourne where his family liveth.
Thomas Hammond, Daniel Hockley.

[81] 'Examinatur', written here in contracted form ('Exitur'), signifies that the entry has been checked by the committee clerk, here named as John Smith: see also Cole MS, fo. 10 n. 20.
[82] See Cole MS, fos. 69–70, for the earlier version of articles against Dr Wilson, and for notes on him and on the deponent John Mead. The present manuscript contains (below) additional articles on the case, and draft warrants for the sequestration and ejection of Wilson from all three of his parishes.

2. That he hath beene Non-resident, ever since he had this Living, being about 12 or 13 yeares, not comeing there for the most part above 4 or 5 times in a yeare, and then but to receive money, or compound for Tythes.
John Mead, William Eldred.
3. That he hath employed a Curate who hath preached for the most part not above once on the Lords day, nor on the Fast day.
Daniel Hockley, William Eldred.
4. That he hath beene a notorious Innovator for he sett up the Rales at his owne proper charges, and that a yeare or two before any Innovations in our Diocesse.
Thomas Hammond, Daniel Hockley.
5. That when the Doctor did come, he used to bow and Cringe towards the East, and at the nameing of Jesus.
William Eldred, Daniel Hockley, John Mead.
6. That hee is a knowne Delinquent, his estate was sequestered, himselfe apprehended, and carryed away but where he is we know not.
Thomas Hammond, John Mead.

Henry Barrington
Thomas Cooke
Arthur Barnardiston
Richard Harlakenden
Robert Crane.

fo. 27

Articles Additionall concerning Doctor Wilson Parson of Depden.[83]
1. Imprimis whether did yow deliver or cause to be sent or delivered to him, or give notice at his house at Fullbourne or elsewhere a Warrant from the Committee of Scandalous Ministers concerning the makeing of his defence and what answer was by him returned, and whether did he cause yow to reade the booke of Liberty, to prophane the Lords day.
John Debnam Curate.[84]
2. Item whether was not the said Doctor for many daies together privately concealed in your house about January twelvemonth, and there at last taken by Captaine Turner and carryed away to London as a Delinquent, and were yow not with, or saw him in the place where he was prisoner, and did he not when he lay in your house privately keepe two horses fitt for service, besides those he usually imployed to ride upon, in the same house moated in, within a parlor or chappell there, and did not his servants or other persons as messengers, much frequent him in the night time, when he lay there, and to what end were the said Horses kept and what became of them.
Richard Baynes.

83 These three articles are interrogatory, asking the individual named to provide further evidence. It was common practice for committees to issue such interrogatories but this is the only case in which the Essex committees' questions (and the answers they received) are recorded. The information is not noted in the Cole MS, but was evidently forwarded to Manchester for his consideration.

84 John Debnam graduated BA 1621, MA 1624 from Emmanuel College, Cambridge, and was curate at Debden throughout Wilson's tenure of the living. It seems unlikely that Hugh Glover, who succeeded Wilson in 1644, had need of his services. Debnam was vicar of Chrishall, 1657–73, when he died: Venn, *Alumni Cantabrigienses*, II, 27.

3. Whether did not the said Doctor employ Thomas Long on the Lords day, in sermon or service time, to fetch wine from Walden, and what moneyes did he deliver to him, to lay out for the same.
Thomas Long.

Arthur Barnardiston Thomas Cooke
Richard Harlakenden Henry Barrington
Robert Crane.

Additionalls to the Depositions above taken at Halsted May 1° 1644 against Dr Wilson.
1. John Debnam to the second article deposeth that he being Curate to the Doctor did acquaint him that a booke was brought to him to be published for allowing

fo. 27v

of Sportes on the Lords day, which he asking him what he should doe about it, he said that he might reade it if he pleased, for otherwise he thought trouble would come of it.
2. Richard Baynes deposeth that he was eight dayes in his house, and did desire to be concealed, and there he saw him taken by Captaine Turner, and carryed away to London.
3. Thomas Long deposeth that his Master Richard Baynes came to him on a Sabbath day in the forenoone, from the Docter with 4 or 5 shillings in his hand, and told him the Docter desired him to go to Walden, being 3 miles of and fetch wine for him, which he did accordingly.
Dr Wilson his Living at Depden is worth 200^{li} per annum, Wimbish 100^{li} per annum, he hath a wife but no childe.

Thomas Cooke
Henry Barrington
Robert Crane
Arthur Barnardiston
Richard Harlakenden.

fo. 28 blank

fo. 28v

Essex
Depositions taken at Halstead May 1 1644 against John Crosse vicar of Gosfeild.[85]
Imprimis he hath beene negligent in preaching, many sabbath dayes not preaching at all, nor any body for him, except of late when the Towne procured one, saying that preaching is but mans invention.
Widdow Dale, Judeth Bacon.
2. Item he read propositions comeing from the king, incouraging men thereupon to give money to maintaine warre against the Parliament, saying if it were never so little, the king would accept well of it.
Richard Clarke, Richard Ruffell.

[85] See Cole MS, fos. 29–31, for the earlier version of the articles against Crosse and notes on Crosse and other matters.

3. Item he reade the booke of Sportes on the Lords day, and exhorted the people to come to heare it read, and to give attention to it, and to observe it, saying it was fit to be reade often, and the booke being lost, he threatened the Churchwardens with the High Commission because they did not buy him another to reade.
Richard Russell,[86] Richard Clarke, Churchwardens.
4. Item he hath usually suffered prophane sportes by the youth on the sabbath, and then did use to sitt and looke upon them, at Stooleball, Barley brake etc without reproofe.
Thomas Nevill, William Syday.
5. Item he said on the sabbath day to this deponent that the sabbath is noe longer to be observed then he is reading Divine service, and that another part of the day, men might take their Liberty and doe what they list, and that Holy dayes are to be kept as well as the sabbath.
Richard Clarke, Robert Digby.
6. Item when the Communion table was to be railed in, and sett Altar waies, this deponent asking him, why he was soe forward to charge the Towne in bringing in an Innovation before it was in other places, he said then wee shalbe the first that shall worshipp.
Richard Ruffle.
7. Item he was very active and strict to observe the Innovations, using to reade service at the Railes where few could heare him, bowing at the name of Jesus, preaching with his surplice, hood and Tippett, without any prayer at the end of his sermon.
Robert Digby, William White.

fo. 29

8. That one Mr Wimms preaching there, he would not suffer him to make any prayer after sermon, but pulled the pullpitt doore open twice, upon which the Cushion lay soe that the Minister was in danger to fall downe and spoyle himselfe.
Robert Digby, William White, John Dyer.
9. That when Godly Ministers preached there, he would usually looke upon them and Jeere and Fleere at them whiles they were in their Sermons.
Elizabeth Webb, William Scot, William Webb.

Arthur Barnardiston
Richard Harlakenden
Thomas Coke
Thomas Honywood
John Ellistone.

fo. 29v blank

[86] This deponent's name is spelled as Ruffell or Ruffle elsewhere in these articles, in Cole MS, fos. 29 and 30, and in the parish's return of those subscribing to the protestation of 1642: in the latter return, Ruffell is listed as one of the constables: Parliamentary Archives, HL/PO/JO/10/1/91/17.

fo. 30

Informations upon Oath taken at Trinity Colledge in Cambridge against Doctor Yong,[87] parson of Haydon and Hadstocke in the County of Essex this 26th day of July 1644.[88]
To the first they say that they inhabite the Towne of Hadstocke and have soe done for these divers yeares and that the said Doctor Yong hath not beene resident to their knowledge uppon the said Living, for the space of one yeare last past.
John Willis, Thomas Carter, John Bawtell.
To the second to their knowledge or memory, the said Doctor hath not preached in the said parish Church for the space of this whole yeare last past, untill the Lords day was senight.
John Willis, Thomas Carter, John Bowsell.
The third affirmed.
John Willis, Thomas Carter, John Bowsell.
Informations upon Oath, upon Articles against Doctor Yong by the Inhabitants of Haydon in the County of Essex the day and yeare formerly.
The first proved by the said John North and Mathew Ashwell.
The second proved by the words was spoken about 3 months since.
The words in the third Article affirmed to be spoken, as in the said Article is contained about a quarter of a yeare since etc.
The fourth affirmed and proved.
The Fifth proved also.
The seaventh proved.
To the Right Honourable the Committee for Scandalous Ministers sitting at Cambridge Articles exhibited against Doctor Yong parson of the parish churches of Hayden and Hadstocke in

87 Edward Young was the eldest of three brothers of a Hertfordshire gentry family who all attended St John's College, Cambridge and became fellows there. Edward graduated BA in 1610, was elected a fellow in 1611, and proceeded MA 1613, BD 1620, DD 1639. In 1617, his uncle and aunt, Richard and Anna Young of Berners Roding, presented him to the rectory of Greenstead by Ongar. He was presented by the crown to the third prebend of Norwich in 1628 and in 1631 to the rectory of King's Ripton, Huntingdonshire. In 1634, he was given a dispensation to hold the livings of King's Ripton and Heydon, but gave up Greenstead by Ongar. The dispensation to hold Heydon with King's Ripton also noted that Young was chaplain to Lord Keeper Coventry, a position in which he could exercise considerable influence in ecclesiastical appointments. In 1638, he resigned King's Ripton and was presented to the rectory of Hadstock, a parish conveniently close to Heydon. He engaged Thomas Punter as curate at Hadstock, an arrangement which lasted until Young was ejected from Hadstock on 23 January 1645. Young was appointed archdeacon of Exeter in 1643 on the mandate of his friend Bishop Brownrigg. Though ejected from Hadstock, Young was able to retain Heydon: Venn, *Alumni Cantabrigienses*, IV, 492; CCEd, Location ID 11269; BL, Add. MS 39535, fo. 37v; CCEd, Location IDs 11293, 7521, 11271, 233121; *Fasti Ecclesiae Anglicanae 1541–1857*, VII, 54 (Norwich), XII, 23 (Exeter). For more about Young's connexions and subsequent career, see Introduction, p. xliv.

88 This case and that against Punter were not heard in Essex by the usual north Essex committee. They were heard in Cambridge by Francis Bacon (of Suffolk), Henry Mildmay (of Essex), John Brewster (of Norfolk), Humphrey Walcott (of Lincolnshire), Robert Vintner (of Huntingdonshire) and Robert Castell (of Cambridgeshire), members of the committee of the Eastern Association which met in Cambridge. That venue would have been more convenient for the witnesses than Colchester or Halstead. Similar arrangements were made in October 1644 to hear the evidence against George Beardsall, minister of Arkesden, another parish in the far north-west of Essex: Holmes, *Eastern Association*, pp. 123–6; *Cambridgeshire scandalous ministers*, pp. 87–9, 119, 149–50.

fo. 30v

the County of Essex xxvj[th] day of July Anno Domini 1644.
Imprimis that the said Doctor Young is a plurallist, he haveing two distinct Cures or Livings, and hath ever beene Non-Resident at Hadstocke aforesaid, being one of them.
John Willis, Thomas Carter, John Bowtell.
Item the said Doctor Yong hath beene very negligent parsonally[89] to officiate there, and for a whole yeare together hath not preached there at all.
John Willis, Thomas Carter, John Bowtell.
Item the said Doctor Yong hath ever since his comeing to Hadstocke which is above 5 yeares since imployed a most Malignant and deboysed Curate to officiate there.
John Willis, Thomas Carter, John Bowtell.
To the Right Worshipfull the Committee for Scandalous Ministers sitting at Cambridge.
Articles Exhibited against Doctor Yong parson of Haydon in the County of Essex this xxvj[th] of July 1644.
Imprimis his Doctrine is very scandalous, for he preacheth that Papists show themselves better subjects to their king then protestants, and that none ought to take up the sword, except he be commanded by the king, and that the sword was given to him by God, and that he that tooke the sword should perish by the sword, which made a poore widdow woeman in the Towne, that has a sonne pressed for the Parliaments service much to bewaile what should become of her sonne because he was constrained to goe against Gods command.
John North, Mathew Ashwell.
Item that upon the sabbath day in the pulpitt he said they hunted the king as a Partridge upon the Mountaines.[90]
John North, Mathew Ashwell.

fo. 31

Item the said Doctor Yong preached that though a king be a Tyrant, we ought to obey him and submitt to him, and that Religion was never knowne to be wonne by force of armes.
John North, Mathew Ashwell.
Item when a Warrant came to warne the said Doctor to goe to Dunmowe to take the Covenant, he went away, and stayed within 4 miles of the Towne for 10 or 12 weekes, and never came to preach in all that time, but sent scandalous Ministers to serve the Cure.
John North, Mathew Ashwell.
Item that the said Doctor would never administer the Covenant to his parishioners.
John North, Mathew Ashwell.
Item that the said Doctor would never reade anything that was sent from the Parliament but onely the first protestation, but when there was a pretended petition for peace, that

[89] *Sic.*

[90] Presumably a reference to 1 Samuel xxvi. 20, the words of David to Saul, king of Israel: 'Now therefore, let not my blood fall to the earth before the face of the Lord: for the king of Israel is come out to seek a flea, as when one doth hunt a partridge in the mountains.' Perhaps Young had preached that parliament's military campaign against the king was a fruitless exercise.

he reade, and exhorted the people to sett their hands to it, and sent it from house to house to have the Townsmen sett their hands to it.[91]
Mathew Ashwell, John North.
Sir,
There hath beene certaine Articles preferred before this Committee against Doctor Younge. The prosecutors themselves, being earnest to have them, we have delivered them, together with Doctor Yong his answer. They are all here enclosed, and commended to your Judgment to acquaint the Earle of Manchester therewith, according as yow shall soe cause.
Cambridge August 30th Sir we are your assured freinds
verso

fo. 31v

Francis Bacon
Henry Mildmay
John Brewster
Humphrey Walcott
Robert Vinter
Robert Castell.
Wee send also the Articles against Punter the Curate as also the answer.
For Mr Good Chaplaine to the Earle of Manchester at Lincolne or elsewhere.
To the Right Worshipfull Committee for Scandalous Ministers sitting at Cambridge.
Articles exhibited against Mr Thomas Punter[92] Curate of the parish church of Hadstocke in Essex 26 of July 1644.
Imprimis that the said Mr Punter is a common Alehouse haunter many times spending the most part of the day and the night there with lewd and ungodly company.
John Bowtell, John Willis.
2. Item the said Mr Punter doth harbour Malignant and dissaffected Ministers and getteth them to preach at our parish and he himselfe did deny the takeing of the first Covenant and did dishearten the parish from takeing of it, saying that himselfe had taken two oaths for the king already, and now he would not goe against him.[93]
John Bowtell, John Willis, Thomas Carter.

[91] For the protestation and the petition for peace, see Introduction, pp. xxx–xxxi.

[92] Thomas Punter, son of a gentleman of Royston (Hertfordshire and Cambridgeshire), was a scholar of Caius College, Cambridge. He graduated BA 1635–6, MA 1639. In 1638, he was appointed curate of Hadstock by Edward Young, who had recently become the rector there. Young had also been rector of the nearby parish of Heydon for some years and he remained resident there. Pluralism was therefore a charge against Young in 1644. It was also alleged that Punter was scandalous but it does not seem to have blighted his subsequent career, which suggests he could be a satisfactory parish minister. In January 1644/5, Young was sequestrated from Hadstock. Sequestration was not appropriate to Punter, who was the unbeneficed curate, but his appointment at Hadstock lapsed, as he was not engaged by Young's successor. By 1646, Punter was appointed rector of Greenstead by Ongar, by the support of the Young family, who had the patronage: see n. 87 above. By 1648, he had moved on to become minister of Linton, Cambridgeshire: the next year he was awarded augmentation and in 1650 the parochial inquisition judged that he was 'an orthodox and godly divine'. He vacated that living in 1660, but regained it in 1663 and kept it until he died in 1684; Venn, *Alumni Cantabrigienses*, III, 407; Newcourt, *Repertorium*, II, 289; Cambridgeshire Archives, P 107/1/1; Shaw, *History of the church 1640–1660*, II, 524; LPL, Comm. XIIa/3; CCEd, Location ID 962.

[93] This refers to the vow and covenant of summer 1643, for which see Introduction, pp. xxxi–xxxii.

3. Item the said Mr Punter is very negligent in keeping the fast dayes, sometimes reading onely a few prayers and a chapter upon the same.[94]
John Willis, Thomas Carter.
4. Item the said Mr Punter did goe to Bartlow upon a Fast day, to buy mault and measure land.
John Webb, Thomas Metcalfe.

fo. 32

5. Item the said Mr Punter did tell one of his parishioners that he might doe any worke upon the Fast day after prayers were ended.
John Webb, Thomas Metcalfe.
6. Item the said Mr Punter did observe the late illegall Innovations in the church, and caused the parishioners to come up to the Railes to take the sacrament.
John Willis, Thomas Carter, John Bowtell.
7. Item the said Mr Punter did tell one of his parishioners that he would give him a sermon at his wedding, and did tell him with what text he would preach, the text was (Occupy untill I come).[95]
8. Item the said Mr Punter did checke one of his parish for using prayers in his house.
John Willis.
9. Item the said Mr Punter did say, he was afraid that Prince Rupert was dead, for he had not heard of him a greate while, and he told one, what would he say and if he did see the Railes sett up again.
John Webb.
10. Item Symon Adams asked Mr Punter of which side the cause went on, the said Mr Punter replyed on the kings side, for one may see how Gods fight against them.[96]
Anne Ellis, Anne Bowtells.
Informations upon Oath against Thomas Punter, Curate of Hadstocke in Essex, July 26 1644.
1. The first Article affirmed by John Bowtell, John Willis, John Webb and Thomas Carter.
2. The second affirmed that the said Mr Punter ~~did~~ used to keepe company with Mr Firman and Mr Griggs and did get Mr Griggs to preach for him, by John Bowtell, and John Willis and John Webb.[97]
That Mr Punter denyed the first Covenant, by John Bowtell and John Willis.
That Mr Punter refusing that Covenant said he had taken two oathes for the king, and now he would not goe

[94] For fast days, see Introduction, p. xxx and n. 120.
[95] Luke xix. 13. No witness is named for this article, which is noted below as 'not proved'. The proponent of this article may have withdrawn through embarrassment at the prospect of being examined on the circumstances.
[96] *Sic*. Punter was asked which side was favoured and he replied the king's side. The final clause is obscure, but presumably was meant to convey that God favoured the king's cause.
[97] It is clear from the text of the second article, printed above, that Firman and Griggs were thought to be ministers. It has not been possible to identify Griggs. Firman might have been John Firmin, rector of Foxearth 1638–56: Venn, *Alumni Cantabrigienses*, II, 140; Smith, *Ecclesiastical history of Essex*, p. 301.

fo. 32v

against it, by Thomas Carter.
3. The third affirmed onely by John Willis.
4. That Mr Punter upon the Fast day asked Thomas Metcalfe the price of Malt, by John Webb and Thomas Metcalfe.
5. The fifth not proved.
6. The sixth affirmed and that it was about three yeares since.
7. The seaventh not proved.
8. The eighth affirmed and that the said Mr Punter checked him, by John Willis.
9. The ninth affirmed by John Webb.
10. The tenth affirmed onely by Anne Ellis.

fos. 33 and 34 blank

---

fo. A3

Here followes his Lordshipps proceedings in the Reformation of the Universitie of Cambridge.

Whereas by vertue of an Ordinance of Parliament I am authorized to indevour the Reformation of this Universitie These are to require you forthwith by this bearer to send unto mee the Statuts of your Colledge together with the names of all the Members of your Society whither Fellowes, Schollers or other officers and alsoe to certifie mee whoe are now present and who absent and to give mee notice of the exprese time of theire discontinuance which are now absent. Dated the 24th of February 1643.

There was 16 of theis warrants sent to all the Colledges in Cambridge.

These are to will and require you upon sight hereof to give speedie advertisment viis mediis et modis to the Master fellowes schollers and offices of your Colledge to repayre to the said Colledge the tenth day of March next ensuing To give an Accompt wherein they shalbe required To answere such things as may be Demaunded be[98] me or such Commissioners as I shall apoynte. Dated the 26th of February 1643.

There was 16 of theis warrants likewise sent to all the Colledges in Cambridge.

Another warrant directed to the Master or President of every Colledge to give in the names of all theire Members who have either left the Colledges or returned since last Catelogue and to send the Records of all Colledge Acts past by the Master and Fellowes for 12 yeares past Dated 11th of March of 1643.

To severall warrants more one to Mr Huddleston of Magdalen hall and the other to Mr Coldmn to send notes of theire prayers and sermons made the 3rd and 10th of March in St Maries Dated 11th of March 1643.[99]

98 *Sic.*
99 Complaints had been lodged about the preaching in the University church of George Huddlestone, fellow of Magdalene and John Coldham, fellow of Queens': see Twigg, *The University of Cambridge*, p. 93, for the outcome.

fo. A3v

By vertue of an Ordinance of Parliament entituled etc giveing mee likwise power to eject such Masters of Colledges as are scandalous in theire lives or Doctrines or that oppose the proceedings of Parliament I doe eject Doctor Cosins from beeing Master of Peeterhouse in Cambridge his opposeing the proceedings of Parliament and other scandalous Acts in the Universitie of Cambridge. And I require you to sequester the profitts of his Mastershipp for one that I shall appoynt in his place and to cutt his name out of the butteries and to certifie mee this your Act in one day. Given under hand and seale this 13th March 1643.

The like warrant for ejectment of Dr Beale of St Johns.
The like for Dr Martyn of Queens Colledge.
The like for Dr Sterne of Jesus Colledge.
The like for Dr Laney of Penbrooke Hall.

By vertue of an Ordinance of Parliament entituled an Ordinance for Regulating the Universitie of Cambridge and for removeing of scandalous Ministers in the seven associated Counties giveing me power to Eject such Fellowes of Colledges as are scandalous in theire lives Doctrins or are ill affected to the Parliament, or refuse obedience to the Parliament, I doe Eject Stephen Hall Batchelour in Devinitie out of his Fellowshipp in Trinity Colledge[100] for refusing to take the solemne league and Covenant. And I require you to sequester the profitts of his Fellowshipp for one that I shall appoynte in his place and to cutt his name out of the Butteries and to certifie mee of this your Act whithine one day after the date hereof.
Given under my hand and seale the 15th day of March 1643.

To the Fellowes of Jesus Colledge in Cambridge.

The like for John Oatway Fellowe of St Johns.

fo. A4

Whereas by vertue of an Ordinance of Parliament for regulating the Universitie of Cambridge etc there was a warrant issued forth in my Name on February 26th last past summoning all the Fellowes of your Colledge to repayre unto the said Colledge to be there resident on the 10th day of March following, I doe hereby declare that if Mr Tunstall and Mr Palgrave do not appeare personally on fryday morning next at the signe of the Beare in Cambridge before those Commissioners whome I have authorized to transact businesses committed to my care in the foresaid Ordinance, or if some person or persons appearing in theire behalfe give not in sufficient reasons for theire absence, I shall proceed to execute such sentence by ejectment or otherwise as by the forementioned Ordinance I am authorized to doe. Given under my hand this 3rd day of April 1644.[101]

[100] As the next entry confirms, Hall was in fact a fellow of Jesus College. He was also vicar of Fordham, from which also he was ejected: Venn, *Alumni Cantabrigienses*, II, 288; Matthews, *Walker revised*, p. 81.

[101] As is clear from the following paragraph, this warrant was issued to Corpus Christi College, of which Robert Tonstall and Edward Palgrave were fellows. Both men also had livings in Lincolnshire, to which they had perhaps withdrawn, and from which they do not seem to have been ejected.

To the Master and Fellowes of Benedict Corpus Christi Colledge in Cambridge, who are required to make due Publication hereof and alsoe to deliver in on Fryday next unto the abovementioned Committee a particular Accompt in writing, of the several fellowes of your Colledge haveing Cure of soules together with the names of parish or parishes and the value of the Benefice.

The like warrant directed to the Master and Fellowes of Gunvill and Caius Colledge, for the appearance of Mr Salter, Mr London, Mr Burton, Mr Pickerell, Mr Colebrand and Mr Haliburton at the same time.

The like warrant directed to the President and Fellowes of St Johns Colledge for the appearance of Mr Ambrose, Mr Greenhall, Mr Peeter, Mr Wrench, Mr Lane, Mr Cleveland, Mr Hay, Mr Rudding, Mr Topping, Mr Spooner, Mr Bullocke, Mr Jones and Mr Whittingham at the same time.

The like warrant directed to the President or senior and other the Fellowes of Queens Colledge for the appearance of Mr Marley, Mr Sparrow, Mr Bryan, Mr Rogers and Mr Hill at the same time.

The like warrant directed to the Provost, Master and Fellowes of Kings Colledge for the appearance of Mr Oley and Mr Carter at the same time.

The like warrant directed to the President and Fellowes of Peterhouse Colledge for the appearance of Mr Tolly, Mr Crashaw, Mr Beamont, Mr Penman, Mr Holder, and Mr Comyn at the same time.

fo. A4v

The like warrant directed to the President and Fellowes of Trinity Colledge for the appearance of Dr Roe, Dr Meredith, Mr Marshall, Mr West sen, Mr Chamberlein, Mr Willis, Mr Bary, Mr Cooke, Mr Croydon, Mr Cowley, Mr Wheeler, Mr Arundell, Mr Stacy, Mr Slater, Mr Cave, Mr Abder and Mr Nicklas at the same time.

The like warrant directed to the Master and Fellowes of Syney Colledge, for the appearance of Bertee at the same time.

The like warrant directed to the Master and Fellowes of Christ Colledge, for the appearance of Mr Honywood, Mr Norton, Mr Wood and Mr Moore senior at the same time.

The like warrant directed to the President and Fellowes of Penbrooke hall, for the appearance of Polcy, Mr Randolph, Mr Aston, Mr Heath, Mr Mapletoft, Mr Franke, Mr Cacott, Mr Lenthall and Mr Bokenham at the same time.

The like warrant directed to the President and Fellowes of Madlen Colledge, for the appearance of Dr Greene, Mr Leech, Mr Pullin, Mr Erskin, Mr Gale and Mr Botteler at the same time.

The like warrant directed to the President and Fellowes of Jesus Colledge, for the appearance of Mr Blackstone, Mr Mason and Mr Malkett at the same time.

fo. A5

Whereas by Ordinance of Parliament Entituled an Ordinance for Regulating the University of Cambridg etc power is given to me to eject such Fellowes of Colledges as are scandalous in theire lives or doctrines of[102] such as have forsaken their ordinary places of Residence within the said Universitie, or that doe or have opposed the proceedings of Parliament, By vertue of the authoritie thereby given to me I doe eject Mr Oley and Mr Carter from being Fellowes of Clare Hall within the said University of Cambridg, for not being Resident in the said Colledge and not returning to the places of theire usuall residence there, upon due summons given to that purpose and for severall other misdemeanours comitted by them.
Which parties are hereby required upon theire returne to Cambridge whensoever not to continue in the said University above the space of three dayes upon payne of imprisonment and sequestration of theire goods, And I doe hereby require you to sequester and collect all and singuler such profitts as belong to theire severall fellowships or other places, to be disposed of to such persons as I shall apoynt in theire roomes and further to cutt theire names out of the butteries and to certifie me within one day after the receipt hereof what you have done therein. Given under my hand and seale the eight day of Aprill 1644.

To the Fellowes of Clare Hall in Cambridge and to every of them.

The like warrant of Ejectment was granted against Mr Norton and Mr Wood of Christ Colledge in Cambridge the same time.

The like warrant of Ejectment was granted against Mr Poley, Mr Mapletoft, Mr Franke, Mr Bokenham, Mr Ashton, Mr Cacot and Mr Lentall of Penbrooke Hall in Cambridge the same time.

The like warrant of Ejectment was granted against Mr Bartee of Sydney Colledge in Cambridge the same time.

The like warrant of Ejectment was granted against Mr Ridding, Mr Greenhall, Mr Wrench, Mr Petter, Mr Cleaveland, Mr Whitingham, Mr Spoonar, Mr Bullocke, Mr Jones of St Johns Colledge in Cambridge the same time.

The like warrant of Ejectment was granted against Mr London, Mr Colebrand, Mr Hallyburton, Mr Pikerell, of Caius Colledg in Cambridg the same time.

fo. A5v

The like warrant of Ejectment was granted against Dr Greene, Mr Leech, Mr Pullin, Mr Ersing, Mr Gale and Mr Botteler of Magdalen Colledge in Cambridge the same time.

The like warrant of Ejectment was granted against Mr Tolly, Mr Beamont, Mr Pemman, Mr Chashawe, Mr Holder, and Mr Comyn of ~~Penbrooke Hall~~ Peterhouse in Cambridge the same time.

The like warrant was of Ejectment was granted against Mr Sparrow, Mr Bryan, ~~Mr Marley~~, Mr Rogers and Mr Hill of Queenes Colledge in Cambridge the same time.

[102] *Sic*: 'or' was intended.

The like warrant of Ejectment was granted against Mr Blacston, Mr Mason and Mr Malkett of Jesus Colledge in Cambridge the same time.

~~The like warrant of Ejectment was granted against Mr Oley and Mr Carter of Clare Hall in Cambridge the same time.~~

The like warrant of Ejectment was granted against Mr Tunstall and Mr Pallgrave of Corpus Christi Colledge in Cambridge the same time.

The like warrant of Ejectment was granted against Mr Sorsby of Edmanuel Colledge in Cambridge the same time.

The like warrant of Ejectment was granted against ~~Mr~~ Dr Roe, Dr Meredith, Mr Marshall, Mr West senior, Mr Chamberlayne, Mr Willis, Mr Bary, Mr Cooke, Mr Wheeler, Mr Cowley, Mr Arundell, Mr Stacy, Mr Cave, Mr Abdy and Mr Nicholas of Trinity Colledge in Cambridge the same time.

fo. A6

Whereas by Ordinance of Parliament entituled an Ordinance for Regulating the University of Cambridg etc power is given to me to Eject such Fellowes of Colledges as are scandalous in theire lives or Doctrines, or such as have forsaken their ordinary places of Residence within the said University, or that doe or have opposed the proceedings of Parliament, By vertue of the authoritie thereby given unto me I doe Eject   from being Fellowes of   within the said University of Cambridge, for refusing to take the soleme League and Covenant for reformation and defence of Religion the Honor and Happiness of the King and the peace and saftie of the three Kingdomes England Scotland and Ireland and for severall other misdemeanours comitted by them, Which parties are required upon theire returne to Cambridge whensoever not to continew in the said Universitie above the space of three dayes upon payne of imprisonment and sequestration of theire goods, And I doe hereby require you to sequester and collect all and singuler such profitts as belong to theire severall fellowshipps or other places, to be disposed of to such persons as I shall appoynt in theire roomes and further to cutt theire names out of the butteries. And to certifie me within one day after the receipt what you have done therein. Given under my hand and seale the Eight day of Aprill 1644.

To the President and Fellowes of   in Cambridg and every of them.

The like warrant was granted against Mr Thornton, Mr Mason, Mr Tyrwhite, Mr Lacy of St Johns Colledge.

The like

fo. A7

Whereas by vertue of an Ordinance of Parliament entituled an Ordinance for Regulating the University of Cambridge etc I have Ejected   Fellowes of your Colledge, These are to give you notice that my purpose is forwith to supply the vacant Fellowships and if there be any in your Colledge whoe in regarde of Degree learning and pietie shall found fitt for such preferment, they shalbe preferred before any others, Therefore

I desire you upon the receipt hereof to send me the names of such Fellowes[103] in your Colledge whome you judge most capeable of Fellowships that they may be examyned and made Fellowes if upon examination they shalbe aproved. Given under my hand this tenth day of Aprill 1644.

I being appoynted and constituted by the right honourable the Earle of Manchester who is authorized thereunto by an ordinance of Parliament to bee a fellowe of Colledge in the University of Cambridge with the approbation of the assembly of Divines now sitting att Westminster doe solemnely and seriously promise in the presence of almighty god the searcher of all harts that during the tyme of my continuance in that charge I shall faithfully labor to promote piety and learninge in my selfe schollers and students that doe or shall beelong to the said Colledge agreable to the late solemne nationall league and covenant by mee sworne and subscribed with respect to all the good and wholesome statutes of the said Colledge and of the Universitye correspendent to the said covenant and shall yeild unto Mr Master of this Colledge all such Respecte and obedience as the statutes of the said house and laudable customes of the Universitye doe require to bee given to the Master and endeavor to procure the good wellfare and perfect reformation both of the Colledge and Universitye so far as to mee apperteyneth.

Whereas in pursuite of an ordinance of Parliament for regulating and reforming the Universitye of Cambridge I have ejected Mr late fellowes of Magdalene Colledge, And whereas Mr have beene examined and approved by the Assembly of Divines now sitting at Westminster according to the said ordinance as fitt to bee fellowes These are therefore to require you and every of you to receive the said Mr as fellowes of your Colledge in roome of Mr formerly ejected and to give them place according to their seniority in the University in reference to all those that are or shall hereafter bee putt in by mee according to the ordinance aforesaid. Given under my hand and seale xi[th] July 1644.

---

fo. A13

Ejectment of Mr Fennicke of Chignall St James
Whereas it appeares that John Fennicke of Chignall St James in the County of Essex is of a scandalous life, an ejectment is granted against him beareing date the day of 1644 the forme whereof is before directed to the Churchwardens and Constables of Chignall St James aforesaid and every of them.

Sequestration of the Tythes of Mr Fennicke of Chignall St James
Whereas it appeares that John Fennicke of Chignall St James in the County of Essex is of a scandalous life, a sequestration is granted against him beareing date the day of 1644 the forme whereof is before directed to .

[103] Thomas Baker suggested that ‘Fellowes’ should be replaced by ‘scholers’.

fo. A14

Ejectment of Mr Lynce of Runwell
Whereas it appeares that Symon Lynce of Runwell in the County of Essex is of a scandalous life and Doctrine, an ejectment is granted against him bearing date the day of 1644 the forme whereof is before directed to the Churchwardens and Constables of Runwell aforesaid and every of them.

Sequestration of tythes of Mr Lynce of Runwell
Whereas it appeares that Symon Lynce of Runwell in the County of Essex is of a scandalous life and doctrine, a sequestration is granted against him bearing date the day of 1644 the forme whereof is before directed to .

fo. A15

Ejectment Mr Goldman of South Okenden
Whereas it appeares that Francis Goldman of South Okenden in the County of Essex is of scandalous Doctrine, an ejectment is granted against him beareing date the day of 1644 the forme whereof is before directed to the Churchwardens and Constables of South Okenden aforesaid and every of them.

Sequestration tythes of Mr Goldman of South Okenden
Whereas it appeares that Francis Goldman of South Okenden in the County of Essex is of scandalous Doctrine, a sequestration is granted against him beareing date the day of 1644 the forme whereof is before directed to .

fo. A16

Ejectment Mr Russell of Chinckford
Whereas it appeares that John Russell of Chinckford in the County of Essex is of a scandalous life, an ejectment is granted against him beareing date the day of 1644 the forme whereof is before directed to the Churchwardens and Constables of Chinckford aforesaid and every of them.

Sequestration tythes of Mr Russell of Chinckford
Whereas it appeares that John Russell of Chinckford in the County of Essex is of a scandalous life, a sequestration is granted against him bearing date the day of 1644 the forme whereof is before directed to .

fo. A17

Ejectment of Mr Dove of Foulnes
Whereas it appeares that Raboshire Dove of Foulnes in the Countie of Essex is of scandalous life and Doctrine, an ejectment is granted against him bearing date the day of 1644 the forme whereof is before directed to the Churchwardens and Constables of Foulnes aforesaid and every of them.

Sequestration of tythes of Mr Dove of Foulnes
Whereas it appeares that Raboshire Dove of Foulnes in the County of Essex is of scandalous life and Doctrine, a sequestration is granted against him beareing date the day of 1644 the forme whereof is before directed to .

fo. A18

Ejectment of Mr Burgis of Canoudon
Whereas it appeares that Elizeus Burges of Canoudon in the County of Essex is a plurallist and nonResident at Canoudon, an ejectment is granted against him beareing date the day of 1644 the forme whereof is before directed to the Churchwardens and Constables of Canoudon aforesaid and every of them.

Sequestration tythes of Mr Burgis of Canoudon
Whereas it appeares that Elizeus Burges of Canoudon in the County of Essex is a plurallist and Nonresident at Canoudon, ~~an ejectment is g~~ a sequestration is granted against him beareing date the day of 1644 the forme whereof is before directed to .

fo. A19

Ejectment of Mr Vicars of South Fambridge
Whereas it appeares that Vicars of South Fambridge in the County of Essex is of scandalous Doctrine, an ejectment is granted against him beareing date the day of 1644 the forme whereof is before directed to the Churchwardens and Constables of South Fambridge aforesaid and every of them.

Sequestration tythes of Mr Vicars of South Fambridge
Whereas it appeares that Vicars of South Fambridge in the County of Essex is of scandalous Doctrine, ~~an ejectment~~ a sequestration is granted against him beareing date the day of 1644 the forme whereof is before directed to .

fo. A20

Ejectment of Mr Holmes of Southchurch
Whereas it appeares that Holmes of Southchurch in the County of Essex is a plurallist and Nonresident at Southchurch, an ejectment is granted against him beareing date the day of 1644 the forme whereof is before directed to the Churchwardens and Constables of Southchurch aforesaid and every of them.

Sequestration tythes of Mr Holmes of Southchurch
Whereas it appeares that Holmes of Southchurch in the County of Essex is a plurallist and non resident at Southchurch, a sequestration is granted against him beareing date the day of 1644 the forme whereof is before directed to .

fo. A21

Ejectment of Mr Kindleton of Magdalen Laver
Whereas it appeares that Francis[104] Kindleton of Magdalen Laver in the County of Essex is of scandalous Doctrine, an ejectment is granted against him beareing date the day of 1644 the forme whereof is before directed to the Churchwardens and Constables of Magdalen Laver aforesaid and every of them.

[104] As noted above (n. 52), Kindleton's forename was George.

Sequestration of tythes of Mr Kindleton of Magdalen Laver
Whereas it appeares that Francis Kindleton of Magdalen Laver in the County of Essex is of scandalous Doctrine, a sequestration is granted against him beareing date the day of 1644 the forme whereof is before directed to .

fo. A22

Ejectment Mr Evett of Yeldham parva
Whereas it appeares that William Evett of Yeldham parva in the County of Essex hath left his Cure there destitute of any to officiate above this twelvemonth, an ejectment is granted against him bearing date the day of 1644 the forme whereof is before directed to the Churchwardens and Constables of Yeldham parva aforesaid and every of them.

Sequestration tythes of Mr Evett of Yeldham parva
Whereas it appeares that William Evett of Yeldham parva in the County of Essex hath left his Cure there, destitute of any to officiate above this twelvemonth, a sequestration is granted against him bearing date the day of 1644 the forme whereof is before directed to .

fo. A23

Ejectment of Mr Strutt of Fawlkbourne
Whereas it appeares that Edward Strutt of Fawlkbourne in the County of Essex is disaffected to the Parliament and a prophane swearer, an ejectment is granted against him bearing date the 17th day of September 1644 the forme whereof is before directed to the Churchwardens and Constables of Fawlkbourne aforesaid and every of them.

Sequestration tythes of Mr Strutt of Fawlkbourne
Whereas it appeares that Edward Strutt of Fawlkbourne in the County of Essex is disaffected to the Parliament and a prophane swearer, a sequestration is granted against him bearing date the 17th day of September 1644 the forme whereof is before directed to Bartholomew Wall and Thomas Herridge.

fo. A24

Ejectment of Mr Frost of Middleton
Whereas it appeares that William Frost of Middleton in the County of Essex is of scandalous life and an enemy too the proceedings of Parliament, an Ejectment is granted against him beareing date the first day of October 1644 the forme whereof is before directed to the Churchwardens and Constables of Middleton aforesaid and every of them.

Sequestration tythes of Mr Frost of Middleton
Whereas it appeares that William Frost of Middleton in the County of Essex is of scandalous life and an enemy to the proceedings of Parliament, a sequestration is granted against him bearing date the first day of October 1644 the forme whereof is before directed to Bartholomew Wall, Edmond Marsh and Vincent Cocke.

fo. A25

Ejectment of Mr Newsted of Swistedd
Whereas it appeares that Christopher Newsted of Swisted in the County of Essex is of scandalous life and Doctrine, an Ejectment is granted against him beareing date the day of the forme whereof is before directed to the Churchwardens and Constables of Swisted aforesaid and every of them.

Sequestration tythes of Mr Newsted of Swistead
Whereas it appeares that Christopher Newsted of Swisted in the County of Essex is of scandalous life and Doctrine, a sequestration is granted against him beareing date the day of the forme whereof is before directed to

fo. A26

Ejectment of Mr Crakenthorpe of Bradwell
Whereas it appeares that George Crakenthorpe of Bradwell in the County of Essex is a Common Tipler and frequently drunke, an ejectment is granted against him beareing date the day of the forme whereof is before directed to the Churchwardens and Constables of Bradwell aforesaid and every of them.

Sequestration tythes of Mr Crakenthorp of Bradwell
Whereas it appeares that George Crakenthorpe of Bradwell in the County of Essex is a Common Tipler and frequently drunke, an ~~ejectment~~ sequestration is granted against him beareing date the day of the forme whereof is before directed to

fo. A27

Ejectment of Mr Long of Fingringho
Whereas it appeares that Joseph Long of Fingringho in the County of Essex is of scandalous life and hath neglected his Cure, an ejectment is granted against him beareing date the day of the forme whereof is before directed to the Churchwardens and Constables of Finringho aforesaid and every of them.

Sequestration tythes of Mr Long of Finringho
Whereas it appeares that Joseph Long of Fenringho in the County of Essex is of scandalous life and hath neglected his Cure, a sequestration is granted against him beareing date the day of the forme whereof is before directed to Wesbram Makon, Samuell Whiting, Robert Theedam and John Nunn.[105]

fo. A28

Ejectment of Mr Clay of Wickam St Paul
Whereas it appeares that Timothy Clay of Wickam St Paul in the County of Essex is of scandalous life, an ejectment is granted against him beareing date the fifth day

[105] Cole MS, fo. 64, has a different list of sequestrators, inserted in error. The list here appears genuine. Samuel Whiting and John Nunn were deponents from Fingringhoe. Wesbram Makon (*sic*) cannot be identified. The family name of the fourth person is only partly legible: Robert 'Theedam' is a conjecture.

of February 1644 the forme whereof is before directed to the Churchwardens and Constables of Wickam St Paul aforesaid and every of them.

Sequestration tythes of Mr Clay of Wickam St Paul
Whereas it appeares that Timothy Clay of Wickam St Paul in the County of Essex is of scandalous life, a sequestration is granted against him beareing date the 5th day of February 1644 the forme whereof is before directed to

fo. A29

Ejectment of Mr Steward of Alphamstone
Whereas it appeares that Rowland Steward of Aphamstone in the County of Essex is of scandalous life an Ejectment is granted against him beareing date the 28th day of January 1644 the forme whereof is before directed to the Churchwardens and Constables of Alphamstone aforesaid and every of them.

Sequestration tithes of Alphamston Mr Steward
Whereas it appeares that Rowland Steward of Alphamston in the County of Essex is of scandalous life, a sequestration is granted against him beareing date the 28th day of January 1644 the forme whereof is before directed to William More, Robert Harrison, Jeoffry Scott and John Scott, and every of them.

fo. A30

Ejectment Dr Wilson of Depden, Wimbish and Fulborne
Whereas it appeares that Doctor Wilson parson of Depden, Wimbish and Fullborne is a plurallist and dissaffected to the Parliament, Ejectments ~~is~~ are granted against him bearing date the day of the Formes whereof is before directed to the Churchwardens and Constables of Depden, Wimbish and Fullborne aforesaid and every of them.

Sequestration tythes of Dr Willson of Depden, Wimbish and Fullborne
Whereas it appeares that Doctor Wilson parson of Depden, Wimbish and Fullborne is a plurallist and is dissaffected to the Parliament, sequestrations are granted against him beareing date the day of the formes whereof are before directed to

fo. A31

Ejectment of Mr Crosse of Gosfeild
Whereas it appeares that John Crosse of Gosfeild in the County of Essex is of scandalous life and Doctrine, an ejectment is granted against him beareing date the 18th day of September 1644 the forme whereof is before directed to the Churchwardens and Constables of Gosfeild aforesaid and every of them.

Sequestration tythes of Mr Crosse of Gosfeild
Whereas it appeares that John Crosse of Gosfeild in the County of Essex is of scandalous life and Doctrine, a sequestration is granted against him beareing date the 18th day of September 1644 the forme whereof is before directed to John Cotten, Richard Ruffle and Thomas Nevill and every of them.

fo. A32

Ejectment Dr Yong of Hadstocke
Whereas it appeares that Doctor Edward Yong of Hadstocke in the County of Essex is a plurallist and Nonresident at his cure of Hadstocke aforesaid, an ejectment is granted against him beareing date the 23th day of January 1644 the forme whereof is before directed to the Churchwardens and Constables of Hadstocke aforesaid and every of them.

Sequestration tythes of Dr Yong of Hadstocke
Whereas it appeares that Dr Edward Yong of Hadstocke in the County of Essex is a plurallist and Non resident at his cure of Hadstocke aforesaid, a sequestration is granted against him beareing date the 23th of January 1644 the forme whereof is before directed to

Bibliography

Manuscripts

British Library, London

Add. MS 4184	Calendar of privy seal warrants, 1654–6
Add. MS 5494	Accounts etc. of delinquents' estates, 1642–8
Add. MS 5811	William Cole's general collections, vol. 10
Add. MS 5829	William Cole's general collections, vol. 28
Add. MS 5852	William Cole's general collections, vol. 51
Add. MS 15669	Commons' committee for plundered ministers
Add. MS 15670	Commons' committee for plundered ministers
Add. MS 15671	Commons' committee for plundered ministers
Add. MS 15672	Cambridgeshire committee for scandalous ministers, 1644
Add. MS 36792	Register of benefices and ecclesiastical preferments, 1649–54
Add. MS 37491	Committee for Essex hundreds of Becontree etc., 1643–54
Add. MS 39534	Dunkin collection, vol. 219: dispensation rolls, 1615–30
Egerton MS 2647	Barrington papers, July–October 1643
Harley MS 6244	Standing committee for Essex, 1649
Lansdowne MS 1038	Bishop Kennett's collections, vol. 104
Stowe MS 189	Letters and papers of Civil War and Commonwealth, 1641–60
Stowe MS 842	Papers relating to Colchester, 1644–84

Cambridge University Library

Mm. 1.38	Baker MS 27
Mm. 1.42	Baker MS 31
Mm. 1.48	Baker MS 37
Mm. 1.53	Baker MS 42
EDR B2/40	Ely consistory court, act book 1623–4

Cambridgeshire Archives

P 87/1/1	Parish register, East Hatley
P 107/1/1	Parish register, Linton

Essex Record Office

D/P 11/1/2	Parish register, Great Dunmow
D/P 14/1/1	Parish register, Finchingfield
D/P 33/1/1	Parish register, Netteswell
D/P 36/1/1	Parish register, Coggeshall
D/P 49/1/1	Parish register, Stisted
D/P 59/1/1	Parish register, West Bergholt
D/P 62/1/1	Parish register, Magdalen Laver
D/P 85/1/1	Parish register, Gestingthorpe
D/P 109/1/1	Parish register, Stansted Mountfitchet
D/P 128/1/2	Parish register, South Weald
D/P 135/1/2	Parish register, Heydon
D/P 140/1/1A	Parish register, Stanford Rivers
D/P 155/1/1	Parish register, Boxted
D/P 206/1/3	Parish register, North Fambridge
D/P 208/1/1	Parish register, Aldham
D/P 212/1/1	Parish register, Twinstead
D/P 213/1/1	Parish register, Wickham St Paul
D/P 214/1/1	Parish register, Belchamp Otten
D/P 243/1/1	Parish register, White Colne
D/P 281/1/1	Parish register, Mount Bures
D/P 299/1/3	Parish register, Terling
D/P 358/1/1	Parish register, Bulmer
D/P 375/1/1	Parish register, Faulkbourne
D/P 408/1/1	Parish register, Belchamp St Paul
D/ACW 14/168	Will of Gabriel Honifold
D/AEW 21/186	Will of John Wright
D/AEW 21/245	Will of Timothy Ottly
D/AEW 23/221	Will of Thomas Aylett
D/AMW 6/252	Will of Robert Calthorp
D/ABA 7	Commissary of bishop of London, Acts, 1634–6
D/ABA 8	Commissary of Bishop of London, Acts, 1636–8
D/ACA 52	Archdeacon of Colchester, Acts, 1637–8
D/ACA 53	Archdeacon of Colchester, Acts, 1638–9
D/ACA 54	Archdeacon of Colchester, Acts, 1639–41
D/ACA 55	Archdeacon of Colchester, Acts, 1663–6
Q/SR 313/74	Sessions roll, midsummer 1641, Castle Hedingham residents
Q/SR 313/100	Sessions roll, midsummer 1641, recognizance of Isaac Wincoll
Q/SR 315/30	Sessions roll, epiphany 1642, recognizance of Robert Chester
Q/SR 321/1	Sessions roll, midsummer 1644, writ of Timothy Middleton, sheriff
Q/SR 321/129	Sessions roll, midsummer 1644, attendance list
Q/SR 322/132	Sessions roll, michaelmas 1644, attendance list
Q/SR 324/26	Sessions roll, easter 1645, indictment showing Middleton sheriff

Q/SR 324/32	Sessions roll, easter 1645, indictment, Sible Hedingham
Q/SR 324/109, 110	Sessions roll, easter 1645, indictments, Sible Hedingham
Q/SR 325/32	Sessions roll, midsummer 1645, indictment of Elisabeth Spurgeon
Q/SR 325/34	Sessions roll, midsummer 1645, indictment of Edward Shephard
Q/SR 325/117	Sessions roll, midsummer 1645, attendance list
Q/SR 329/158	Sessions roll, midsummer 1646, attendance list
Q/SR 334/84	Sessions roll, michaelmas 1647, attendance list
Q/SR 400/30	Sessions roll, easter 1664, indictment of Maidstones
Q/Sba 2/57	Sessions bundles, 1645, examination of Edward Shephard
D/DU 293/103	Deed, manor of Newton Hall, Great Dunmow
D/DU 472/18	Deed, manor of Little Dunmow
D/DAV 56	Deed, manor of Eastham Burnels
D/Y 2/7/4	Letter of William Atwood
D/Y 2/7/5	Letter of William Atwood
D/DBa E14	Letter, Dame Joan Barrington to Robert Calthorp
D/DMs C2	Letter, Stephen Marshall to Carew Mildmay
D/Dmy 15M50/233	Warrant for swearing John Wright as JP
D/B 5 GB4	Colchester assembly book, 1647–66
T/A 42/1	Transcript of state papers (domestic) 15/358 (ship money)
T/Z 151/113	Transcript, monumental inscriptions, Bradwell-juxta-Coggeshall

Lambeth Palace Library

Comm. XII	Commonwealth, parliamentary surveys

University of Leicester Library

Special Collections, MS 31	Reformation of the University of Cambridge and Essex ministers, 1644

Lincolnshire Archives

LCL 5456	Proceedings of commissioners for scandalous ministers, Lincolnshire
LCL 5458	Proceedings of commissioners for scandalous ministers, Suffolk

London Metropolitan Archives

DL/B/A/002/MS 09537/015	Second visitation of William, bishop of London, 1637

The National Archives

E 179/112/646	Subsidies of 1641, Essex, Hinckford hundred

SP 16	State papers, England
SP 28/227	State papers, orders of county committees, Essex
C 231/6	Crown dockets, commission of the peace, Essex, 1644
PROB 11/173/77	Will of John Knopp of Middleton
PROB 11/197/603	Will of Sir Edward Bullocke of Faulkbourne
PROB 11/206/442	Will of John Simson, rector of Mount Bures
PROB 11/225/288	Will of John Elliston of Gestingthorpe
PROB 11/225/598	Will of Daniel Falconer, rector of Aldham
PROB 11/232/21	Will of Thomas Wilson, rector of Debden
PROB 11/283/306	Will of John Elliston of Little Coggeshall
PROB 11/306/2	Will of William Jones, rector of Ashen
PROB 11/389/300	Will of John Russell, rector of Chingford

Oxford, Bodleian Library

MS 324	Commons' committee for plundered ministers
MS Tanner 290	Letter of William Alanson to Bishop Wren
MS J. Walker c.1–c.11	Papers of John Walker

Parliamentary Archives

HL/PO/JO/10/1/91/1–44	Protestation returns, Essex, Hinckford hundred
HL/PO/JO/10/1/112	Essex petition re Ireland, safety of kingdom, 20 Jan. 1642
HL/PO/JO/10/1/141	Essex petition for peace, 4 Jan. 1643
HL/PO/JO/10/1/150–1, 153	Papers re Christopher Newstead and the parish of Stisted
HL/PO/JO/10/1/211	Petition of 6 Aug. 1646 for Matthew Elliston's appointment
HL/PO/JO/10/1/219	Papers re appointment of John Chamberlin to Bulmer

Suffolk Archives

HA517/C15	Title to manor of Overhall, Gestingthorpe, Essex

Primary printed sources

Unless otherwise specified the place of publication is London.

A calendar of the docquets of Lord Keeper Coventry 1625–1640, ed. Jan Broadway, Richard Cust and Stephen K. Roberts (4 vols., List and Index Society, 2004)

Acts and ordinances of the interregnum 1642–1660, ed. C. H. Firth and R. S. Rait (1911)

Allen, D. H., *Essex quarter sessions order book 1652–1661* (Chelmsford, 1974)

Barrington family letters 1628–1632, ed. Arthur Searle (Camden fourth series, vol. 28, 1983)

Calamy, Edmund, *An abridgment of Mr. Baxter's history of his life and times* (1702)

Calendar of state papers domestic 1625–49 (23 vols., 1858–97)

Fragmenta genealogica, ed. F. A. Crisp (13 vols., 1889–1909)

HMC, *7th Report, Part I* (1879)
Journals of the House of Commons (1507–)
Journals of the House of Lords (1509–1767)
Le Neve, J., *Fasti Ecclesiae Anglicanae 1541–1847*, ed. J. Horn *et al.* (13 vols., 1969–2013)
Massachusetts Historical Society, *Winthrop papers* (6 vols., Boston, MA, 1863–92)
Mather, Cotton, *Magnalia Christi Americana* (2 vols., Hartford, 1853)
Mercurius rusticus, or, the countries complaint of the barbarous outrages committed by the sectaries of this late flourishing kingdom (1685)
Middle Temple records, ed. Charles Henry Hopwood (4 vols., 1904–5)
Minutes and papers of the Westminster Assembly 1643–1653, ed. Chad Van Dixhoorn (5 vols., Oxford, 2012)
National prayers: special worship since the Reformation, I: *Special prayers, fasts and thanksgivings in the British Isles, 1533–1688*, ed. Natalie Mears, Alasdair Raffe, Stephen Taylor, and Philip Williamson (with Lucy Bates) (Church of England Record Society, 2013)
Nettles, Stephen, *An answer to the Jewish part of Mr Selden's history of tithes* (Oxford, 1625)
Newcourt, Richard, *Repertorium ecclesiasticum parochiale londinense* (2 vols., 1708–10)
Original records of early nonconformity under persecution and indulgence, ed. G. Lyon Turner (3 vols., 1911–14)
Proceedings in the opening session of the Long Parliament: House of Commons, ed. Maija Jansson (7 vols., Rochester, NY, 2000–7)
Roll of alumni in arts of the university and King's College of Aberdeen, 1596–1860, ed. P. J. Anderson (Aberdeen, 1900)
Stuart royal proclamations, ed. J. F. Larkin and P. L. Hughes (2 vols., Oxford, 1973–83)
Suffolk and the great rebellion 1640–1660, ed. Alan Everitt (Suffolk Records Society, 1960)
The Cambridgeshire committee for scandalous ministers 1644–45, ed. Graham Hart (Cambridgeshire Records Society, 2017)
The constitutional documents of the puritan revolution 1625–1660, ed. S. R. Gardiner (Oxford, 1906)
'The Cromwellian decimation tax of 1655, the decimation lists', ed. J. T. Cliffe, in *Camden Miscellany XXXIII* (Cambridge, 1996)
The diary of Ralph Josselin 1616–1683, ed. Alan Macfarlane (Oxford, 1976)
The division of the county of Essex into severall classes: together with the names of the ministers and others fit to be of each classis. Certified by the standing committee of that county, etc. (1648)
The journal of William Dowsing: iconoclasm in East Anglia during the English Civil War, ed. Trevor Cooper (Woodbridge, 2001)
The letters of George Davenport 1651–1677, ed. Brenda M. Pask with Margaret Harvey (Woodbridge, 2011)
The pension book of Gray's Inn 1569–1669, ed. Reginald J. Fletcher (1901)
The records of Lincoln's Inn, admissions, ed. W. P. Baildon (2 vols., 1896)
The records of Lincoln's Inn, the black books, ed. W. P. Baildon *et al.* (6 vols., 1897–2001)
The register of admissions to Gray's Inn, 1521–1889, ed. J. Foster (1889)

'The royalist clergy of Lincolnshire', ed. J. W. F. Hill, in *Reports and Papers of the Lincolnshire Architectural and Archaeological Society* (new series), vol. 2, part 1 (1938, published 1940), pp. 34–127
The Suffolk committees for scandalous ministers 1644–1646, ed. Clive Holmes (Suffolk Records Society, 1970)
Visitation articles and injunctions of the early Stuart church, II, ed. Kenneth Fincham (Church of England Record Society, V, 1998)
Visitations of Essex, ed. Walter C. Metcalfe (2 vols., 1878–9)
Visitations of Suffolk, ed. Walter C. Metcalfe (Exeter, 1882)
Walker, John, *An attempt towards recovering an account of the numbers and sufferings of the clergy* (1714)
White, John, *The first century of scandalous, malignant priests, made and admitted into benefices by the prelates, in whose hands the ordination of ministers and government of the church hath been* (1643)

Thomason Tracts

E.30[4]: England and Wales, Parliament, *Two ordinances of the Lords and Commons assembled in parliament* (1644)
E.40[34]: Whitby, Daniel, *The vindication of a true protestant, and faithfull servant to his church, Daniel Whitby, rector of Thoyden-Mount in Essex* (1644)
E.88[16]: Vic[c]ars, John, *The opinion of the Roman judges touching imprisonment, and the liberty of the subject, or, A sermon preached at the Abby at Westminster, at a late publique fast, Jan. 25. 1642* (1643)
E.92[1]: Vic[c]ars, John, *A discovery of the rebels* (1643)
E.105[23]: Anon, *A remonstrance of the Commons in parliament* (1643)
E.166[4]: Gulter, Giles, *The archbishops crueltie, made knowne in a true story of one Mr. Edward Rood, who was minister at Saint Helens in Abingdon, and dismissed of his meanes and ministery by him* (1641)
E.242[32]: Rupert, prince, Count Palatine, *Prince Rupert his declaration* (1642)
E.339[11]: Anon, *The humble petition of the ministers of the counties of Suffolke and Essex, concerning church-government* (1646)
E.589[4]: Fairclough, Samuel, *The prisoners praises for their deliverance from the long imprisonment in Colchester* (1650)
E.1048[1]: Russell, John, *The solemn league and covenant discharg'd. Or St. Peter's bonds not only loosed but annihilated* (1660)
669.f.6[35]: Paget, William Paget, Baron, *The copie of a letter sent from the right honourable the Lord Paget, unto the honourable house of parliament, declaring the reasons of his departure from the parliament, unto the kings most excellent majesty at Yorke* (1642)

Secondary printed sources

Unless otherwise specified the place of publication is London.

A biographical register of St John's College, Oxford, 1555–1660, ed. Andrew Hegarty (Woodbridge, 2011)

A history of the county of Essex (12 vols., Victoria County History, 1903–2022)
Aston, Margaret, *Broken idols of the English Reformation* (Oxford, 2016)
Aston, Margaret, *England's iconoclasts*, I: *Laws against images* (Oxford, 1988)
Auger, Peter, 'Attribution of three works to John Viccars (*c.* 1604–53?)', *Notes and Queries*, 61 (2014), 362–6
Barclay, Andrew, *Electing Cromwell: the making of a politician* (2011)
Beavan, Alfred P., *Aldermen of the city of London temp. Henry III – 1912* (1908)
Bendall, Sarah, Brooke, Christopher and Collinson, Patrick, *A history of Emmanuel College Cambridge* (Woodbridge, 1999)
Bewes, W. A., *Church briefs* (1896)
Bowen, Lloyd, 'Royalism, print and clergy in Britain, 1639–1640 and 1642', *Historical Journal*, 56 (2013), 297–319
Braddick, Michael, *God's fury, England's fire* (2008)
Brod, Manfred, *Abingdon in context: small-town politics in early modern England, 1547–1688* (Peterborough, 2010)
Bullock, Llewellyn C. W., *Memoirs of the Bullock family, A.D. 1166 to 1905* (Rugby, 1905)
Champion, Justin and McNulty, Lee, 'Making orthodoxy in late Restoration England: the trials of Edmund Hickeringell, 1662–1710', in *Negotiating power in early modern society*, ed. Michael J. Braddick and John Walter (Cambridge, 2001)
Clarke, Samuel, *The lives of sundry eminent persons in this later age* (1683)
Complete baronetage, ed. George E. Cokayne (5 vols., Exeter, 1900–6)
Copinger, W. A., *The manors of Suffolk* (7 vols., 1905–11)
Cressy, David, 'Purification, thanksgiving and the churching of women in post-Reformation England', *Past & Present*, 141 (1993), 106–46
Donagan, Barbara, 'The clerical patronage of Robert Rich', *Proceedings of the American Philosophical Society*, 120 (1976), 388–419
Donagan, Barbara, *War in England, 1642–1649* (Oxford, 2010)
Dougall, Alistair, *The devil's book: Charles I, the book of sports and puritanism in Tudor and early Stuart England* (Exeter, 2011
Durston, Christopher, 'For the better humiliation of the people: public days of fasting and thanksgiving during the English revolution', *The Seventeenth Century*, 7 (1992), 129–49
Emmison, F. G., *Elizabethan life*, I: *Disorder* (Chelmsford, 1970)
Erwin, Lucy Lane, *Ancestry of William Clopton of York County, Virginia* (Rutland, VT, 1939)
Fincham, Kenneth, and Lake, Peter, 'The ecclesiastical policies of James I and Charles I', in *The early Stuart church, 1603–1642*, ed. Kenneth Fincham (Basingstoke, 1993), pp. 23–49
Fincham, Kenneth and Taylor, Stephen, 'Episcopalian conformity and nonconformity 1646–60', in *Royalists and royalism during the interregnum*, ed. Jason McElligott and David L. Smith (Manchester, 2010), pp. 18–43
Fincham, Kenneth and Taylor, Stephen, 'Episcopalian identity, 1640–1662', in *The Oxford history of anglicanism*, I, ed. Anthony Milton (Oxford, 2017), pp. 457–82
Fincham, Kenneth and Taylor, Stephen, 'Vital statistics: episcopal ordination and ordinands in England, 1646–60', *English Historical Review*, 126 (2011), 319–44
Fincham, Kenneth, and Tyacke, Nicholas, *Altars restored: the changing face of English religious worship, 1547 – c. 1700* (Oxford, 2007)

Flather, Amanda, 'Gender, agency and religious change in early Stuart England' in *Popular culture and political agency in early modern England and Ireland*, ed. Michael J. Braddick and Phil Withington (Woodbridge, 2017), pp. 145–63
Fletcher, Anthony, *The outbreak of the English Civil War* (1981)
Foster, J., *Alumni Oxonienses: the members of the University of Oxford 1500–1714* (4 vols., Oxford, 1891–2)
French, H. R. and Hoyle, R. W., *The character of English rural society: Earls Colne, 1550–1750* (Manchester, 2007)
Gardiner, S. R., *History of the great Civil War 1642–1649* (4 vols., 1893)
Gibson, J. and Dell, A., *The protestation returns 1641–42 and other contemporary listings* (Bury, 2004)
Green, Ian, *The Christian's ABC: catechisms and catechizing in England c. 1530–1740* (Oxford, 1996)
Green, Ian, 'The persecution of "scandalous" and "malignant" parish clergy during the English Civil War', *English Historical Review*, 94 (1979), 507–31
Gyford, Janet, *Public spirit: dissent in Witham and Essex 1500–1700* (Witham, 1999)
Hessayon, Ariel, '*Gold tried in the fire': the prophet TheaurauJohn Tany and the English revolution* (Aldershot, 2007)
Hill, Christopher, *Economic problems of the church: from Archbishop Whitgift to the Long Parliament* (Oxford, 1956)
Hodson, W. W. and C. F. D. Sperling, *A short history of the borough of Sudbury in the county of Suffolk* (Sudbury, 1896)
Holmes, Clive, *The Eastern Association in the English Civil War* (Cambridge, 1974)
Hoyle, David, *Reformation and religious identity in Cambridge, 1590–1644* (Woodbridge, 2007)
Hunt, W., *The puritan moment: the coming of revolution in an English county* (Cambridge, MA, 1983)
Ingram, Martin, *Church courts, sex and marriage in England, 1570–1640* (Cambridge, 1987)
Jones, Thomas Wharton, 'The pedigree of Alliston or Elliston of Essex and Kent', in *The herald and genealogist*, V, ed. John Gough Nicholls (1870), 24–6
Kyle, Chris R., '"A dog, a butcher and a puritan": the politics of Lent in early modern England', in *Connecting centre and locality: political communications in early modern England*, ed. Chris R. Kyle and Jason Peacey (Manchester, 2020)
Laurence, Ann, *Parliamentary army chaplains 1642–51* (Woodbridge, 1990)
McCall, Fiona, *Baal's priests: the loyalist clergy and the English revolution* (Farnham, 2013)
Matthews, A. G., *Calamy revised, being a revision of Edmund Calamy's account of the ministers and others ejected and silenced, 1660–62* (Oxford, 1934)
Matthews, A. G., *Walker revised, being a revision of John Walker's sufferings of the clergy during the grand rebellion, 1642–60* (Oxford, 1948)
Merritt, J. F., 'Religion and the English parish', in *The Oxford history of anglicanism*, I, ed. Anthony Milton (Oxford, 2017), pp. 122–47
Millstone, Noah, *Manuscript circulation and the invention of politics in early Stuart England* (Cambridge, 2016)
Milton, Anthony, 'Anglicanism and royalism in the 1640s', in *The English Civil War: conflicts and contexts, 1640–49*, ed. John Adamson (Basingstoke, 2009)
Milton, Anthony, *England's second reformation: the battle for the Church of England, 1625–1662* (Cambridge, 2021)

Morant, P., *History and antiquities of the county of Essex* (2 vols., 1768)
Nuttall, W. L. F., 'Sir Thomas Barrington and the puritan revolution', *Transactions of the Essex Archaeological Society*, third series, 2, part 1 (1966), 60–82
Opie, Iona and Opie, Peter, *Children's games with things* (Oxford, 1997)
Oxford Dictionary of National Biography (60 vols., Oxford, 2004; online 2008)
Parker, Kenneth L., *The English sabbath: a study of doctrine and discipline from the Reformation to the Civil War* (Cambridge, 1988)
Phillimore, Sir Robert, *et al.*, *Ecclesiastical law of the Church of England* (2nd edn, 2 vols., 1895)
Pocock, D. C. D., 'Some former hop growing centres', *Agricultural History Review*, 13 (1965), 17–22
Preston, Arthur E., *The church and parish of St Nicholas, Abingdon* (Oxford, 1935)
Round, J. H., 'Colchester during the Commonwealth', *English Historical Review*, 15 (1900), 641–64
Royal Commission on Historical Monuments, *An inventory of the historical monuments in Essex* (4 vols., 1916–23)
Seaver, Paul, *The puritan lectureships* (Stanford, 1970)
Shaw, W. A., *A history of the English church during the Civil Wars and under the Commonwealth, 1640–1660* (2 vols., 1900)
Sier, L. C., 'The Wyncoll family', *Transactions of the Essex Archaeological Society*, 12 (1913), part 1, 1–13
Sitwell, H. D. W., 'Royal sergeants-at-arms and the royal maces', *Archaeologia*, 102 (1969), 213–14
Smith, Harold, 'Some Essex royalist clergy – and others', *The Essex Review*, 33 (1923), 82–3
Smith, Harold, 'South Ockendon clergy 1640–60', *The Essex Review*, 33 (1923), 8–13
Smith, Harold, *The ecclesiastical history of Essex under the Long Parliament and the Commonwealth* (Colchester, 1933)
Smith, Harold, 'The sequence of Essex clergy, 1640–1664', typescript, 2 vols., ERO
Spraggon, Julie, *Puritan iconoclasm in the English Civil War* (Woodbridge, 2003)
Stone, Lawrence, 'The size and composition of the Oxford student body 1580–1909', in Lawrence Stone (ed.), *The university in society*, I (Princeton, 1975)
Suffolk manorial families, ed. J. J. Muskett (3 vols., Exeter, 1894–1914)
Tatham, G. B., *Dr John Walker and the sufferings of the clergy* (Cambridge, 1911)
The Book of Common Prayer: the texts of 1549, 1559, and 1662, ed. Brian Cummings (Oxford, 2011)
The history of parliament: the House of Commons, 1604–1629, ed. Andrew Thrush and John P. Ferris (6 vols., Cambridge, 2010)
The history of parliament: the House of Commons 1640–1660, ed. Stephen K. Roberts (9 vols., Woodbridge, 2023)
The knights of England, ed. W. A. Shaw (2 vols., 1906)
Tolmie, M., 'Thomas Lambe, soapboiler, and Thomas Lambe, merchant, general baptists', *Baptist Quarterly*, 27 (1977), 4–17
Twigg, John, *The University of Cambridge and the English revolution* (Woodbridge, 1990)
Tyacke, Nicholas, *Anti-Calvinists: the rise of English Arminianism c. 1590–1640* (Oxford, 1987)
Vallance, Edward, *Revolutionary England and the national covenant: state oaths, protestantism and the political nation* (Woodbridge, 2005)

Venn, J. and Venn, J. A., *Alumni Cantabrigienses: a biographical list of all known students, graduates and holders of office at the University of Cambridge, from the earliest times to 1900. Part I: from the earliest times to 1751* (4 vols., Cambridge, 1922–7)

Wadmore, J. F., *Some account of the worshipful Company of Skinners of London* (1902)

Walker, R. R. A., 'John Elliston and John Sparrow', *Notes & Queries* 167 (1934), 312

Walter, John, '"Affronts and insolencies": the voices of Radwinter and popular opposition to Laudianism', *English Historical Review*, 122 (2007), 35–60

Walter, John, 'Confessional politics in pre-Civil War Essex: prayer books, profanations and petitions', *Historical Journal*, 44 (2001), 677–701

Walter, John, *Covenanting citizens: the protestation oath and popular political culture in the English revolution* (Oxford, 2017)

Walter, John, 'Popular iconoclasm and the politics of the parish in eastern England, 1640–42', *Historical Journal* 47 (2004), 261–90

Walter, John, *Understanding popular violence in the English revolution: the Colchester plunderers* (Cambridge, 1999)

Webster, Tom, *Godly clergy in early Stuart England: the Caroline puritan movement c. 1620–1643* (Cambridge, 1997)

Unpublished theses

Cliftlands, William, 'The "well-affected" and the "country": politics and religion in English provincial society, c. 1640–c. 1654', Ph.D. thesis, University of Essex, 1987

Hart, Graham, 'The parish clergy of the diocese of Ely and their parishioners, c. 1630–1650', Ph.D. thesis, University of Essex, 2015

Quintrell, B. W., 'The divisional committee for southern Essex during the Civil Wars and its part in local administration', MA dissertation, University of Manchester, 1962

Quintrell, B. W., 'The government of the county of Essex, 1603–1642', Ph.D. thesis, University of London, 1965

Shipps, K. W., 'Lay patronage of East Anglian puritan clerics in pre-revolutionary England', Ph.D. thesis, Yale University, 1971

Index

Names of people and places in **bold** refer to the Essex clergy against whom charges are made in the manuscripts and their parishes.

'The object of the Society shall be to advance knowledge of the history of the Church in England, and in particular of the Church of England, from the sixteenth century onwards, by the publication of editions or calendars of primary sources of information.'

PUBLICATIONS

1. Visitation Articles and Injunctions of the Early Stuart Church. Volume I. Ed. Kenneth Fincham (1994)

2. The Speculum of Archbishop Thomas Secker: The Diocese of Canterbury 1758–1768. Ed. Jeremy Gregory (1995)

3. The Early Letters of Bishop Richard Hurd, 1739–1762. Ed. Sarah Brewer (1995)

4. Brethren in Adversity: Bishop George Bell, The Church of England and the Crisis of German Protestantism, 1933–1939. Ed. Andrew Chandler (1997)

5. Visitation Articles and Injunctions of the Early Stuart Church. Volume II. Ed. Kenneth Fincham (1998)

6. The Anglican Canons, 1529–1947. Ed. Gerald Bray (1998)

7. From Cranmer to Davidson. A Church of England Miscellany. Ed. Stephen Taylor (1999)

8. Tudor Church Reform. The Henrician Canons of 1534 and the *Reformatio Legum Ecclesiasticarum*. Ed. Gerald Bray (2000)

9. All Saints Sisters of the Poor. An Anglican Sisterhood in the Nineteenth Century. Ed. Susan Mumm (2001)

10. Conferences and Combination Lectures in the Elizabethan Church: Dedham and Bury St Edmunds, 1582–1590. Ed. Patrick Collinson, John Craig and Brett Usher (2003)

11. The Diary of Samuel Rogers, 1634–1638. Ed. Tom Webster and Kenneth Shipps (2004)

12. Evangelicalism in the Church of England c.1790–c.1890. Ed. Mark Smith and Stephen Taylor (2004)

13. The British Delegation and the Synod of Dort (1618–1619). Ed. Anthony Milton (2005)

14. The Beginnings of Women's Ministry. The Revival of the Deaconess in the Nineteenth-Century Church of England. Ed. Henrietta Blackmore (2007)

15. The Letters of Theophilus Lindsey. Volume I. Ed. G. M. Ditchfield (2007)

16. The Back Parts of War: The YMCA Memoirs and Letters of Barclay Baron, 1915–1919. Ed. Michael Snape (2009)

17. The Diary of Thomas Larkham, 1647–1669. Ed. Susan Hardman Moore (2011)

18. From the Reformation to the Permissive Society. A Miscellany in Celebration of the 400th Anniversary of Lambeth Palace Library. Ed. Melanie Barber and Stephen Taylor with Gabriel Sewell (2010)

19. The Letters of Theophilus Lindsey. Volume II. Ed. G. M. Ditchfield (2012)

20. National Prayers: Special Worship since the Reformation. Volume I: Special Prayers, Fasts and Thanksgivings in the British Isles, 1533–1688. Ed. Natalie Mears, Alasdair Raffe, Stephen Taylor, Philip Williamson and Lucy Bates (2013)

21. The Journal of Bishop Daniel Wilson of Calcutta, 1845–1857. Ed. Andrew Atherstone (2015)

22. National Prayers: Special Worship since the Reformation. Volume 2: General Fasts, Thanksgivings and Special Prayers in the British Isles, 1689–1870. Ed. Philip Williamson, Alasdair Raffe, Stephen Taylor and Natalie Mears (2017)

23. The Further Correspondence of Archbishop Laud. Ed. Kenneth Fincham (2017)

24. The Household Accounts of William Laud, Archbishop of Canterbury, 1635–1642. Ed. Leonie James (2019)

25. The First World War Diaries of the Rt. Rev. Llewe llyn Gwynne, July 1915–July 1916. Ed. Peter Howson (2019)

26. National Prayers: Special Worship Since the Reformation. Volume 3: Worship for National and Royal Occasions in the United Kingdom, 1871–2016. Ed. Philip Williamson, Stephen Taylor, Alasdair Raffe and Natalie Mears (2020)

27. The Restoration of the Church of England: Canterbury Diocese and the Archbishop's Peculiars. Ed. Tom Reid (2022)

Forthcoming Publications

The Papers of the Elland Society 1769–1818. Ed. John Walsh and Stephen Taylor

The Correspondence of William Sancroft. Ed. Grant Tapsell

The Sermons of John Sharp. Ed. Françoise Deconinck-Brossard

The Correspondence and Papers of Archbishop Richard Neile, 1598–1640. Ed. Andrew Foster

Birkenhead, All Souls, and the Making of Herbert Hensley Henson: The Early Journals, 1885–1887. Ed. Frank Field and Julia Stapleton

Shaping the Jacobean Religious Settlement: The Hampton Court Conference, 1604. Ed. Mark Byford and Kenneth Fincham

The 1669 Return of Nonconformist Conventicles. Ed. David Wykes

The Correspondence of Francis Blackburne (1705–1787). Ed. G. M. Ditchfield

The Letters and Papers of William Paley. Ed. Neil Hichin

Charles Simeon's Letters: A New Collection. Ed. Andrew Atherstone

The Diary of an Oxford Parson: The Reverend John Hill, Vice-Principal of St Edmund Hall, Oxford, 1805–1808, 1820–1855. Ed. Grayson Carter

National Prayers: Special Worship since the Reformation. Volume 4: Anniversary Commemorations, Additional Material, 1533–2023, and General Index. Ed. Philip Williamson, Natalie Mears, Stephen Taylor and Alasdair Raffe

Suggestions for publications should be addressed to Dr Gareth Atkins, General Editor, Church of England Record Society, Queens' College, Cambridge CB3 9ET, or at ga240@cam.ac.uk.

Membership of the Church of England Record Society is open to all who are interested in the history of the Church of England. Enquiries should be addressed to the Membership Secretary, Professor Hilary Carey, coersmembers@gmail.com.